ROAD
SONG

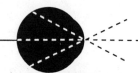

**This Large Print Book carries the
Seal of Approval of N.A.V.H.**

ROAD SONG

Natalie Kusz

Thorndike Press • Thorndike, Maine

Library of Congress Cataloging in Publication Data:

Kusz, Natalie.
    Road song / Natalie Kusz.
        p.   cm.
    ISBN 1-56054-138-5 (alk. paper : lg. print)
    1. Kusz, Natalie—Childhood and youth. 2. Alaska—
Biography. 3. Alaska—Social life and customs. I. Title.
[CT275.K898A3   1990b]   90-27649
979.8'05'092—dc20   CIP
[B]

Thorndike Press Large Print edition published in 1991
by arrangement with Farrar, Straus & Giroux.

Cover design by Wendell Minor.

The tree indicium is a trademark of Thorndike Press.

This book is printed on acid-free, high opacity paper. ∞

For my father, Julius Kusz,
and for Frank Soos,
with profound thanks

What we have been becomes
The country where we are.
— Wendell Berry
"An Anniversary"

Acknowledgments

Any full-length work would be too exhausting to complete without the support of many people. Some of those to whom I owe tremendous gratitude are the following:

For early encouragement and continuing moral support: Raymond Lane, Jerah Chadwick, Karen Minton, Jane Leer, Robin Lewis, Lisa Chavez, John Fannin, Helen Harrel, Alma Davis, Ann Kalinak, Patrice Melnick, Susan Blalock, Patricia Monaghan, Roland Wulbert, Michael Spooner, Shannon Greaves, Peggy Shumaker, Leonard Michaels, Wendy Lesser, Lynne Sharon Schwartz, James Tate, Jim Hall, Thomas Becknell, Don Postema, Wayne Roosa, Joy Longley, and Shirley Becknell.

For editorial advice and extraordinary patience: Jonathan Galassi, Gail Hochman, Kathleen Anderson Mooney, and Frank Soos.

For financial encouragement: the Mrs. Giles Whiting Foundation, the General Electric Corporation, and the Council of Literary Magazines and Presses.

For clerical assistance: Kathy McGill, Janine McFarland, and Nancy Busse.

For exhaustive interviews and courageous honesty: Julius, Leslie, and Ian Kusz and Bethel Spooner.

For her invaluable written memories, upon which most of this book was based, thanks to the memory of Verna Lane Kusz.

And special gratitude is owed to Charity Kusz, who lived with this book more closely than anyone, and who waited a very long time to go to the zoo.

Prologue

To write of those years, I climb a high bluff and look down. From this height, only shapes are visible, broad green swaths of pattern and sequence, with moments like small white houses pricking the edges. I focus in on one and it leaps to the lens, sharp and distinct, full of color, and I swing the lens left to another, and another. And when several have passed, I look out, and see them again over distance, counting them, mapping where they fall on the plain. The view from here is strange, and I find myself disoriented, like a child flying over her neighborhood for the first time, seeing her house not alone but among a thousand other houses, all alike and all different, and so much space all around. I notice, too, the streets and their crosswalks, many heading away, many more returning.

ROAD
SONGS

Our first months in Alaska, that one long summertime before I was hurt, were hard — in the way, I think, that all immigrants' lives must be hard — but they were also very grand, full of wood fires and campgrounds, full of people and the stories they told at night when we ate all together, full of clean dust that we washed from our bodies with water carried home from cold springs. My family — Mom and Dad and we four children — had driven up from Los Angeles in a green Rambler station wagon, our clothes and plants and water jugs packed and pulled behind us in a twelve-foot travel trailer with two beds. We were going for an adventure, Mom and Dad had told us, to a place where we could play as loud as we wanted to, where neighbors were far away and everyone minded their own kinds of business. During the 1968 recession, my father had been laid off from his computer job, and he and my mother had seen this as

11

their chance to break away, to act upon wishes we had made among ourselves for years, there at our table in the city. No more feeling jealous when Mom's sisters wrote from Oregon and Idaho, telling of apples in the trees and cows in the barn. We would write them now from country more raw and more our own than any Sheryl or Cara could tell of. And though the new place we came to was hard, we had come to it exhilarated and hopeful, expecting roughness and finding it, when we arrived, more to our taste than all we had relinquished behind us.

These were the things my parents had shed us of, shrugging up out of them like clothing grown too small around their shoulders: a house on southeast L.A.'s Chester Street, tall and white from its days as a farmhouse, sitting on a double city lot with outbuildings, a play-house, a garden, magnolias and roses and fenced-in grass; blackberry vines I hunted through for ripeness while Mom talked to a neighbor over the fence; chinning bars hung from the trees where Leslie and I played, shouting our voices over car sounds on the boulevard one block over; a mortgage that Mom and Dad paid by having one or two jobs each, working different shifts when they could to save sending their children into the care of my grandmother; city people with good clothes and white teeth and deftly styled hair, smiling in church and mixing about afterward, speaking of dishwashers and diets and how to keep oil stains off the driveway.

We were gone from these things long before we moved away, living our days through my father's Polish songs and my mother's spoken dreams, through stories Dad told at night of Europe, of the war, of times when people survived picking mushrooms and roasting whole pigs to render off the fat of them. He protected us children, in those early days, from the hard parts of war, referring instead to the land. He spoke his father's name, and those of his brothers, telling of the trees outside the prison camps, the berries growing at their feet, the times when, after escaping one camp or another, he and his brothers grabbed handfuls of these, filling their mouths and sucking their fingers clean. And the people there, he said, the people of the land . . . Far back in the woods, with no one but family nearby, a man might walk the yard in his underwear, just because he could. Through the stories my mother, and then we all, had turned nostalgic for places we had never seen, countries full of trees and cold rivers and neighbors far apart. My father's privilege as an airline worker was to fly us low-cost just about anywhere, and we went as often as we could, and as far. Dad showed us France, and England, even Germany, visiting small villages there to give thanks to the one or two masters who had been kind to him back when he had been a Polish boy-prisoner on their farms. I played there on brick pavement with children who spoke none of my language but who could teach me their games just as well. My special friend in Germany was Heidi, a blond child with a face like a heart, wearing pointed shoes and old jeans and a checked flannel shirt tucked in. She was the granddaughter of the man who had used Dad's brother Pietrek on his farm — the only man in the village, Dad told us later, who had not been a Nazi then.

In the middle of hopscotch, Heidi would tell her friends to wait, and pull me down the alley. "Come on," she said, for it seemed to me then that I understood her speech, and we went into a candy store with glass counters taller than I was, and lights shining down on licorice and hard candy and more chocolates than I had ever seen in my life. Heidi knew the shopkeeper there, standing in his thick white apron and belly, and she spoke to him, grabbing my arm and pointing to me, making the introductions. I held up a hand and waved, and Heidi flashed a hand toward the glass case. What did I want, she asked. I pointed out my choice, and the round man packed up a pile of chocolate disks with white sprinkles, and later, when I showed the bag to my father, he murmured, "Ah, *bon-bons*. I remember." We sat on the bed and shared them, my father biting down and beginning a new story — telling, not of the beatings he received as a prisoner there, but about candy, about *bon-bons* snuck into the hay and eaten there in secret with his brother. Later, back in the States, when my mother drove the freeway at rush hour, she said to me, or to herself, I couldn't tell, "It's hard to get used to this again, isn't it. This enormous number of people." Young as I was, I understood her, wondered how she had heard me thinking of Europe, of Heidi's tall brick house and its trees, the goats wandering there, the flowers not planted but wild. So, over time, my parents' hunger to leave the city became my own, appeased but never satisfied by short trips and by stories of lives they had led long ago.

But mostly it was the imagination tales, and not the real ones from way back, that pushed us forward out of those days. My parents read to us from New England realty catalogues, and then from books on Alaska, discovering in them moose and snowshoe hares, fish in silted rivers, squirrels so bold that they ran through your feet. Arriving home after work, Mom would drop her coat at the door and call, "Look. I picked this up today," and she would hold open a catalogue with her hand, sitting at the table among us, pointing out a farm cottage in Maine — "A creek and twenty acres," Dad said. "I like that one" — or another farther south, all of them green and raw in our minds, all distilled into hope. My mother had moved to California from Vermont when she was very young, and what she remembered of the wild — berry jam on the stove, swallows out the window — and what my father remembered for himself became the skeletal narrative of our future, and we filled it in with log houses heated by firewood and standing alone in the center of miles and miles of land. Ours was a storytelling family even in pleasing times, and in those days my parents looked on words as our sustenance, rich in their flavor and wholesome for the soul.

They had come, my parents said later, to distaste for civilization — for its people, its small and self-absorbed borders — and to impatience as well, a churning in their bellies to be elsewhere, in places much newer and still greatly older than this. Over years, they had observed in themselves a continuing unlikeness to their society, a growing unease during pinochle parties or church potlucks. Before we children had arrived, they had sampled and cast aside all the lives they could find in that place, and by the time we left for Alaska, my parents had run through what options the city had for them, performing light opera and theater, going to college, training in computers and business and even — for Mom — flight attendance. My father had played handball but hated to talk it with his friends. "A game," he would say, "is not a religion." My mother had shocked the neighbors by bearing a child one evening and coming home to weed the pomegranates and to tend her other children next morning. She said, "It's the women giving birth in the rice paddies and getting on with the job. They're putting us to shame." She despised sewing and cleaning and housewife domesticity, and she furnished the house with secondhand things, again to the shock of the churchfolk.

When they spoke at card parties of their wish to move north, someone would say, "Oh, pass the corn chips. Such IDEAS, you two." Or, "Look what you have here," people told them. "A big house, grass for the kids, good jobs. You can visit anyplace on the airline. There's no need, you know, to MOVE anywhere."

It was a fine existence, my parents agreed, but it was not a life. Perhaps my mother's roaming urge had grown through the stories

17

my father told of other places, but then she had always — even growing up — salivated over other people's slide shows, their dinner-time shots of fishing trips and excursions into the hills. Perhaps, too, she had begun already to notice how even her marriage was peculiar here; whereas an average and comfortable existence left her and Dad flailing separately toward air, a hard time threw them into each other, backs together, faces toward the fire. Their marriage was, as was anyone else's, a companionship, yes, but mainly it was an alliance, and a too-long time of peace might make it grow lazy, the treaty dusty and forgotten. As for my father himself, and his impetus to move far away, he had seen human bondage and come to know freedom, and he could not recognize in that city or its people a concern for either one.

And their unrest in California increased until, when they had four children and a job and a half each, there arrived the days of our running-away trips abroad, of dreaming aloud every evening and looking at real-estate books. The stories themselves did not begin here, I think, for I remember always having heard them; but now they were told with a note of intensity, before and after each trip, as if the idea of wilderness was becoming for them, not a wish, but the real future.

So they listed the house with an agent, and sold all our things, buying with the money a twelve-foot travel trailer and spare parts for the car, and they shopped in junk stores for a log stripper, for a two-man saw, for paper plates and mosquito spray and rifles and hatchets and knives. In all this, they made certain to involve us children, leading us down aisles and demonstrating the proper use of each thing they touched. "A log stripper," my father told us, squatting down to our height, "takes the bark off like this. And when all the logs are done, we build the house. Bedrooms with windows and the sun coming in." Their voices lifted, it seemed, the very air around us, and we children asked questions — "Can we have a tree house there" — and spoke our own plans: fishing, and tiny gardens of our own, and letters back home to our grandfather, telling him all about snowmen.

In the interest of space, we children each had to leave some dear things behind: tricycles, favorite toys, a small wicker rocking chair my sister Leslie had sat in. At our moving sale, Leslie ran after the man who bought her rocker, screaming, "Mommy, he's stealing my chair," and Mom picked her up and consoled her, smiling at the man and waving him away. Before we left, then, when we still were packing up the trailer, Mom took us secondhand shopping, helping each of us to choose an overnight bag to call his or her "treasure chest." I was six, the oldest child, and my treasure chest, I thought, was the most grown up: tan leather with brass, and a mirror in the lid. Leslie's was square-cornered, burgundy Naugahyde, and she filled it with four-year-old things: a mirror, a comb, dolls, crayons, picture books. My brother, Ian, was three, and his treasure chest opened from the side with shiny metal buckles; it was gray-and-white-plaid molded plastic, and looked like him, I thought. Bethel was just one, so we voted together on hers: a miniature square suitcase of denim over hard sides. When we bought them, Mom told us to choose carefully what we put inside, to keep only things that were really treasures, because these chests were all we could afford room for on the trip. We selected with great care the things for our cases, holding up doll clothes to the light, folding our possessions down inside. Among my own things were a rabbit-fur collar beaded with pearls — a gift once from Mom — and an India-rubber porcupine Dad gave me for having my tonsils out, which squeaked when you buried a finger in its quills, and assorted European coins from our trips overseas.

After garage sales and a great many trips to Goodwill, each of us was left holding to his or her belly that small suitcase, that finite and intimate collection of all we had picked out ourselves, and we loaded them softly into the trailer, solemn then at the thought — and full of wonder, too — that for the first time each of us owned something, had sorted through the cosmos and chosen out what jewels we could find that would fit within the space of our hands. Mom punched out our names on label tape and stuck them on our treasure chests, and later, during the trip, we would open them in our laps, or lean our heads against them when we slept. At church that last time, Mom stood in a bathroom stall while at the sinks a woman spoke to two others, saying, "I mean, *Alaska!* It's so hilarious, like they're off to be pioneers. Or missionaries, or hippies, or something even worse . . ." And then Mom exited the stall and stood smiling — unsure, she said later, why she felt no wound.

But there were others at the last, neighbors and real friends, who came to say goodbye, telling Mom and Dad to make good, bidding them godspeed. It was March, and kindergarten was not yet out for me, so people brought over books, saying to read them on the way. My grandfather came to fill his eyes with us, looking hard and slow, and my father's brother Pietrek swore at this mad parting and drew my father aside, saying, "I know this was your wife's idea." He shook his head then and moved to his car, pulling out coats and wool blankets and handing them over, making his final pronouncement: "You'll be back in two months." Dad laughed at Pietrek, kissed him on both cheeks, and spoke Polish words into his ear. "When I see you, brother, you'll be guest in a house I built from scratch with my own trees."

And then we were gone, body and spirit. It was Saturday, and while the neighborhood slept in, before it was time for cartoons, my father bent over the wheel and gave thanks, asking guidance, safety, good fortune. It was the shortest prayer we had ever heard him make — no call for peace to the hungry, no mention of imprisoned saints — and when he was finished, Dad rolled down the window and stuck out his bugle, sounding the charge to battle. We were out of sight before the neighbors could reach their doors.

We were heading toward Alaska, Mom told us, but only toward it; if, on the way, some-place else possessed us, we would stay there and begin living. It hardly seemed likely, even then, that having studied Alaska so faithfully we would stop just short of it, but it was the spirit of the day to abandon certainty, and her words sounded good in our ears, and full of command.

We had prepared for this road trip as we had for all the others, the weekend drives to Mexico, the "explorings" into mountains, the rides to look at Death Valley, where we had stood together listening to the vast, breathless sound of infinite space. We readied ourselves first by choosing food: packing hard rolls and butter in a bag, buying mustard and onions and cheese or some ham, adding at the last apples, cold soda, a thermos of water. When it came time to eat, Dad passed his pocketknife to Mom and she slit open rolls, filling them first and then passing them back to us children, and we all shared the same soda, drinking from the bottle and wiping off the rim. On those old drives we had felt temporarily whole and apart, our food and money measured to last out the trip, and whatever we'd brought we used up completely, for it would have seemed unfaithful somehow to save anything, to arrive back home still holding a part of what we had promised ourselves we could squander.

But this new trip was indefinite; for we carried forth the same spirit of the road but no sense of its ending. And the road itself became a new tale, one we would retell over dinner for years. We made stops on the way in northern

California, in Oregon, in Idaho to see my mother's sisters, and each of them in turn sent us off, gladly or not. In Marysville, Nora and Bob asked were we sure, did we know what we were about, and when Mom and Dad nodded yes — "I never want to see another potato bug," Mom said — Bob opened a drawer, saying, "Then you'll need this." He handed my mother a tin flour sifter, the old kind that you shook back and forth and back, spilling silk-white clouds. It was his second-to-last gift. In the morning, as he drove us junking for a flat-iron, he turned up the radio, and the announcer said, "All right, folks, let's hear it for Julius Kusz, just passing through on his way to Alaska. Here's a favorite of his from a hitch at Fort Bliss, Texas — 'I'm in the Jailhouse Now.' You all have a safe trip, hear?" Bob doubled up and swerved, laughing into his chest, and my father moaned; he loathed Country-and-Western songs, this one most of all. It had been all he could get on the radio from El Paso his first six months there in the army.

Then, before we headed north again, Nora stood grinning, and Bob said, "Keep your hearts growing; most of us never get the chance to start over." His liver would kill him before we could see him again, but until then he would send letters full of passionate encouragement, wishing us well.

We saw Cara and Vince in Oregon, watching Vince's construction business put up houses such as we wanted someday; but even their farm, once part of my parents' desire, seemed too cultivated to us now, too close to the city and far from the land. And last we stopped in Idaho to find Sheryl and Ed, the final piece of family of whom to take leave.

It was nightfall, and we were coughing out dust from the road, and rain was starting down in blurred force. Against my shoulder, Bethel slept, sucking unconsciously on her bottle, and Leslie and Ian shifted and moaned, finding no comfortable position. "Verna," my father said, "do you know where they live?"

My mother pushed up her glasses. "Not really. Maybe we should wait till morning."

So Dad turned in at a sign, "Camper Spaces: Vacancy," and without warning the wheels of the station wagon ground into the mud. Up the drive, a man looked out of a trailer window, light falling out past him on the dirt. My father said, "I'll call in a tow from the office," and Mom started singing to us children, all grown fretful now and asking for dinner.

Dad came back with a blond woman, having recognized her accent, and he spoke to her now in German, lifting up his hands. The man we had seen in the trailer walked down toward us.

In English, the woman said, "Hey Fred, you think your truck would get this out? It's that same old pothole," and having spoken nothing, the man went for his keys. When he had gotten us out, rocking forward and revving the engine, Fred slapped my father's back, and the woman lectured, "Don't be afraid to ask for help. People won't offer, but they're glad to be asked." She got us a camping space and gave German directions to Sheryl's house, and then we loaded ourselves into bed, listening to the rain.

We were delayed in Idaho for days, partly because the roads were flooding in British Columbia, but mostly because Uncle Ed was sure he could talk my parents out of their foolishness. Truckers came from up north all the time, he said, each with a different bad story. "Cold," he said, "and ice fog. It gets so they have to sleep in the truck, because if they got out they'd be lost just three feet away." Ed spoke of bears, of wolves chewing down through the roof to feed on whole families. It was not, he said, the sort of place to take children.

"But Ed," my mother said, breaking in. "What about humans. Thirty-three years I've lived in cities, and I've seen people I'm much more afraid of than bears." But Ed continued, ignoring her voice, and those evenings in the

26

trailer, as Mom and Dad sacrificed their blankets to take the chill off the rest of us, he would pound on the door and remind them, "It'll be worse in Alaska." It was to become a family refrain, repeated loudly and often whenever a prickly wind, a leaden snowfall, or a damp woolen boot liner inconvenienced us.

Ed offered Mom and Dad his second house free, if they would stay and help out on the farm. He took them driving over graveled roads, bounding too fast over ruts and large rocks, repeating, "Alaskan roads will be worse." He drove them to a back-to-earth hardware store because they asked him to, and he stood as they picked through broadaxes and saws and old-fashioned household tools. "It's primitive," he said, looking over at them. "Get back in this century." But my family scarcely heard him, laughing now and imagining specific futures where we stood all together under trees, putting these treasures to use.

Our final purchase there in Idaho was one we gave thanks for then and long thereafter. In the back of the same junk store Ed had shown us, partly dismantled and buried in piles of dust and old metal parts, was a cast-iron wood cookstove at least eighty years old. Finding it first, my mother stood saying nothing, touching it with her fingertips here, and there, calling finally for my father to come see.

The smith who had made the thing had taken great care, forming intricate scrollwork on warming racks and handles, on the overhead bread boxes, on the nickel-plated sternwheeler spanning the oven door. Across the hull of the boat, the imprint *Majestic,* and this would be our name for it. While Mom gave the dealer the thirty dollars he asked, Dad tied the stove on the roof of the station wagon, praying hard for our overloaded clutch; that evening, my parents assembled the *Majestic* in Sheryl's driveway, shining it up with stove black and lighting inside it our first fire.

We stood all around warming ourselves, Sheryl and Ed a little step out from the rest of us, and after silence and time my father said, "We cooked on these in Poland." He seemed somehow to awaken then, perhaps throwing off the final damp spirit of Ed's many lectures, and he bent forward and showed us the stove, the grates which reversed for coal or wood, the ash box like the one his own mother would empty and scatter on the garden, the oven door she pulled open to check into, releasing out past her shoulders the rye-and-wheat steam of hot bread. And not, he said, the airy stuff our family now used for toast, but real, solid bread, dense and substantial and seedy inside. He would teach us one day to bake like that, to break off the heel and butter it, to slice into the loaf with long knives.

It must have been then that Ed knew he would not dissuade us, that we were further into lunacy than he had first supposed; when we packed up our things the next day to drive off, he said, "You surely are crazy," but the venom had gone, and the energy. We waved and called out to him, and then, pulling our heads back inside, we began once again to sing road songs, choosing our favorites and shouting them out: "Wayfaring Stranger," "My Lord, I'm on My Journey," and every Russian and Polish verse my father had ever taught us.

For us, the children of the family, who remembered Mom and Dad only since they began traveling away with us, songs on the road were tradition, as much our habit as were stories from my parents' growing up, or the huge illustrated Bible they read to us at nap time. A song began with one voice — Mom's or Dad's opening out for two notes. By the third, the rest of us had it and added our parts, Mom switching to alto and taking me sometimes with her, the children's voices and the adults' mixing and widening out, a cappella.

My father's head dipped side to side, like a swimmer leaning into his strokes, bellowing out tenor and baritone from the deep, ringing caverns of himself. Mom lifted up her face, taking in air, moving back into the melody, and from her we children learned our own sopranos, the true and unmuffled phrasings, the tones directed by breath and sustained until our very bones and their hollows resonated and increased with the joy of them.

And as the stories all along had kept us whole in ourselves, the songs and the words in my father's own tongues drew in now, it seemed, the rest of the world, those alike and those unlike, but all somehow familiar friends. In Alberta, having driven one hundred miles with the trailer hitch barely holding on, we pulled up to a machinist's shop in a Polish mining town, and while a man welded another full brace onto the tongue, my father stood in the street and spoke loud hilarity with his countrymen. The town, it seemed, had not changed in five decades, and the men there spoke of "renting" local women at the saloon, paying them cash on the spot if they would dance and drink for the evening. "They wear nice clothes," the men said. "And hair, too. A man needs that kind of company." In the end, the machinist charged just eight dollars, and was astonished that my parents had expected to pay much more. "I only charge what's fair," he huffed. "I'm not some guy from the States, sticking it to you like a thief. That hitch should get you where you're going now."

Elsewhere on the way, there were Slavic shopkeepers and German grocers, many of whom handed candy to us children and accepted no payment, all of whom were glad enough to talk to my father, to speak their old language out loud. My mother listened for the words she could recognize, keeping up as best she could with the conversation, and what she didn't get, my father filled in for us later as we drove.

But there were other good people, too, English-speakers not drawn to us by language, or by song, or by anything visible we could name; and soon it was clear that this fresh sort of kindness was new, not to the world, but only to us, and that my parents were seeing what they had imagined in their stories all along: people more our kind than we were ourselves. There were young men alone in small trucks who pulled us up steep hills or fiddled under the hood when our engine gave out, waving us on our way and grinning. At Liard Hot Springs, we met a Cherokee man named Bob with degrees in mining and geology, who spent summers in Alaska and winters in Florida and who lived year-round in a camper on back of his pickup. He would tell us anything we wanted to know about the road, and offer any help, but he would refuse my parents' offer of a tiny heater for his camper; it was as if, my mother wrote later, a cup of coffee he could accept as hospitality, but a slice of bread might obligate him, or give one the right to tell him what to spread on it. My parents' hearts warmed to him, and much later he would drink coffee with us again at the Fairbanks campground, and would drive with us out to see the land we had bought, scouting it over with my father and approving it with a grand gesture of his arm.

We met Dick and Esther there on the road, on an evening when we had pulled into a shaded campground, nursing a weary clutch. Having unloaded the trailer to make room for us on the beds, my family ate dinner and Dad got out his guitar. "Hey, Julius," Mom said, "look over there." She pointed across the way to a school bus painted white, with Alaskan license plates and "Destination: Adventure" painted in black over the windshield. Beside it at the picnic table, a man like Santa Claus and a red-haired woman and two children drank something out of mugs, warming their hands around them. My father got up and walked over, still strumming, and the rest of us followed.

"Are you Alaskans?" Dad asked, and the children of our families said hi to one another, handing our names around: from us, Natalie, Leslie, Ian, and the baby, Bethel, and from them, a girl my age named Toni, and a boy Leslie's age called Barry.

"As much Alaskans as anything else, I suppose," the man said. "Wait a second." And he stepped into the bus and brought out a guitar. He joined in the tune my father was still playing, and while Esther, his wife, told my mother their story, Dick and my father made music, each beginning songs the other had never heard, while the other picked them up and varied the tune. They played cowpoke songs and pop ballads, European folk music and medleys of all sorts, moving up and down the frets for long stretches, then strumming for a bit while they took up the conversation. The talk and the music lasted into the night, long after bedtime for us children, but the adults indulged us and let us play, luxuriating as they were in one another's company.

Dick and Esther had a cabin in Fairbanks, having once lived there steadily for thirteen years. Now they spent mostly summers in Alaska, working road construction, but Dick was also a postcard photographer, a piano tuner, a bona fide sourdough, and a man who played almost as many instruments as my father did. Whereas Dad had learned his music out of necessity as a four-year-old in war, when he and his father and brothers had been minstrel violinists playing on German streets for small coins, Dick apparently had just loved his gift and developed it, experimenting with and mastering whatever instrument he ran across in the way. Winters now, he ran a photography studio in Phoenix, and he had had to restrain himself that first night, he said later, from capturing our "unloading act" on film. Until he mentioned it, we hadn't noticed the comic nature of our evening ritual; as we moved in and out of the trailer with boxes and plants and garage-sale relics, piling them on the ground and going back for more, and more, and still more, we must indeed have looked like the "Laugh-In" gang, spilling out ten at a time from a VW bug. Wanting not to risk offense, Dick never got our photograph, but for all the jokes we made of it over years, he might as well have shot a whole roll. For this family, too, became one of our own, part of the collection of friends we carried forward with us into summer, into winter, into years where our best times were those when we told the old stories.

It was hard parting in the morning, though

we promised to meet again in Fairbanks. Before that, Dick and Esther would be pressing fast toward Dawson Creek — "Piano-tuning jobs," Dick said — and we would be taking more time, nursing the car along, ogling the land. The road had been hard on the station wagon, hard on the trailer hitch, hard on us all, even kept alive as we were by my parents' gestures at all we drove by, and their continued imaginings of the end of the journey. They had prepared as well as they could for the trip, stocking a cache of spare parts and extra blankets, but even so there was much they had to cope with on the way.

Not the least of this was their parcel of children. In my memory, we were all exceptionally good, and my parents claimed later that this was true. Still, I recall a great deal of ingratiating talk on my mother's part, her head turning back toward us as she spoke in a bright voice, calming us. The car engine died one day without warning, and my father pulled to the shoulder, looking up and down the road, seeing no other travelers. In the back seat, Ian and I were looking out windows, and Leslie was poking through her treasure chest, holding up things for the baby to see.

"Hang on," my father said to Mom. "I'll open the hood." He got out and raised it, and my mother turned around to us, saying, "A little patience, while Daddy fixes the motor." It was this call for good behavior which, at least for me, brought perversely and immediately to mind the fact that I was uncomfortable. My legs were starting to numb, and my face itched. I shifted in my seat, straightening my legs and bumping the children next to me down the row. Ian felt the crush last, for he was at the other end, and he stopped looking outside, saying, "Mommy, the sun is too hot. It's burning me through the window."

"Roll the window down, then, and lean away from the light."

"No, it's the back windows," Leslie said. "The ones that don't open."

"Hold on until we get going again. Be patient." Mom called out to my father, "Is it the battery?" She always asked this, about any mechanical problem.

My father's face leaned around the hood, wearing that look, my mother said later, "that would have chilled flowing lava." "If it is," he said, "we're in trouble. Let's see, we have a new generator somewhere. I'll try changing that."

"Oh-h-h," Mom drawled, and her voice sounded long and ingenuous, the way it commonly did for jokes. "What a good rule of thumb. 'When in doubt, see what you've brought.' "

My father laughed and batted her through the window, passing by toward the trailer. Mom spoke again to us children, pacifying us while my father worked, and when he looked around the hood and called, "Verna, try starting it," she did, and the engine came right on. In the back, we children jumped up and down on the seat, shouting, "Hooray," and Mom said, "Now we'll leave the windows open for some wind, but only for a minute, or the dust will get all over us."

Another time, just before the trailer hitch had been repaired, my father had been driving far into the night, wincing as the hitch dragged bottom at every slight bump, hoping to come across a town. My mother was shining a light on the Milepost in her lap, trying to make out where we were, and finally she said, "I can't tell how far we've come since that café. I don't know. Maybe we'd better stop."

"Yeah, okay." My father slowed the car. "We'd better. I can hardly focus on the road anymore." He pulled again to the side, but it was so dark beyond the headlights that he and my mother could not be sure they were fully off the highway. "The children are mostly asleep," Mom whispered. "Let's not set up the trailer."

My father went for our pillows and blankets, shivering out loud breaths when he slid back under the wheel. "It's a good thing," he said, "that this seat makes into a bed. We'll have to share body heat." In the folded-down back seat, I heard him, and watched for a minute at the sudden absence of headlights before I fell asleep again.

Leslie and the others woke me up in the morning, pushing up against me and crying miserably. My feet in their socks were chilled through, and across my shoulders Ian pressed the cold cloth onto my skin, making me jump. "Daddy," I yelled, "turn on the heater. Please, hurry." The others were still crying, and Mom groaned, "Yes, do. It's freezing." She leaned over and turned the ignition herself, flipping on the heater switches.

Mom stiffened and grabbed on her glasses. "Oh, good grief," she said. "Julius, look outside."

My father sat up and said nothing for a moment, and began slowly to laugh, building it up to a roar. Leslie rolled away to see out the window — pulling the blankets with her and making Ian cry — and she asked, "What's so funny, Daddy."

"Of all the places," my father said. "I had to park in a refrigerator." Now I sat up myself and looked at what had been there last night in the darkness. Everything was white, even the trees, and mountains angled steeply upward on both sides of the road. In front of us, the highway itself was snow-on-gravel, and it bent around to the right, lost behind the nearest mountain. "Children," my mother said, "let's wait for the heater to work, and we'll eat breakfast in the car." We had rolls and cold oranges and pieces of cheese, and Dad promised us tea when we could find a place with hot water.

And then the last day came. All morning we had sung songs, expending all the air inside us; the loud cacophony of our tires pulling over gravel was so familiar now that we hardly heard it, it had always been there, we would always shout like this to be heard. I was leaning my neck back into the seat, and the jolting of my head up and down was like my mother bouncing Bethel on her hip. For an hour now or longer, Dad had been asking, "How much farther," and Mom had been answering, her finger in the Milepost, "Any time, I think. I can't tell, but soon."

Then: "There it is," my father shouted, and we all looked, seeing, a thousand feet ahead, a small brown sign, its white letters reading, "Welcome to Alaska, The Last Frontier."

Later, none of us could say who started it; it seemed, in fact, that we all began together. However it was, a countdown began, and Ian joined in more strongly than usual, for this was the astronauts' song. "TEN," my father shouted, louder than any of us, and we raised our volume to his level. And "nine, eight . . . seven," slowing down the numbers, making them come out even until, just as we passed the sign, we hollered, "One . . . ALASKA," and we slapped all the knees, our own and each other's.

But we were startled immediately into silence, shocked at the loudness of ourselves. For at the border the road changed to pavement, and after we jounced through the few rocks spilled over on the asphalt, a vivid smoothness spread out underneath us, and the car seemed to go faster, the trailer become lighter on its hitch, and my father's hands looser on the wheel. At my mother's word, we opened the windows wide for the first time in weeks, blowing the dust out behind us.

POSSESSING
THE LAND

We had taken our time and not reached Alaska until May. All along the way, we had collected friends like Dick and Esther, strange and interesting people traveling in revamped school buses or vans or Volkswagens, all of them heading for Alaska as we were, and we arranged to camp in the same spots, and to meet ourselves together at the end.

The end for us would be Fairbanks, for my parents had studied the guidebooks and decided against Anchorage; it was a bigger city, they said, and likely another suburbia. "And besides," Dad told us, grinning while he drove. "Besides. Fairbanks is right in the middle, farthest away from the edges." After the border, it would be a long day's drive to get there, so first we stopped in Tok, pulling in close to a laundromat built inside a huge old water tank. There were showers there and we all had one, soaping our chests and watching brown foam run off us down the drain. All

41

our clothes, every pillow, every blanket, were filled with road dust, and while Mom stuffed them all into washers, we children watched Dad hose down the trailer, shooting water on the windows so we could see through them again. While he worked, Dad pointed out the trees for us, naming black and white spruce, thin birches and willows by the Russian and Polish names he remembered: *sosna, brzoza, wierzbina.* "And you can make syrup from birch," he said. "Like maple, only lighter. But it takes a lot of boiling, steams up the whole house."

After showers and laundry, it was already 7 p.m., and Mom and Dad packed our linens into the station wagon, afraid to dirty them again on the dust inside the trailer. We found a campground with water spigots, and in the morning while Leslie and Ian and I made fairy countries on miniature moss hills, Bethel put rocks in her mouth and swallowed some before we caught her; our parents cleaned out the trailer, washing dishes and sponging walls and holding drawers out the door, tapping out the dust. Dad untacked the cardboard from the trailer's front window, for on the paved road there was less danger of flying rocks. "Just in case, though," he told Mom, "let's leave the rubber mat under the gas tank." We children got bored watching, and we asked to go walk on the trails, standing close to the door while we spoke and putting our heads inside. "Not yet," Mom said. "We'll all take a walk later. Right now go as far as that fence, but stay where we can see you." She pointed to the edge of the camp, to the string of logs stretched between upright posts, marking a boundary through the woods. "Natalie, you're in charge."

"Can we sit on it?" I asked, and Dad looked out. "Okay," he said, "and watch Bethel."

"Yay," Leslie called, "Ian, let's run," and they raced bouncing on new moss, waving their arms and falling down. We all lay against the fenceposts, talking, then Ian climbed up and bent his body over, hanging from his waist and looking at us upside down. "You look funny," he said.

"You do, too." Leslie reached through the logs and grabbed a dry grass growing on the other side. She broke it off long and put the stalk in her mouth, looking at me over the feathery end. "I'm a farmer," she said, laughing, looking silly, and then the rest of us were reaching for grasses, holding our feet on the near side so as not to break Mom's rule, straining our torsos through the posts.

"Stay off the fence." It was a man's voice through the trees, and we all stopped, searching him out. He was, it turned out, a Bureau of Land Management chief, wearing polished boots and a hat in the woods, and he told us, "This is not a playground."

I was afraid and looked back toward the trailer, but Mom and Dad were inside somewhere out of sight. "We just wanted a piece of that grass," I said to the man. "It doesn't grow on this side."

"That grass is not part of the campground. Leave it alone."

I picked Bethel up and led the others to the trailer, and by the time we got there Leslie and Ian were crying. My voice wavered when I told the story, and I finished, "We weren't doing anything wrong, Daddy, really." Our father pulled us in together and said, "It's okay, you're not in trouble," and then I started to cry, for I never could help it when he hugged me. Mom stood alongside, looking out toward the fence. She spoke, quiet and angry: "They get their bureaucrats from the Lower 48. We're obviously too close to the border." In an hour, we were back on the road to Fairbanks.

We arrived there at midday, stopping in the center of town on Lacey Street next to the Rexall Co-op Drug Store. The streets — one main one and four or five perpendicular — were roughly paved, but there were no curbs yet or sidewalks, and Dad drove

44

slowly into the gravel parking lot, easing the trailer over canyon-deep potholes. "Let's walk around awhile," he said, turning off the car. "Give the shocks a rest." We walked along Cushman Street holding hands, and we found a J. C. Penney's, a Ward's and a Sears catalogue outlet, a Woolworth with a lunch counter, and a Safeway grocery store next to the post office. The people we passed were dressed just like us, in work clothes and plain hair cut with kitchen scissors, driving trucks and cars nearly as muddy as ours before we had washed it. The pickups were full of coal or lumber, and straw brooms and snow shovels stuck up like flags from the holes along the truckbed sides. A man passed us on foot, grinning and waving hello, and we children smiled back, staring at the beard reaching down to his chest. Back at the Co-op we all went inside, and while Dad paid for ice cream cones, Mom asked about campgrounds to park a trailer in.

"There's only one yet," the woman said, "unless they've opened the site out at Chena River. You're a couple weeks ahead of most campers, so you should find a spot just fine."

"We won't need it long," Mom told her, taking a cone. "Just till we get some land."

The woman grinned. "Yeah, well, that's one thing we got a lot of."

So we collected in Growden Park, free in those days to travelers and full always of people arriving and those going away. We stayed there under trees, meeting people, and every day when someone new arrived, Mom had them over to our picnic table, asking them their stories, breathing in all this history. Dad unhitched the trailer and set up the stabilizers, and we stacked our things alongside under tarps. We took the car along all the roads we could find, driving faster now without the trailer's weight, and left a note on Dick and Esther's cabin, telling them where to find us. Cherokee Bob drove in from the highway, and so did other old traveling friends, and we had small reunions outside at the tables, cooking over fires and spraying bug dope on our skin. The men and single women looked for work during the days and played guitars and violins and concertinas in the slow times, laughing at how bright the sun stayed, even at two in the morning. At night, I sat on a log and listened to the talk, to stories and jokes made there and carried on for years, and long after I went to the trailer for bed, I could still hear my father laughing or arguing in German, Polish, or Serbo-Croatian to those around us who spoke with such tongues.

On an evening when the laughter was very

good, and the mosquitoes and gnats very thick in the air, I sat at the picnic table closest to my father, spreading chili on a bun. A man walked up close then, smiling, showing a chipped tooth in a clean, wide face, and he held out a hand to Dad, asking what was his accent, it sounded familiar. "Polish," my father said, and he grabbed the man's hand, shaking it hard. "That's where I came from. What's yours?"

Oscar was Roumanian, he said, last name of Daum, and although I had never been able to hear my father's accent, having grown up so close to it, I could hear Oscar's and thought it was magic, pronounced with a tongue held softly behind the teeth. Oscar had seen our California license plates when he had pulled in with his family, and now he and my parents compared notes, finding that we were here from similar parts south, with similar stories of the road. Oscar would bring his brother, wife, and kids to meet us, he said, when they came back from getting groceries. My father made introductions all around, and Oscar winked at me. "Those blue eyes," he said, "where'd you get them?" He sat down and accepted coffee in a Styrofoam cup, with two sugars and a cream. Was Dad looking for work, he asked.

My father nodded. "Oh, yeah."

"Carpenter's Union is hiring."

"I don't know carpentry," Dad said. "Wish I did."

Oscar grinned and his forehead moved back. He drank some coffee, laughing over the rim. "No problem. The union steward's Polish — you got an in right there. Say a few words in the language, and you're on."

We all laughed then with our heads back, and Mom passed Oscar the coffee. Dad joked, "Hey, if the building goes up crooked, they just blame it on the Polack. They shake their heads and they say, 'But you can't fire him. He speaks so pretty.' " My family was not quick to use the word *friend*, but we counted Oscar as one from that first day, and later, when his family drove up honking in a jeep, we took them as part of us as well.

Vic was Oscar's brother, but no one would have known that just by looking. Where Oscar was tall and broad, Vic was short and mousy, darker of skin, and with a much more throaty accent. But Vic had the same thick fingers, the same prankster's eyes, the same way of pulling my ears and chuckling when he made a joke. He had in common with Oscar, too, and also with my father, a driving sense of family, the outcome of too many years of war, of being citizens dispersed and wandering across Europe, fleeing the Nazi invasions.

Though it was still early in the summer, Vic was already homesick for his wife, daughter, and sons, chafing to make his summer income and to take it back to them in California. First thing he would do back home, he said, was put on a T-shirt and take his boys four-wheeling in the desert. Vic's favorite thing was to play verbal war with Oscar's wife, Jean, teasing at her for small things until she slapped him with her shoe.

Jean was English, a lover of small comforts like running water, and she had come along this year only after Oscar had gotten some Alaskan friends to write her, describing moose and rabbits, and hundreds of unpolluted lakes, and sky so blue it made the eyes raw. Until Jean came to the park, Mom had been the one we called "mosquito feast," because, no matter how many of us there were around a fire, the bugs all went straight for her. Now Jean deserved the name, too, even doused with repellent, and she and Mom called us children over from the trees to count who had the most scabs around her ankles. It was always about even.

Their daughter, Nicky, was my age, and Tyrone about Leslie's, and we spent our days and nights sharpening wooden spears and going off into combat. Our enemies were the leeches in the pond; we made up fierce tales

49

about them and the ways they treated prisoners, and we stood at the water's very edge, stabbing down into the blackness, careful never to get ourselves wet. If we did, we were captured, and if we lost a spear, that too was a casualty of war, and we called time out then while we ran to the woods for more sticks.

When the Daums had left California, their favorite commercial was one where a polo player introduced himself as Rodney, and droned on in a Harvard accent how he had everything in life and would "hahdly" use any mouthwash but Listerine. Now anyone who had more than Jean did was "Rodney" to her, and although the joke was hers originally, we all carried it through to its limits. It started out that the Airstream caravans that came through were full of Rodneys. My family of six slept inside a bare twelve feet of trailer; Oscar and Jean and their two kids were in a barn-red makeshift on wheels; and Vic slept in his jeep, so anyone had to be a Rodney who shared a thirty-foot Airstream with only one other person. After that, a Rodney was someone with bath fixtures or a portable toilet. And later, when winter was closer, "Rodney" made its way down to people already prepared with parkas and mukluks. "What a Rodney," someone would say, and the rest of us would straighten up our necks, looking superior.

I suppose we were all very poor. Until the forest fires started and the men went off to fight them, we lived on what little we'd brought with us, dishing it out for each other and sharing what we had. On the road, Dick and Esther had taught us to make Russian Tea, mixing Tang and cinnamon and powdered tea in a jar, and before they arrived in Fairbanks, we taught it to all the others, drinking it nights at the tables. We wore our clothes threadbare, made friends with a go-go dancer and her children, with two women in a van, with a college student who braided my hair in loops around my ears. Linda could make blueberry jam, too, the way the Eskimos did it, and I watched and got in her way when she tanned another camper's moose hide. The go-go dancer offered us her malamute and Mom looked sideways and said, uh, she didn't know. "Oh, please, Mommy," we all said. "He's not mean at all. Look. He's afraid of *everything*. He gets scared if you even look like you're mad. And we need a dog if we go live in the woods." Finally, Mom took him, and she named him Hobo and played howling games with him in the evenings.

When the city became restless with the squatters in the park, we all moved on to a campsite by the river, and everyone worked at small jobs to earn money for land. Once a day, a sternwheeler churned by, filled with tourists, and we all stopped talking to hear the captain broadcasting insults over the loudspeaker. "And here are the gypsies," he would intone. "These people have squatted on every free acre in the state. We're hoping they don't take a shine to City Hall." After the riverboat was past, Mom would snort and clean her glasses. "Huh," she would say. "Rodneys."

Oscar and Vic got a private contract building A-frames for a widow, and they offered to split the take with Dad if he wanted to help. It wasn't much money, especially divided three ways, but the brothers said they were glad to have Dad, and pretended it was too much work for just the two of them. And later they introduced Dad to foremen on union jobs, setting him up so he could make a living on his own. My father learned that summer to fight fires, to build houses, and to construct roads, and my mother learned powdered milk and to keep her children from drowning in the river.

My family did buy land, a hundred miles away in Delta Junction with no road in, 258 acres of spruce, birch, and willow. Mom's Uncle Ray wired up money, half enough for the down payment, and on the phone Mom thanked him, saying, "You're not rich, either.

And I don't know exactly when we can pay you back."

"It's okay," Uncle Ray said. "Your dad and I, we're brothers. We have to look out for family." Whenever my parents could afford it, he told her, then they could talk about repayment; for now, buy the land and prosper, and take pictures when she could, and let him know how the place looked. It was the first of many times he would come to our aid, and long after, when I was grown, he would send me checks every year, saying, "Divide this however you see best; you know who in the family needs what right now."

We bought the land sight unseen, and Bob told my parents this was foolish, it might be swamp, for all they knew. So we all drove to Delta one day and Bob came along, and he stood on a hill among trees, looking around and approving. We wrote happy thanks to Uncle Ray, borrowing a camera and sending him photos. Oscar and Vic bought land closer to Fairbanks, and when the river flooded too high to make the campground safe, they talked my parents into moving our trailer onto their place. It was too late in the summer to build for ourselves in Delta, so we accepted the offer, and our families spent a week raising walls for a room onto the trailer, digging space for an outhouse with two seats for company and no front wall. Summer work ran out, so the men were always at home, or hunting rabbits for dinner, or catching union calls in town. My mother hauled water from the Fox River spring fifteen miles off, and my father stood out in morning frost, playing reveille on his bugle. Until the outhouse was built over its hole, I got up early every day to climb down inside and rescue what lemmings had fallen in during the night. It was the best mousetrap I could imagine, and I was glad to stroke the tiny, pumping chests before I reached up and put the animals out of the pit. Later, after the outhouse was done, two of us would sit there — myself, and Toni or my sister Leslie — hanging our wrists over our knees, looking out at the woods and telling stories; we were careful to listen and to scream warning if we heard footsteps coming around through the leaves.

The air was beginning to chill now, and frost covered the morning trees. Cranes and Canadian geese flew southward through the air, their calls falling down around us even when the birds were too high to be seen. Beginning this first fall, the flight of birds would forever signal this urgency in our bellies, this earnest race to finish the project of setting our family up for winter. It was August already, and the trailer addition had no windows, to save heat leaking out, but it had no insulation, either, and before the real cold came, we had to have a woodstove. Over the summer Oscar and Vic had shown us the Army Surplus Store, had helped us carry home bunk beds, and folding chairs, and mosquito netting for the trailer door. Now we made more trips, for winter things this time, buying a tent stove that burned both oil and wood, a length of stovepipe, a great stainless-steel freezer box to keep bears out of our food. From hardware stores came kerosene lamps and a yellow chainsaw so heavy that only the men could lift it. These things weren't expensive, but they cost as much as we had; my father's forehead took on many lines, and his eyes looked hard at my mother when he opened his wallet and showed her the inside.

And then Oscar discovered the dump.

He drove up the road fast one day, honking the horn and waving. He had just taken our trash to the landfill. "Hey, Julius," he called, "get in the jeep." My father looked up from cleaning the chainsaw, and over by the trailer I looked up, too. Oscar's nose was opening and closing the way it did when he told a Polish joke and tried not to laugh. He wiggled his hand. "Julius, get in. I've got something to show you."

"Show me what?" Dad said.

Oscar pounded the seat. "Will you just get in?"

Dad put the chainsaw inside the cabin door, wiping his hands on a rag, and he climbed in beside Oscar. To my mother, Oscar called out, "We'll be back. I'm showing Julius how to get to the new dump."

The Fairbanks landfill was small and filling up, so the Post Commander had started letting civilians into the army dumpsite; the distinction between military and non-military was not that great anyway, since, during floods and fires and such, everyone worked salvage together. And because so many civilians' clothes were army surplus, people could not even be told apart by what they wore. This was fine with us; olive drab didn't get rust stains from hard water.

Oscar and Dad were gone a long time. When they got back, Dad was grinning, and there were no lines in his forehead. He stepped down from the jeep, calling, "Verna," and he reached behind his seat, pulling out a thick stainless-steel hand basin, weighing it up and down in his hand.

We were all there by then — Jean, and Vic, and us children — and my mother said, "Where . . ." Then Dad and Oscar were unloading other things, clothes in my size and "bunny boots" in theirs, and they were telling the story of the dump, mounded high, it seemed, with good things that people just threw out. Rather than ship their goods when they moved, folks would toss them away, and for years after that day, my family salvaged at the dump, taking home dishes, and blankets, and clothing, even food: C rations, beans, outdated cold cuts frozen and still in their packing cases. After we found a full ton of bagged flour, we called the place the "flour mill," and what we couldn't use we took to friends, and to the missionaries who ran a radio station off the highway.

Years later, after Fairbanks shopkeepers complained that they were losing business to the dump, Dad would be arrested just before Christmas when he went there without us, would be taken in and questioned by the M.P.s. "It's not for me only," he would say then. "There are people at the mission with kids and no money. They can use whatever clothes I can bring them." The provost there listened to Dad and interrupted. "Really? What sizes?" "Any," said Dad, and the provost went on, "My wife has all these boxes for Goodwill . . . wait here." He called together some men, and while Dad sat in the metal chair, he and they went to their quarters and brought back boxes and bags of clothing — men's and women's and children's and babies' — and told Dad to take them, and not to get caught again at the dump.

But all that was not for a long time yet; for now, standing by the jeep and pulling out trash bags, we knew only to be happy. And that evening Dad told us the story of the ravens, how Elijah sat on a mountaintop with no human help to call on, and God sent the ravens to him carrying meat, and then bread, more than enough to keep him alive.

When the outhouse and trailer addition finally were done, and we had collected together most of what we needed for winter, we stood all together in front of our cabin, looking at it. Face-on, it pretended to be nothing other than itself: a tiny trailer with bulging, fly-eyed windows, attached to a plywood wanigan with a tar-paper roof and a secondhand door. In front, an army field tent stood low to the ground, covering tools and storage boxes, and against the cabin's side wall, the big metal freezer chest and two oil barrels on stilts. Smoke rose out of the stovepipe, blowing away in the wind. My father puffed breath out his cheeks, and my mother held out her arms and said, "Ah, look. It's the Rodneys." That night there was a bonfire and fresh rabbit, and my father brought out the instruments and handed them around.

Then it was time. Vic and Oscar and their

family loaded what they had into their cars, making ready to drive back Outside. Vic hugged my father around the neck, and said he wished he would have Dad's bugle around when he took his boys four-wheeling. Dad ran inside and back again, and pushed the bugle through Vic's open window, saying, "Here. You can tell your kids where this has been." Vic said no, he could not take this, it was not right, he had nothing to exchange for it. My father pushed out his lips for a minute, looking at his friend, and he said, "Okay, we'll trade. You promise you'll read the Bible through once, and I give you my horn." Fair deal, Vic said, and he shook my father's hand. And now it was time. Our friends gave hugs all around and wished my father luck in finding a job. Stay here as long as we needed, they said, or stay forever, and next summer they'd all find new work together. And we would see these people again in a year, would have a whole new batch of Polish jokes; but by then other things would have changed, and the story of my family's first cold season would not be the one we had expected to tell.

My mother described the next months as the time she learned winter. At twenty below, she found, Jell-O set in half an hour, but it would freeze inward from the edges at $-40°$. Metal clung to the hands at that temperature and left burn marks on skin at −60°. Propane would still flow to the stove even at fifty below if you wound heat tape around its tank or built around it a box with a 100-watt bulb inside. The same gas dryer you put in your car's tank would keep heating oil flowing from its barrel. And some of the best places to find winter clothes were the Salvation Army and the Army Surplus Store. Oscar had said, and other friends had agreed, that in winter every person should keep a full set of clothes in the car in case of a breakdown, and bags of sand in the trunk for extra traction. All of these came from thrift stores, too, and even with the summer money running out, Mom and Dad seemed glad to buy them, because it made our stake in this place appear somehow more substantial.

Still, there was nervousness in the looks my parents gave each other, and in the breathless way my dad hurried to the car every morning on his way to the union hall in town. Our summer friends had said to prepare for a jobless winter, to earn what we could before snowfall, because no one built houses or put through any roads in the cold. Yet our own building materials and car repairs had cost my parents most of what they had had to spare, and now that November had come, and the thermometer read −41°, there was almost nothing left for stove oil or for food. During this time, I was the only one of us sure of getting a fully balanced meal every day; my first-grade teacher had sent home an application for free hot lunch after she had noticed me asking for credit several days in a row. Leslie and Ian learned to be happy with anything — oatmeal, egg noodles, fresh rabbit when there was some — and while they ate, Mom put powdered milk in Bethel's bottle, and fed her the soft food with a spoon.

Our nearest neighbors through the trees were the Horners, two cabins of cousins whose sons went to my school. Paul was in my class, Kevin was a year ahead, and both their families had moved here, as we had, from California, escaping the city and everything frightening that lived there. Kevin had a grown brother in L.A. who was comatose now since he'd been hit on the freeway; his mother, Geri, had come with her brother-in-law's family to Alaska to get well, she hoped, from her own mental breakdown, and to keep herself as far as she could from automobiles.

Paul and Kevin Horner were my best friends then, and we played with our dogs in the cousins' houses, or in the wide snowy yard in between. On weekends or days off from school, my parents took us sledding and to the gravel pit with our skates. Sometimes, if the day was long enough, Paul and Kevin and I followed rabbit tracks through the woods, careful not to step right on the trails for fear of leaving our scent there — for fear, that is, that the rabbits would abandon them. We mapped all the new trails we could find, and my mother gave me orders about when to be home. Bears, she said, and we laughed, said didn't she know they were asleep, and we could all climb trees anyway. We were not afraid, either, when Mom warned of dog packs. Dogs got cabin fever, too, she said, especially in the cold. They ran through the woods, whole crowds of them, looking for someone to gang up on.

That's okay, I told her. We carried pepper in our pockets in case of dogs: sprinkle it on their noses, we thought, and the whole pack would run away.

In December, the day before my birthday, when the light was dim and the days shorter than we had known before, Dad got a break at the union hall, a job at Prudhoe Bay that would save us just in time, before the stove oil ran out and groceries were gone. Mom convinced us children that he was off on a great adventure, that he would see foxes and icebergs, that we could write letters for Christmas and for New Year's, and afford new coats with feathers inside. In this last, I was not much interested, because I had my favorite already — a red wool coat that reversed to fake leopard — but I would be glad if this meant we could redeem from the pawnshop Dad's concertina, and his second violin, and mine, the half-size with a short bow, and the guitar and mandolin and rifles and pistol that had gone that way one by one. Whether I played each instrument or not, it had been good to have them around, smelling still of campfires and of songfests in the summer.

It was cold after Dad left, cold outside and cold in our house. Ice on the trailer windows grew thick and shaggy, and Leslie and I melted handprints on it and licked off our palms. There had been no insulation when the add-on went up, so frost crawled the walls there, too, and Mom had us wear long johns and shoes unless we were in our beds. Paul and Kevin came for my birthday, helped me wish over seven candles, gave me a comb and a mirror. They were good kids, my mother said, polite and with good sense, and she told me that if I came in from school and she was not home, I should take Hobo with me and walk to their house. You're a worrywart, Mommy, I said. I'm not a baby, you know.

I wish now I had been tolerant of her fears, and perhaps even shared them. Alaska was a young place when we moved to it, much larger than it seems now, with more trees and thicker ice fog, and with its few people more isolated in the midst of them. During the very deep cold, car exhaust came out in particles rather than as gas, and it hung low and thick in the air, obscuring everything, so that even traffic lights were invisible to the car which was stopped right beneath them. In the middle of ice fog, a person was isolated, muffled and enclosed apart from anyone else on the road. Radio stations ran air-quality bulletins, warning asthmatics and old people to stay indoors, and most folks stayed home anyway, knowing how easily a fan belt would shatter in the cold. To us California-bred children, the rolling dense fog that billowed in our open door was a new and thrilling thing; but to my mother, who siphoned stove oil into the fuel barrel five gallons at a time, and who scavenged deadwood and sticks from under snow, that fog must have seemed formidable, the visual symbol of all one must fight against in this place. She kept the lock fastened even when we were home, and she looked and listened with her head out the door for long seconds each time she had to go out to the ice box. I remember her steps outside, slow and controlled on the bottom stairs, hitting faster and harder toward the top, and I remember her gasp as she lurched inside, her glasses clouding up with frost, Baggies of frozen berries falling down from her arms.

The morning after my birthday, Mom woke up and couldn't stand. She shivered and sweated, and when I helped her sit up she said the room was tilting away from her, and could I mix Bethel up a bottle. It was her tonsils, she said. They were tight in her throat and she couldn't swallow around them. Her skin was hot and wet under my hand; the sweat sat on her forehead and soaked into hairs that fell into it when she tried to lift her neck. "Stay there and I'll make some Russian Tea," I said. "Okay, Mommy? Maybe you can drink some tea?" Mom moved her head. She made a grunting noise as she swallowed, and her lips drew far back from her teeth.

Bethel had been sucking air from an empty bottle, and now she started to cry, dangling the nipple from her teeth and pulling herself up onto Mom's bed. Mom's eyes stayed closed, but her hand lifted off the mattress and patted limply at Bethel's shoulder. I breathed hard, and my eyes stung inside their lids. I picked my sister up and carried her into the trailer room, telling her, "Come on in here, Bethel. Let's make some milk and tea."

Leslie and Ian had their treasure chests out on the floor, and Leslie looked up. "Mommy's really sick, isn't she," she asked.

I said yes, she was really sick.

I stayed home all week from school, making macaroni from boxes and saying everyone's prayers at night. Mom moved from bed to honeybucket and back and had me read Psalms at bedtime until she was strong enough again to see the words. The honeybucket in the corner was a five-gallon plastic paint can with a toilet seat on top, and under its red cloth drape it filled up, for Mom was too weak to carry it to the outhouse pit. I poured in more Pine Sol than usual each time someone used it, and the cabin filled with the fecund smell of pine oil and waste, a scent we would still loathe years later when we got a real toilet and electricity and began to boycott pine cleaners. The days got shorter all the time, and with no windows in the wanigan, we seemed to move in twilight, squinting at one another between four dark walls. I felt snappish and breathless, and I bossed Leslie and Ian until they cried. Finally, my mother was better and I went back to school, and she met me at the bus stop afternoons, walking me home down the road, shining the flashlight ahead of us.

Christmas passed, and Mom went into town every day — for water, or to do laundry, or to get the mail — but no check arrived from my father. He wrote often, including short notes to each of us, and he said he had sent his first paycheck down just two weeks after he started work. It was good money, he wrote, enough for stove oil and groceries and for the instruments in hock. When he came home, we would finish my violin lessons, and we'd start on the younger kids, too, and we would play together the same songs we had sung on the way up the Alcan and then after that at the campgrounds all summer long.

That first check never did come. Mom wrote back that it must have been lost, and could he get them to print another. When was the next one due, she asked. She would try to stretch things out until it came.

The redemption time was running out on all our things at the pawnshop. We had one violin left to pawn, the one my grandfather had given to Dad before I was born, when Dad had driven from L.A. to New York and brought the old man home with him. In Polish, it was a *Benkarty*, a wide, barrel-chested French violin, aged reddish-brown under its lacquer. It was for a master, made to play fast and ring loudly, its neck rounded and thinner than most, the back of its body all a single piece of maple. The wood and varnish had aged and crystallized so smoothly that when my father tuned it and began to play, each string he stroked resonated acutely with the sounds of the others. To pay the interest on the other things in hock, my mother took the *Benkarty* in to the pawnbroker, telling him she would be back for it soon. "It's my husband's," she said, trusting this Russian man to keep the violin safe, if only for sake of the old country and my father's Slavic tongue. She could not know then that the man would sell the *Benkarty* before its redemption date, or that she and my father would never get it back. At the time, the clearest thing for her was the extra cash she got for it, and the powdered milk and the gas she was able to buy that afternoon.

Mom arranged her days carefully around the hours I was in school. Her glasses had broken across the bridge one morning when she had come inside and set them to thaw on the woodstove, so she walked me to the bus stop wearing prescription sunglasses and then fastened my sisters and brother into the truck and drove into town, scraping ice from the windshield as she steered. I know from her journal that she was afraid, that she padlocked the cabin door against the vandalism recently come into town, that she counted her time out carefully so she would be home in time to meet my afternoon bus. She reminded me and made me promise that, should she be late one day, I would take Hobo to Paul and

Kevin's and wait there until she came for me. "Okay, Mommy," I said then, and turned to pull Hobo's ears.

"No, listen to me, Natalie." Mom held my arm until I looked up. Behind the dark lenses her eyes were invisible, but her cheeks were white, and her lips very nearly the same color. "This is not a joke," she said. "Now don't forget what I'm saying. You must go to the boys' if I'm late. This is very important."

"It's okay," I repeated. I looked into her glasses. "I'll remember."

On January 10, only Hobo met me at the bus stop. In the glare from school-bus head-lights, his blue eye shone brighter than his brown, and he watched until I took the last step to the ground before tackling me in the snow. Most days, Hobo hid in the shadow of the spruce until Mom took my bag, then he erupted from the dark to charge up behind me, run through my legs and on out the front. It was his favorite trick. I usually lost my balance and ended up sitting in the road with my feet thrown wide out front and steaming dog tongue all over my face.

Hobo ran ahead, then back, brushing snow crystals and fur against my leg. I put a hand on my skin to warm it and dragged nylon ski pants over the road behind me. Mom said to have them along in case the bus broke down,

69

but she knew I would not wear them, could not bear the plastic sounds they made between my thighs.

No light was on in our house.

If Mom had been home, squares of yellow would have shown through the spruce and lit the fog of my breath, turning it bright as I passed through. What light there was now came from the whiteness of snow, and from the occasional embers drifting up from our stovepipe. I laid my lunchbox on the top step and pulled at the padlock, slapping a palm on the door and shouting. Hobo jumped away from the noise and ran off, losing himself in darkness and in the faint keening dog sounds going up from over near the Horners' house. I called, "Hobo. Come back here, boy," and took the path toward Paul's, tossing my ski pants to the storage tent as I passed.

At the property line, Hobo caught up with me and growled, and I fingered his ear, looking where he pointed, seeing nothing ahead there but the high curve and long sides of a Quonset hut, the work shed the Horners used also as a fence for one side of their yard. In the fall, Paul and Kevin and I had walked to the back of it, climbing over boxes and tools and parts of old furniture, and we had found in the corner a lemmings' nest made from chewed bits of cardboard and paper, packed under the curve of the wall so that shadows hid it from plain sight. We all bent close to hear the scratching, and while Paul held a flashlight I took two sticks and parted the rubbish until we saw the black eyes of a mother lemming and the pink naked bodies of five babies. The mother dashed deeper into the pile and we scooped the nesting back, careful not to touch the sucklings, for fear that their mama would eat them if they carried scent from our fingers.

It seemed that we had spent most of the fall looking out just like that for shrews and lemmings. Oscar and Vic had cats, and Paul and Kevin had three German shepherds, and one or another of them usually found a rodent to play with. Oscar's cats would catch a shrew in their teeth, holding tight to skin behind its neck until its eyes swelled out and it stopped breathing. The boys and I squeezed the cats' jaws, screaming, "You're not even *hungry*," until the teeth parted and the shrew dropped into our palms. If we were fast enough, it was still alive, and we pushed its eyes back in and let it go. The dogs worried a lemming in their mouths, dropping it out on occasion and catching it back into the air, over and over again until it couldn't move and was no longer any fun. When we caught the dogs doing this, we beat their ears with walking sticks, but usually we were too late and had to bury the thing under moss.

The dogs were loud now beyond the Quonset, fierce in their howls and sounding like many more than just three. Hobo crowded against my legs, and as I walked he hunched in front of me, making me stumble into a drift that filled my boots with snow. I called him a coward and said to quit it, but I held his neck against my thigh, turning the corner into the boys' yard and stopping on the edge. Paul's house was lit in all its windows, Kevin's was dark, and in the yard between them were dogs, new ones I had not seen before, each with its own house and tether. The dogs and their crying filled the yard, and when they saw me they grew wilder, hurling themselves to the ends of their chains, pulling their lips off their teeth. Hobo cowered and ran and I called him with my mouth, but my eyes did not move from in front of me.

There were seven. I knew they were huskies and meant to pull dogsleds, because earlier that winter Paul's grandfather had put on his glasses and shown us a book full of pictures. He had turned the pages with a wet thumb, speaking of trappers and racing people and the ways they taught these dogs to run. They don't feed them much, he said, or they get slow and lose their drive. This was how men traveled before they invented snowmobiles or gasoline.

There was no way to walk around the dogs to the lighted house. The snow had drifted and been piled around the yard in heaps taller than I was, and whatever aisle was left along the sides was narrow, and pitted with chain marks where the animals had wandered, dragging their tethers behind. No, I thought, Kevin's house was closest and out of biting range, and someone could, after all, be sitting home in the dark.

My legs were cold. The snow in my boots had packed itself around my ankles and begun to melt, soaking my socks and the felt liners under my heels. I turned toward Kevin's house, chafing my thighs together hard to warm them, and I called cheerfully at the dogs to shut up. Oscar said that if you met a wild animal, even a bear, you had to remember it was more scared than you were. Don't act afraid, he said, because they can smell fear. Just be loud — stomp your feet, wave your hands — and it will run away without even turning around. I yelled "Shut up" again as I climbed the steps to Kevin's front door, but even I could barely hear myself over the wailing. At the sides of my eyes, the huskies were pieces of smoke tumbling over one another in the dark.

The wood of the door was solid with cold, and even through deerskin mittens it bruised my hands like concrete. I cupped a hand to the window and looked in, but saw only black — black, and the reflection of a lamp in the other cabin behind me. I turned and took the three steps back to the ground; seven more and I was in the aisle between doghouses, stretching my chin far up above the frenzy, thinking hard on other things. This was how we walked in summertime, the boys and I, escaping from bad guys over logs thrown across ditches: step lightly and fast, steady on the hard parts of your soles, arms extended outward, palms down and toward the sound. That ditch, this aisle, was a river, a torrent full of silt that would fill your clothes and pull you down if you missed and fell in. I was halfway across. I pointed my chin toward the house and didn't look down.

On either side, dogs on chains hurled themselves upward, choking themselves to reach me, until their tethers jerked their throats back to earth. I'm not afraid of you, I whispered; this is dumb.

I stepped toward the end of the row and my arms began to drop slowly closer to my body. Inside the mittens, my thumbs were cold, as cold as my thighs, and I curled them in and out again. I was walking past the last dog and I felt brave, and I forgave him and bent to lay my mitten on his head. He surged forward on a chain much longer than I thought, leaping at my face, catching my hair in his mouth, shaking it in his teeth until the skin gave way with a jagged sound. My feet were too slow in my boots, and as I blundered backward they tangled in the chain, burning my legs on metal. I called out at Paul's window, expecting rescue, angry that it did not come, and I beat my arms in front of me, and the dog was back again, pulling me down.

A hole was worn into the snow, and I fit into it, arms and legs drawn up in front of me. The dog snatched and pulled at my mouth, eyes, hair; his breath clouded the air around us, but I did not feel its heat, or smell the blood sinking down between hairs of his muzzle. I watched my mitten come off in his teeth and sail upward, and it seemed unfair then and very sad that one hand should freeze all alone; I lifted the second mitten off and threw it away, then turned my face back again, overtaken suddenly by loneliness. A loud river ran in my ears, dragging me under.

My mother was singing. *Lu-lee, lu-lay, thou little tiny child,* the song to the Christ Child, the words she had sung, smoothing my hair, all my life before bed. Over a noise like rushing water I called to her and heard her answer back, Don't worry, just sleep, the ambulance is on its way. I drifted back out and couldn't know then what she prayed, that I would sleep on without waking, that I would die before morning.

She had counted her minutes carefully that afternoon, sure that she would get to town and back, hauling water and mail, with ten minutes to spare before my bus came. But she had forgotten to count one leg of the trip, had skidded up the drive fifteen minutes late, pounding a fist on the horn, calling me home. On the steps, my lunchbox had grown cold enough to burn her hands. She got the water, the groceries, and my brother and sisters inside, gave orders that no one touch the woodstove or open the door, and she left down the trail to Paul's, whistling Hobo in from the trees.

I know from her journal that Mom had been edgy all week about the crazed dog sounds next door. Now the new huskies leaped at her and Hobo rumbled warning from his chest. Through her sunglasses, the dogs were just shapes, indistinct in window-light. She tried the dark cabin first, knocking hard on the windows, then turned and moved down the path between doghouses, feeling her way with her feet, kicking out at open mouths.

Dark lenses frosted over from her breath, and she moved toward the house and the lights on inside.

"She's not here." Paul's mother held the door open and air clouded inward in waves. Mom stammered out thoughts of bears, wolves, dogs. Geri grabbed on her coat. She had heard a noise out back earlier — they should check there and then the woods.

No luck behind the cabin and no signs under the trees. Wearing sunglasses and without any flashlight, Mom barely saw even the snow. She circled back and met Geri under the windowlight. Mom looked toward the yard and asked about the dogs. "They seem so hungry," she said.

Geri looked that way and then back at my mother. "No. Paul's folks just got them last week, but the boys play with them all the time." All the same, she and Mom scanned their eyes over the kennels, looking through and then over their glasses. Nothing seemed different. "Are you sure she isn't home?" Geri asked. "Maybe she took a different trail."

Maybe. Running back with Geri behind her, Mom called my name until her lungs frosted inside and every breath was a cough. She whistled the family whistle my father had taught us, the secret one he and his family had used to call one another from the woods in Nazi

Germany. *"Dodek, ty-gdzie,"* the tune went, "Dodek, where are you?" She blew it now, two syllables for my name, high then low, then a lower one, quick, and another high slide down to low. Her lips hardly worked in the cold, and the whistle was feeble, and she finished by shouting again, curling both hands around her mouth. "Come on," she said to Geri. "Let's get to my cabin." The three younger children were still the only ones home, and Mom handed them their treasure chests, telling them to play on the bed until she found Natalie. Don't go outside, she said. I'll be back real soon.

Back at the Horners', Geri walked one way around the Quonset and Mom the other. Mom sucked air through a mitten, warming her lungs. While Geri climbed over deeper snow, she approached the sled dogs from a new angle. In the shadow of one, a splash of red — the lining of my coat thrown open. "I've found her," she shouted, and thought as she ran, Oh, thank God. Thank, thank God.

The husky stopped its howling as Mom bent to drag me out from the hole. Geri caught up and seemed to choke. "Is she alive?" she asked.

Mom said, "I think so, but I don't know how." She saw one side of my face gone, one red cavity with nerves hanging out, scraps of dead leaves stuck on to the mess. The other eye might be gone, too; it was hard to tell. Scalp had been torn away from my skull on that side, and the gashes reached to my forehead, my lips, had left my nose ripped wide at the nostrils. She tugged my body around her chest and carried me inside.

VITAL
SIGNS

I had little knowledge of my mother's experience of the accident until many months afterward, and even then I heard her story only after I had told mine, after I had shown how clearly I remembered the dogs, and their chains, and my own blood on the snow — and had proven how little it bothered me to recall them. When I said I had heard her voice, and named for her the songs she had sung to me then, my mother searched my face, looking into me hard, murmuring, "I can't believe you remember." She had protected me all along, she said, from her point of view, not thinking that I might have kept my own, and that mine must be harder to bear. But after she knew all this, Mom felt she owed me a history, and she told it to me then, simply and often, in words that I would draw from long after she was gone.

She said that inside the Horners' cabin she had laid me on Geri's couch, careful not to jar the bleeding parts of me, expecting me to wake in an instant and scream. But when I did become conscious, it was only for moments, and I was not aware then of my wounds, or of the cabin's warmth, or even of pressure from the fingers of Paul's grandfather, who sat up close and stroked the frozen skin of my hands.

Geri ordered Paul and Kevin to their room, telling them to stay there until she called them, and then she stood at Mom's shoulder, staring down and swaying on her legs.

Mom looked up through her glasses and said, "Is there a phone to call an ambulance?"

Geri was shaking. "Only in the front house, kid, and it's locked." She held her arms straight toward the floor, as if to catch herself when she fell. "Karla should be home in a minute, but I'll try to break in." She tugged at the door twice before it opened, and then she went out, leaving my mother to sing German lullabies beside my ear. *When morning comes,* the words ran, *if God wills it, you will wake up once more.* My mother sang the words and breathed on me, hoping I would dream again of summertime, all those bright nights when the music played on outside, when she drew the curtains and sang us to sleep in the trailer. Long years after the accident, when she felt healed again and stronger, Mom described her thoughts to me, and when she did she closed her eyes and sat back, saying, "You can't know how it was to keep singing, to watch air bubble up where a nose should have been, and to pray that each of those breaths was the last one." Many times that night she thought of Job, who also had lived in a spacious, golden land, who had prospered in that place, yet had cried in the end, "The thing that I so greatly feared has come upon me." The words became a chant inside her, filling her head and bringing on black time.

The wait for the ambulance was a long one, and my mother filled the time with her voice, sitting on her heels and singing. She fingered my hair and patted my hands and spoke low words when I called out. Paul's grandfather wept and warmed my fingers in his, and Mom wondered where were my mittens, and how were her other children back home.

Geri came back and collapsed on a chair, and Karla, her sister-in-law, hurried in through the door. Geri began to choke, rocking forward over her knees, telling Karla the story. Her voice stretched into a wail that rose and fell like music. "It's happening again," she said. "No matter where you go, it's always there."

Karla brought out aspirin and gave it to Geri, then turned and touched my mother's arm. She whispered, "She's remembering her boy." She said that as soon as Geri was quiet, she would leave her here and fetch my siblings from the trailer.

"Thank you," Mom told her. "I'll send someone for them as soon as I can." She looked at Geri, wishing she had something to give her, some way to make her know that she was not to blame here; but for now Mom felt that Geri had spoken truth when she said that sorrow followed us everywhere, and there was little else she could add.

The ambulance came, and then everything was movement. I drifted awake for a moment as I was lifted to a stretcher and carried toward the door. I felt myself swaying in air, back and forth and back again. Paul's whisper carried over the other voices in the room, as if blown my way by strong wind. "Natalie's dying," he said; then his words were lost among other sounds, and I faded out again. A month later, when our first-grade class sent me a box full of valentines, Paul's was smaller than the rest, a thick, white heart folded in two. Inside, it read: "I love you, Nataly. Pleas dont die." When I saw him again, his eyes seemed very big, and I don't remember that he ever spoke to me anymore.

It was dark inside the ambulance, and seemed even darker to my mother, squinting through fog on her sunglasses. She badgered the medic, begging him to give me a shot for pain. The man kept working, taking my pulse, writing it down, and while he did, he soothed my mother in low tones, explaining to her about physical shock, about the way the mind estranges itself from the body and stands, un-blinking and detached, on the outside. "If she does wake up," he said, "she'll feel nothing. She won't even feel afraid." When Mom wrote this in her journal, her tone was filled with wonder, and she asked what greater gift there could be.

At the hospital, there were phone calls to be made, and Mom placed them from outside the emergency room. First she called Dick and Esther Conger, two of the only sum-mertime friends who had stayed here over winter. After our first meeting on the road, there where Dick and my father had played music together, the Congers had arrived after us in Fairbanks, and sometime during the summer, during cookouts when we shared the same campfires, the children of our fam-ilies had become interchangeable; Toni and Barry were in the same age group as we were, and discipline and praise were shared equally among us all. It was never shocking to wake up in the morning and find Toni or Barry in one of our beds; we just assumed that the person who belonged there was over sleeping in their bus. Now, as my mother explained the accident to Dick, our friend began to cry, saying, "Oh, Verna. Oh, no," and Esther's voice in the background asked, "What's happened? Let me talk to her." Mom asked the Congers to drive out for my brother and sisters, to watch them until my father came.

Leaning her head to the wall, Mom telephoned a message to the North Slope. She spoke to Dad's boss there, explaining only that "our daughter has been hurt." Just now, she thought, she couldn't tell the whole story again, and besides, the worst "hurt" my father would imagine could not be this bad. The crew boss said a big snowstorm was coming in, but they would try to fly my father out beforehand; if not, they would get him to the radiophone and have him call down. A nurse walked up then and touched Mom's shoulder, telling her, "Your daughter is awake, and she's asking for you." A moment before, Mom had been crying, pressing a fist to her teeth, but now she closed up her eyes like a faucet and walked after the nurse, pulling up her chin and breathing deeply in her chest. She had trembled so that she could hardly wipe her glasses, but when she moved through the door and saw the white lights, and me lying flat on a table, she was suddenly calm, and the skin grew warmer on her face.

Mom positioned herself in front of my one eye, hoping as she stood there that she wasn't shaking visibly, that her face was not obviously tense. She need not have bothered; as I lay staring right to where my eye veered off, the room was smoky gray, and I was conscious only of a vicious thirst that roughened the edges of my tongue, making them stick to my teeth. I was allowed no water, had become fretful, and when my mother spoke to me, I complained that the rag in my mouth had not been damp enough, and that these people meant to cut my favorite coat off me. I have to think now that my mother acted courageously, keeping her face smooth, listening to me chatter about school, about the message I had brought from my teacher, that they would skip me to the second grade on Monday. Mom's answers were light, almost vague, and before she left the pre-op room, she told me to listen to the nurses, to let them do all they needed to; they were trying to help me, she said. A little later, after I was wheeled into surgery, a nurse handed her the things they had saved: my black boots, and the Alice in Wonderland watch Mom had given me for Christmas.

My mother made more phone calls, to

86

churches in town and to ones in California that we'd left behind, telling the story over again, asking these people to pray. Old friends took on her grief, asking did she need money, telling her to call again when she knew more. These people knew, as my mother did, that money was not so much the question now, but it was something they could offer, and so they did. And for months and years after this they would send cards, and letters, and candy and flowers and toys, making themselves as present with us as they could. For now, on this first night, they grieved with my mother, and they said to go lie down if she could, they would take over the phones. And each of these people made another call, and another, until, as my mother walked back to the waiting room, she knew she was lifted up by every friend we had ever made.

The Horners had arrived, and for a little while they all sat along the waiting-room walls, stuffing fists into their pockets and closing their eyes. None of them wanted to talk about the accident, or to wonder about the progress in surgery, and when my mother said to Karla, "I just talked to some people in California who would never *believe* the way we live here," her words seemed terribly funny, and started the whole room laughing. It wasn't so much, she wrote later, that they were forgetting why they were there; in fact, they remembered very well — so well that, compared to that fact, everything else was hilarious. And they could not possibly have continued for long as they had been, she said, pressing their backs to the walls and waiting. So for hours after Mom's joke, and far into the night, the adults invented names for our kind — "the outhouse set," "the bush league" — and they contributed stories about life in Alaska that would shock most of the people Outside. They joked about Styrofoam outhouse seats — the only kind that did not promote frostbite; about catalogues that no one could afford to buy from but whose pages served a greater purpose; about the tremendous hardship of washing dishes from melted snow and then tossing the gray water out the door. Mom told the story about "Rodneys," which everyone considered superb, and they spent long minutes discovering more and more absurd definitions. From time to time, Geri got up from her seat to walk alone in the hall, but when she came back in, she was ready again to laugh.

My father arrived about midnight, dressed in a week's growth of beard and in an army-surplus parka and flight pants. Mom met him in the hall and stood looking up; Dad dropped his satchel to the floor, panting, and he watched my mother's face, the eyes behind her glasses. He spoke first, said his was the last plane out in a heavy snowstorm. Then: "How did it happen?" he said. "Did she fall out the door?"

My mother waited a beat and looked at him. "It wasn't a car accident, Julius," she said, touching his arm. She started telling the story again, and my father looked down then at the blood crusted on her sweater, and he closed his eyes and leaned into the wall. My mother told him, "You can't appreciate how I feel, because you haven't seen her face. But I wish that when you pray you'd ask for her to die soon."

Dad opened his eyes. "That must seem like the best thing to ask," he whispered. "But we don't make decisions like that on our own. We never have, and we can't start now."

Sometime after 2 a.m., my three surgeons stepped in. My mother said later that had they not still worn their surgical greens, she would not have recognized them; during the night, she had forgotten their faces.

The men sagged inside their clothes, three sets of shoulders slumped forward under cloth. I was still alive, they said, but only barely, and probably not for long. I had sustained over one hundred lacerations from the shoulders up, and had lost my left cheekbone along with my eye. They'd saved what tissues they could, filling the bulk of the cavity with packings, and what bone fragments they had found were now wired together on the chance that some of them might live.

My father groped for a positive word. "At least she doesn't have brain damage. I heard she was lucid before surgery."

Dr. Butler brushed the surgical cap from his head and held it, twisting it in his hands. His eyes were red as he looked up, explaining as kindly as it seemed he could. A dog's mouth, he said, was filthy, filthier than sewage, and all of that impurity had passed into my body. They had spent four hours just cleaning out the wounds, pulling out dirt and old berry leaves and dog feces. Even with heavy antibiotics, I would likely have massive infections, and they would probably spread into my brain. His voice turned hoarse and he looked across at Dr. Earp, asking the man to continue.

Dr. Earp rubbed hard at the back of his head and spoke softly, working his neck. For now, Dr. Earp said, they had been able to reconstruct the eyelids; that would make the biggest visible difference.

On my parents' first hourly visit to intensive care, Mom stopped at the door and put her hand to my father's chest. "No matter how she looks," she said, "don't react. She'll be able to tell what you're thinking."

The nurse at the desk sat under a shaded lamp, the only real light in the room. She stood and whispered that mine was the first bed to the left. "She wakes up for a minute or so at a time," she said. "She's been asking for you."

"First one on the left," my father repeated, a little too loudly for that place, and from somewhere inside a great rushing river I heard him and called out, thinking he had used the family whistle when really it was just his voice. At my bed, Mom watched him as he stood looking down, and when the lines in his face became deeper, she turned from him, pinching his sleeve with her fingers. She walked closer to me and held the bed rail.

My appearance after surgery was not truly better than before, but it was, my mother thought, more orderly. My head seemed much too large, covered mostly in white dressings, and the exposed parts of my face were black, with a maze of stitches so thick that even my mouth was barely visible among them. An intravenous tube carried clear nourishment into one ankle; I had bled when the needle went in, and the red was crusted over on my foot.

"We're here, Natalie," Mom whispered. "We'll see you again in an hour."

91

I never saw in my face what my mother had. By the time I found a mirror, weeks had gone by, and my face was stitched and healing, and even the one or two photos I have from the early days are not so bad to look at. The pictures are mostly full of bandages, and the small slit of an eye, and the thin line of lips pieced together and smiling. My father, too, and our friends, saw only the after-effects of the accident, but it was enough for them to hear the story and to know that whatever hard things happened to us afterward, the accident itself had been the most terrible to see.

And however difficult were the places my parents walked through, there were others who walked with them, offering what they could. With my father once more out of a job, Dick and Esther housed, fed, and cared for my younger siblings during the days, then sat up long nights over their breakfast bar, listening to progress reports and news from the hospital. My mother told me later that she could tell the stories more easily than either Dick or Esther could absorb them, and these friends sagged over the counter, wanting to undo all this aching. My parents' struggles became theirs, and their hope increased as ours did, as I grew stronger, as my stitches came off, as I moved from the ICU into a regular room. Dick and Esther called in new friends, and friends of friends, all who, in this small town, had heard of the little girl from Badger Road, and who came to ask what we needed. And when my parents looked warily on all this concern, wondering if it could be real, these people ignored them, preparing what help they could and asking nothing.

Rod and Lynn Smith were A.A. friends of Dick and Esther's nearest neighbors. They had heard from somewhere that I needed to fly Outside for more surgery, and that my doctors and people from the churches had called everyone they could think of for help and had found none. So Rod and Lynn phoned a Shriner friend in Clear, Alaska, and between them they made over twenty calls to the States, and in the evening they came to my mother to say that it was all arranged. I was scheduled in at Seattle University Hospital, and the Shriners in San Francisco would pay airfare for all of us. Mom stood up from her chair then and thanked these people, telling them, "I don't know what we can do . . ."

Lynn waved a hand, shaking her head. "We have a proverb in A.A.: what alcoholics don't need is another obligation. So when we help someone out, we don't need paying back. We just say, 'Do as much for the next guy.' " My mother and father would use that phrase countless times in the coming years, always

93

telling of the night when they first heard it.

To raise quick cash for the trip, my parents advertised a yard sale on local radio. The announcers all knew the story, knew what the sale was for, but my parents made them swear just to announce it, and not to grovel for handouts on our behalf. And the disc jockeys kept their words, never mentioning the cause behind the yard sale; they just announced the fact of the sale itself — on the hour every hour, and ten or twelve times in between. Our tent went with my father's chainsaw. The 30-06 rifle, they sold to a gun dealer at Cabin Inn. No one wanted the hand-crank cream separator, but my father had coveted and bought it from a small shop on our way up the highway, and would have felt brokenhearted to part with it anyway. When the radio men called to ask if the sale was a success, my mother said emphatically yes, and thanked them in a wide voice.

And these were the people we found ourselves with. Yes, there would be those less sympathetic: impatient relatives, neighbors who built spite fences, careless flight attendants hurrying toward takeoff and nearly knocking me out of my wheelchair. But these were the sorts of foolish people anyone could have known, in any place. Who counted most were Dick and Esther, with their motto,

"There's always room for one more," and Oscar and Vic and Jean, who wrote now every week, reminding us of last summer, and who would be back with us the next warm season, as if nothing had changed, and all those besides them, who made my parents believe that, in spite of all that had happened, we had been right to come here. Later, after long months in Seattle, my mother would take all of her children on a train to visit relatives in California. There, she would find that already she had outgrown that place, that people she had once known were now uncomfortable around her.

We were oddities in California, people who wore secondhand clothes grown dingy from wood ashes, and who had lived in the woods with no water. My brother relieved himself into the philodendrons, making the neighbors complain, and at dinnertime my sister held up her plate and said, "Look, Mommy. It's not paper." Mom borrowed her sister Paula's car and drove us all out for a look at our old house, to see the magnolias and rosebushes and the swings in the yard; one more viewing, she said, just to see how things still looked. But when we got there, we saw that it all was very different now: the new family had let the weeds take over, the blackberry vines go to seed, and all across the hot concrete there was a tremendous noise: a construction crew preparing to widen the street. As we stopped for a moment next to the curb, Mom looked across at the place and said, "Well, I'd like to take it back with us, but I don't miss it enough to stay here."

We visited our old church, our old neighbors, my grandparents. Most of the people grinned, said it was great to see us again, but when my mother told her stories of Alaska, their eyebrows came together over their smiles, and they looked at Mom strangely, as if she were speaking of flying saucers. She should have expected this, she told me later; she should have known not to mention outhouses to people who bevel the edges of their lawns. No, my mother thought, the beaches were nice, and the sunshine very good to look at, but on the whole, she was ready to go home. We all were.

The evening before we left, there was a loud pounding on my aunt's front door, and Paula left the back patio to answer it. I was sitting on the concrete with my treasure chest open and spread out around me, and I heard Paula call, "Verna, could you come to the door." In a second, Mom was back again, and behind me she said, "Hey. Look who's here."

It was Oscar and Jean, and Nicky and Tyrone, come a hundred miles from the desert;

and for a few minutes we all went insane, collapsing into each other and laughing about nothing. In the frenzy, Jean tripped over my treasure chest, and Bethel was knocked down and she started to cry, and Oscar held me up in the air to keep my face from getting knocked. That night, we borrowed my aunt's barbecue and roasted hot dogs outside, eating once again with our hands under open air. We made Russian Tea and retold stories from the summer before, reminiscing about flood threats and pet burials, about Oscar racing out in morning frost while my father played reveille on his bugle. We talked, too, about next summer, planning new jobs, new places to live. In the middle of it all, Oscar put his hands under my arms and lifted, bringing my face up to his. He looked at me for a long moment, taking in the gauze and the scars and the one remaining eye, spreading his smile wide. "Well, Natalie," he said, "you've got one left. And it's still mighty blue." When I laughed at him, he squeezed me to his chest, and over his shoulder I could see Jean and my mother, smiling and talking fast between breaths, waving their hands in the air.

THE

FEAR

The response I hear first from nearly everyone who asks about my missing eye is, "So, I suppose now you're afraid of dogs?" And it is true that on the night I lost my eye Dr. Earp told my parents that I was not likely to live more than a day or so, yet if I did survive I would forever be subject to grotesque nightmares and an unreasoning fear of dogs. So I do not find this question ridiculous when it is put, although I have never reacted badly to dogs and in fact have owned several in my lifetime. No, what I wonder at is the fact that, when I say that my mother seemed to have lost more in the accident than I did, people look at me from the sides of their eyes, questioning.

But those who are truly insightful will know this fact: that the greatest injuries are never those of the body. The people who feel uncomfortable when I mention my mother are the ones interested more in gruesome detail than in stories of heroism or pain. Like children in a schoolyard, they want to know what was my accident, how much did it hurt, and what did I look like afterward. I want to stare squarely back at these people, to have them answer for their urge to reduce heartache to a piece of hearsay, examined and set apart from the people who endured it.

I am not the only person I have known who has encountered emotional sightseers. I have a friend whose husband died slowly of brain cancer, and who during those three years managed all the business that his dying entailed. She drove him in for myriad appointments and treatments, filled his prescriptions and administered drugs, arranged counseling for him and reasoned with him herself when he was lucid for it, and all the while she held up her children, a toddler and a schoolboy, preparing them gradually for the finish.

People who knew her said she was brave, and shook their heads at her strength, but when she met any of these in a store or on the street, she was sent home with messages mostly to her husband. "Tell John," they said, "that we're all pulling for him. Tell him we miss him at work." Those who did ask her how she was doing herself grew uncomfortable and walked quickly away if she said the truth, or anything other than "Fine. And yourself?" — and I don't recall that anyone ever asked after her children. Like me, she found that few people who asked really wanted to know of pain, or of anything that would involve them in unpleasantness; their tastes ran more to stories of laser surgery and chemotherapy, things which belonged to a world far different from their own. My friend learned early on to do her grieving in private, at night while her sons were in bed, and to speak very little of her situation except to the two or three friends closest by. My friend's husband was insulated and secure from all this, and in any case he lost so much of reality as his mind deteriorated that he needed less and less protection, while his family, those who must survive after him, grew to need more and more. The truth is, I think, that the casualties among us include not just those who are dying, or bleeding, or recovering from injury, but also the caretakers around the edges whose selves fall sacrificed to their charges.

It had to happen eventually, that I found a mirror and looked in. For the first days after my accident, I had stayed mostly in bed, leaning my bandages back on the pillow and peeling frostbite blisters from my hands. The new skin was pink, and much thinner than the old, as sensitive to touch as the nail beds I uncovered by chewing down to them. I had taken to running two fingers over stitches standing up like razor stubble on my face, then over the cotton that covered the right side and the rest of my head. The whole surgical team came in daily to lift me into a chair and unwind the gauze, releasing into the room a smell like old caves full of bones. And all this time I had never seen myself, never asked what was under there, in the place where my left eye belonged.

I had asked my mother once if I would again see out of that eye. It was an hour after my dressings had been changed, and the smell of hot ooze still hovered in my room. The day before, Mom and Dad had brought the other children to the hospital, explaining in bright voices, "We're going to visit Natalie." It had been, I think, a move to include the young ones in this new life, for though my parents had explained a little about the accident, and a little of the place where I was now, it was hard to know how much the others understood, for Leslie was not quite five, and the younger ones just two and three. So while Mom had sat in a waiting room watching them, Dad had lifted me to a wheelchair and taken me from my room, holding a hand against the bandages as my weak neck sagged to the side. I had smiled going in through the waiting-room door, and Bethel had cried, not recognizing me. Ian had held back, and Leslie touched my knee, looking timid but curious, talking about small things until Mom had explained to Bethel that this really was Natalie.

All this had been enlightening for me, had pointed out how large were the changes in my face, had brought me then to ask my mother, "Will I get to see out of this eye again?" Mom stood up and adjusted my bed rail. "Do you want your feet a little higher," she asked. "I can crank them up if you like."

I pressed, "Mommy, my eye. Will I be able to see from it?"

"Hang on," Mom said. "I need to use the little girls' room." She started to the door and I screamed after her, "Mommy, you're not answering me." But she was gone, and after that I did not ask.

Later, when the light was out, I lay back and looked far right, then left, concentrating hard, trying to feel the bandaged eye move. I thought I could feel it, rolling up and then down, ceiling to floor, matching its moves with my other eye. Even after I was grown, I could swear that I felt it blink when I pressed my two lids together.

Men from down the hall visited me during the day, rolling in on wheelchairs or walking beside their IV racks. They all wore two sets of pajamas, one wrong way forward so their backsides were covered. The hospital floor was old, its tiles starting to bubble, and the wheels on my friends' IV racks made rumbling sounds as they passed over. If a nurse walked by the door and looked in, the men waved her away, saying, "It's all right, dear. I'm visiting my granddaughter." For a kiss they gave me a sucker and a story about bears, or they carried me to a wheelchair and took me around to visit. In this way, I passed from room to room, brushing at the green curtains between beds, pouring water into plastic glasses, gathering hugs and learning to shake hands in the "cool" way. I signed plaster casts in big red letters, and I visited the baby room, pressing my chin to the glass.

On a day when I felt at my smallest and was in the bed still sleeping, one of my favorite men friends checked out, leaving on my nightstand a gift and a note that said he would miss me. The gift was a music box lined in pink satin, with a ballerina inside who pirouetted on her toes when I wound the key. And behind her inside the lid, a triangular looking glass not much bigger than she was.

My mother came in behind me as I was staring into the mirror, holding it first from one angle, then from another, and she stood by the bed for a moment, saying nothing.

When I turned, she was looking at me with her shoulders forward, and she seemed to be waiting.

"My eye is gone, isn't it?" I asked.

She kept looking at me. She said, "Yes it is."

I turned again and lifted the box to my face. "I thought so. Those dogs were pretty mean."

I didn't understand, or was too small to know, what my mother thought she was protecting me from. It must be something very bad, I thought, for her to avoid every question I asked her. "Mommy," I said once, "I don't *feel* like I'm going to die."

She looked up from her book and the light shone off her glasses. She said, "Oh, no. You're certainly not going to do anything like that."

"Then will I be blind?"

"Well," she said, "you can see now, can't you?" And when I pressed her with more questions, she looked toward the door and said, "Shh. Here comes your lunch tray."

It all made me wonder if my wounds were much worse than everyone said — and of course they were, but there were long years of surgery still ahead, and no one wanted me to feel afraid. I was angry, too — as angry as a seven-year-old can be — that Mom patted my cheek with her palm and said she'd be taking my malamute to the pound before I came home. I stared at her then with my head up and sputtered out a peevish tirade, telling her I didn't hate all dogs, or even most dogs, but just the ones who bit me. It didn't occur to me until my own daughter was seven, the same age I was when I was hurt, that Mom might have been sending my dog away for her own sake.

For a very long time after the accident, my brother and sisters and I were not allowed outside the range of Mom's eyes. I was the oldest, and perhaps the only one of an age to feel constrained, especially since my parents did all they could to make us satisfied to stay close by. We had moved, after I was hurt, from a twelve-foot trailer on Oscar's piece of forest to a plywood cabin we built four miles away on a road between neighbors. Through all the building times, the children's job was to haul away brush the grownups chopped out, piling it to the side and going to get more. Or we brought them nails when they called for them, or stood on the edge when Dad dug the outhouse pit, waiting as he threw the dirt up and out, then spreading it around with our feet. Mom took pictures of us all at our jobs, including her children in the party atmosphere, hoping to content us and hold us nearby.

And we did love the building, the way our

houses were like most Alaskan ones, built one room at a time over years, patchwork additions added on in squares like blocks laid together by babies, the corners never quite matching. We loved, too, the way a well was pounded down, for our parents and their friends had invented the method, and Dad had gone hunting the tool. He found a heavy round track roller from a Caterpillar tractor and had a man weld it to a long steel bar like an axle; and for a long day the adults stood one-inch galvanized pipe on its pointed end, inserted the bar of the well-pounder, lifted the roller and slammed it down, driving the pipe into earth. The first feet were quick, for the top ground was soft, and permafrost was still a little way down. At each hard slam of the well-pounder, the woods echoed back the iron ringing, and my father grabbed a pipe wrench, twisting the well a quarter turn. It went this way for a single long stretch of hours, slam and turn, slam and turn, for if we stopped overnight for sleep, the earth would seize up around the pipe, cementing it there for good. We children passed time by singing slave boat songs, the lurching rhythms adding strength to grownups' arms. At twenty-seven feet the works hit water, and at thirty-three the pounding stopped. Dad screwed a red hand pump to the top of the well, and we primed the pump with water from cups, working the handle fast, up and down, until it drew red iron spillage from the ground.

We built our houses on oil barrels, enclosing the bottoms with plywood to trap the warm air, and it all was so new that for a time we children were glad to stay close, there where our mother could see us. Mom hung a chalkboard in the room where we slept, and when we were outside building tree forts, Dad wrote us messages, signing them "The Shadow" or "The Phantom." "Where are the cookies?" the words read. "Only the Shadow knows." We would hunt then through the cabin, looking behind the woodstove and under beds, pulling out finally a bag of cookies from Dad's pillowcase, saying, "Daddy, you wrote that message. You're the Shadow."

"How can you say that?" Dad looked surprised. "I was outside with you." It became a game to catch him writing, and though we always knew he did it, he managed to leave messages always at moments when we would swear he had been with us the whole time.

And we had treasure hunts to find the paperweight Dad hid in plain sight; this was the rule, it had to be visible, but the paperweight was clear acrylic with three jade stones inside, and when our father laid it in a wall against the fiberglass insulation, the crinkles in the foil showed through the "treasure," blending it utterly in. We took turns hiding it and Mom and Dad pretended wonder at how hard they had to look when it was their turn to hunt.

My family made friends of the boys next door, and since my parents owned the slough between our properties, we had space enough for sledding in the winter, tree forts in the summer. A huge culvert four feet wide fed into the slough, and we played inside it, throwing in rocks to hear the echo, sitting there under the road and listening to cars driving over. In winter, Dad dug a trench in the snow and we slid down it, screaming and holding up our hands, and Bethel once had a tooth knocked out when she crashed up her sled at the bottom. My father built a playhouse, two stories, with a ladder to the flat roof, and Mom stained it red, built furniture from scrap lumber, put up curtains inside. The veins in Mom's hands pushed up under her freckles as she stood back, holding a hammer against her little flat bottom. Her cheeks got red when she worked like this, and when her nose started to sweat, she held wide round glasses on the end of it by pushing her lips out in a kiss. She hung two tire swings away from the outhouse, put together a teeter-totter, taught us to balance the sides: the two middle children — Leslie and Ian — on one end, I and Bethel, the little one, at the other. At night, we stood behind Mom's chair and combed out her hair, plucking out stray white strands from among the black.

For the most part, I was happy, and so were we all. Kenny Mezzulo next door was my best friend, and my first crush, and he and I made Tang in paper cups, or skated on the road when the ice was down. When Mom bought me a box of tools, I sawed fallen willows and Kenny thought of things to build with them: a doll swing, a chair, a walking stick with the diamonds carved out. Much later, Kenny would outgrow my company, would prefer to play with boys of his own age, four years older and with bigger muscles. But these first years were good ones, and I was sorry to go away the times when I was scheduled at the hospital.

Eventually, I grew into friendships with classmates at school, and it was when I started asking to spend nights away that I noticed how large my mother's eyes had become. All along, Mom had quietly placed herself wherever her children were, had chopped underbrush out from the trees while we played, or given us orders to make our games together in front of the cabin window. It had been all right for us to play with the Mezzulos; they kept us nearby and within protective range. But now, when I wanted to go other places, Mom found a thousand excuses for me not to, and I realized that up until now, or at least since my accident, she had always been where I was, always within my peripheral vision. When I had wanted to go to Kenny's house, or down to the frog hole, or into a store, there had always been a reason for Mom to come, too. The times I had insisted that she let me go without her, or had pointed out strong reasons for her to stay, I had had to take all my siblings along, and Mom had been on the road with her glasses pushed up when we came back in sight of the house.

Now, when I asked to go away for the night, she looked all around with her eyes and said she didn't think the car would start, or tomorrow was a busy day. I used to wail, "No, you just don't want me to go. I never get to do ANYthing," and she started saying yes more often; but even after I was in high school and was free to spend whole weekends away, Mom would watch TV all night by the window when any one of us was gone.

By the time I was old enough to be my mother's friend, she had come most of the way out of her black time, that long expanse where fear filled her chest like a black wind blowing. She spoke to me then about fear, how it grew from inside you outward, how it dried out your eyes. She said that mothers had a thousand thoughts to get through with

110

in a day, and that most of these were about avoiding disaster. A mother learned early to turn pan handles in toward the stove, to keep roller skates off the steps, to lock the medicine chest. And it would seem, she said, that if you got through enough days where your children were not eaten by bears, did not fall down the outhouse pit, did not lose more than half a finger to frostbite, you would begin to relax a little, and to worry less in your sleep. It was natural; no one could foresee every possible danger, and eventually most mothers decided not to try. But because of her own history, she herself had never relaxed, had thought her thousand thoughts and more, and somehow she had lost me anyway. When the black time came after my accident, she watched herself become obsessed with us children, and she defined this obsession as illness, directing its face toward what she feared most of all: that she had her mother in her.

I think I was vaguely aware, long before my accident, that there was some problem between my mother and my grandmother, but I was not cognizant enough to ask about it. My impressions came mostly from glances exchanged between my parents back in California, and from my mother's quick shuffle toward the car as my grandmother called after her, "Verna, wait. I was telling you about Paula." But until I was much older I never knew what it was my mother was hurrying away from.

When I was very young — five or so — and we lived in Los Angeles, my parents both worked during the day and we children stayed at Grandma's house until dinnertime. Her rooms smelled close, I remember, with dust motes hanging in the light, and we napped covered with knitted afghans in my grandfather's study. I usually wet the bed. In the afternoons, Grandma let me go next door to Mrs. Mealer's, or to Mrs. Durkee's house on the other side, and they sat with me on the porch, fed me cookies, gave me a white Easter bonnet with elastic under the chin. I preferred the neighbors' houses to my grandmother's, partly because they baked thick, sugary things, and partly because when they spoke to me it was never to complain that I was loud.

Grandma seemed very old, even then, though she must not have been more than seventy. She had a raspy, questioning voice, and air sounded out between her words. At lunchtime, when she used her apron to mop up our spills, the voice rose in pitch, and she said, "I make you special juice, and you pour it on the table." She wore cotton print dresses with short sleeves, and over varicose veins, stockings running up to a garter belt. When she walked through the house, she placed her hands on pieces of furniture, using them like canes as she swung each hip in front of her. Her rocker was padded, with a skirt around the bottom, and she sat herself into it by bending over her knees and falling backward with a loud sigh.

We had to be very careful at my grandmother's house. Although we were rarely spanked except in cases of grave misbehavior, Grandma's words could make us feel just as bad. When my sister stuck her hand in the fish tank, Grandma snatched her up and made her run to the bathroom, crying, "Your mother trusted me to keep you here, and now you're getting yourself fish-poisoned. You're making your mommy hate me." My grandmother could make us feel responsible for all the wrong that came about in the world, and we never dared tell Mom or Dad, because of what might happen if they found out how bad we were.

Still, everything there was not unpleasant for us. Grandma put in our barrettes, gave us bologna on bread, let us read my grandfather's books. She had a glass table with shells in the bottom, and if we were careful we sometimes could take these in our hands, blowing off the gray dust, putting our ears to the holes. If Grandpa was home he would tell us their names: conch, nautilus, abalone; and if he was not, we would use them as telephones, speaking to mermaids inside. For the most part, we children played among ourselves while Grandma watched, staying as much as we could out of her way, and we wore Kool-Aid mustaches and captured grasshoppers in the yard.

In the evenings, after Mom had gotten us home, Grandma would call on the phone, and Mom would stretch the cord as far through the kitchen as she could, trying to get dinner ready. Her attitude then was strange to me; she spoke differently to Grandma than to other callers. The conversations were long ones, an hour at least, and I can hardly remember Mom speaking during them, though I'm sure she must have. What I recall is that she held the receiver up with her shoulder and said little, just a low "M-m-m" now and then, opening cupboards and getting out pots and pans all the while. When she needed something that the phone would not reach, she gestured to Dad or to me with her hands. The look on her face was not stern, but neither was it pleasant — her lips met in too small a line, her eyebrows sat too low on her forehead.

Mom usually said several times that it was time for her to go before she really did hang up. Her face looked brighter, more polite, when she said this, and fell together tiredly each time my grandmother kept talking. (Once, the phone disconnected itself accidentally, and Grandma's line was still ringing busy an hour later. After Mom got back through to her, Grandma said she had just noticed that no one was on the other end.) When she rang off, Mom would lean her head down and say to my father, "Julius, she makes me so tired."

It was only after I was much older that my mother described to me what these conversations were about. Mostly, she said, Grandma called either to complain about other relatives — the wrongs they had done her, the suspicious glances they had cast — or to tell Mom that she herself was guilty of mistreating the mother who had raised her. But to explain my grandmother's nature, Mom said, she could not describe the phone calls only, but had to explain all about her mother, all the history and all the context, and she spoke to me then in a light voice, looking away and back again.

From earlier times than Mom could remember, Grandma had always seemed somehow "bent." She would look at you every day, Mom said, from somewhere behind her eyes, and inside that look you were judged good or evil, for her or against her. If you were against her, it might just be that you had asked to wear a barrette instead of pigtails as she saw best. If you were for her, if you had accepted the braids without speaking, you were also a silent partner in her hatred, expected to stand touching her while she screamed rejection at whoever had chosen barrettes. "See?" she would say with tears running out. "Your sister likes braids. She knows I know what's pretty, and you would, too, if you weren't so selfish." Her logic didn't always make sense, and if you corrected her or stuck up for her "enemy," you became one, too, suddenly and without compromise. Grandma would slump and look up at you through mist, saying, "I'm alone now. You're all against me. I have no one on my side."

And this seemed most important to her — that she have someone on her side. When Mom and her sisters were in California high schools, Grandma would phone their friends' mothers if one of the daughters was an enemy that day, and she had most parents believing that her children were evil. At home, it was impossible to predict the emotional weather, it changed so rapidly. Grandma might smile when Mom brought a friend home, or she might grab the friend's collar and throw her out the door. She hurled brushes and drinking glasses when she was angry, and then said into her handkerchief, "Why do you hurt me like this?" She was obsessive about money, for the family was poor, and she hoarded it in secret places, feeling menaced when anyone asked after it. At the same time, she humiliated her husband over finances, asking him could he still feel like a man when his wife wore cotton stockings and his daughters all needed shoes. The sisters learned to pick their friends from those who asked the fewest personal questions. They learned, too, never to bring their friends home, or even to let Grandma know their names.

Even when Grandma was "for" you, Mom said, it hurt. She might call up your date, pretending to be you, and say, "I don't think you know what a favor I'm doing by going out with you. And you've never once bought me flowers." Or she would circulate anonymous letters, sometimes for and sometimes against you, among your friends' families or with the people at church. The oldest daughter, Paula, almost lost a job when Grandma wrote the boss a letter in Paula's name, speaking bitterly against her low wages. It seemed that Grandma wanted more money for babysitting, and knew that Paula couldn't afford it, but she never admitted to writing that letter or any of the others; and certainly no one confronted her, afraid as they were of what it might cost them later. The daughters were all mortified this way at one time or another, and long before they left home they all stopped letting Grandma know who they were seeing or where they worked. Later, when my parents lived in New York, Mom would rewrite whole pages home to delete a friend's or landlord's last name, fearing what could come if Grandma ever wrote to these people.

Although she always knew that Grandma wasn't "right" somehow, it wasn't until she was eighteen that Mom got anyone to answer her why. She was engaged then to Eddie, a hometown boy just out of army boot camp and stationed at his first duty assignment out of town. When the wedding was less than two months away, Grandma wrote Eddie a letter signed with the name of Mom's best friend. In it, she shredded him for not leaving his car with Mom, for being insensitive, for being much less than Mom deserved. Thinking that Mom had started the complaints, and hoping he could appease her, Eddie went AWOL, until some friends found him and brought him back. Mom didn't hear about the letter until then. When she did, she wrote Eddie her own letter, apologizing for her mother, breaking the engagement off.

The day after, Mom told me, her head kept threatening to roll off her neck, and she barely got through the day at work. Riding home, she lay across the back seat of her father's car, closing her eyes on the seat cover. She decided that it was all right about the wedding, that she had been less in love with Eddie than with the family nights at his house, but it was not all right that she continue on this way, not knowing what it was that she faced.

"What's wrong with Mother," she said into the air, and when her father spoke softly around the subject, she said, "Daddy, no. Just say the truth." Without looking around, my grandfather started talking, telling out a history that Mom actually had lived before she was old enough to carry it in her mind.

My grandmother's poison pen had come to light first on the East Coast, when my grandfather was pastor of a Baptist church in Maine. Until then, Grandma had appeared "regular," the plainer-faced of twin sisters, married at twenty-eight to a man who spoke so gently that you had to bend close to make out his words. They had five daughters, of which my mother was second to youngest, and at the time when Grandma's mind went wrong, the children were spread from ages two to ten.

My grandfather didn't say how he found out about the letters, only that they were said to come in the morning mail and were never signed. The words were inked on plain paper in Grandma's writing, and they went out mostly to women in the church, complaining of many things: that the preacher visited help on every parish family while his own front steps needed fixing, or that this or that woman was turning eyes against the preacher's wife. The letters defended Grandmother against rumors that no one had ever spread, rumors that Grandma was dull or frigid, or that she didn't know how to keep house.

Grandpa was afraid, he said, in the face of this thing he did not recognize. He checked Grandma into a mental hospital for two weeks' observation, and he waited sadly, the way that an advisor waits for advice. He studied at home for his sermons, fed his daughters three meals, and told them their mother was sick but would be home in a little while. He visited Grandma and watched her cry out, asking him how could he do this to her, how could he believe these lies, she had written no letters at all. In the end, her doctors diagnosed her a paranoid schizophrenic. Hopelessly so, they said.

They said he should leave her there, Grandpa told my mother, that she could only do hurt at home. No one, no matter how close, could reason her out of this, could go behind her eyes and make her know the world as it really was. No one could teach her about people, that they had no knives in their pockets, that they didn't follow her as prey. No one, probably, could make her remember even sending those letters.

But he could not do that, Grandpa said, did Mom see? He wept for the years his children had paid for, but he could not have left his wife there in a place she would never be free of, could not confine her body to where her mind was said to belong. So Grandpa had taken her home, had resigned as pastor in Vermont, had moved his family far west to a place with new air, knowing as his daughters grew older that they would breathe their mother's breath for the rest of their lives.

And Grandpa was certainly right, at least with regard to my own mother. Once she had a name, a tag for the corners and oily blind alleys Grandma looked out from behind, Mom took that name to the L.A. library and for a weekend she read gluttonously, piling books and journals around on the floor, the chair, the table, feeding herself through her own eyes the knowledge she'd needed all along. She found it some comfort to read finally and know that to help her mother was a thing well wished for, but far outside her own power.

It was good to know, too, that she need not admire a woman like that, or feel somehow to blame for Grandma's fear that her daughters were always just ahead and waiting to seize her. These consolations were good, my mother told me, and healthy for the spirit, but they could not overpower a new sad thing, a clinical study showing that Grandma's vision could pass on, could live inside the skulls of her children. This news was hard, urging that my mother watch herself like an enemy, and the fear of having children became after that a sourness Mom carried on her skin every day.

My father first met Mom during this period, when he was still a recent immigrant, still growing disillusioned with the falseness and self-importance of American citizens. It was 1953, just before Dad was to be drafted into the army, and when a church singles group in Los Angeles organized a skating party Dad went, spotting Mom there first thing and asking her to be his partner. Mom was seventeen and also, Dad said later, the only person he saw there who withdrew from the spotlight, who was comfortable laughing at other people's stories without demanding they listen to a better one of hers. "She was real," he would tell his children. "Your mom, even in that place, she was real."

"You vantoo skate," Dad had asked, and

Mom said all right, with that thin smile, I imagine, that she wore pointed toward the floor in all the photos. She held his hand around the bend for "The Mexican Hat Dance," laughing kindly all the times he fell off his wheels and pulled her down after him. "My ferry first skating," Dad shouted, getting up and smiling around at the strangers, all of them making a path around him. Later, in the parking lot, he tried to kiss her (years afterward my mother said, "Your dad was all hands"), and Mom pushed him away, rigid and afraid and refusing his request for a date. My father was too loud for that place, and too ingenuous — certainly far too conspicuous; for Mom had learned strong reserve and shyness, growing up with her mother, and this honest and vivid young Pole was too much for her.

But my father wrote letters from his army post, sending word through other friends to "say hello to that girl." He felt drowned in the service, but stopped short of writing that, despairing alone over the vast inhumanity around him. It was the McCarthy era, and people — military ones especially — looked dangerously askance at Europeans, at my father himself without even U.S. citizenship to speak for him. "The people there," he said much later, "were like Nazis. Everyone hear-

ing McCarthy, everyone hating us foreigners."
He walked the sidewalks alone at night, thinking. His letters to my mother, though, were
merely lonely, describing his Christmas, his
dinner, the church he went to. She wrote him
back once or twice, speaking only of the small
things, never mentioning her mother, her history, the bleak despair in her own mind. She
told instead of her own holidays, describing
the weather there, saying, "I hope things are
going better for you." This continued a year
or more, and my mother's friends laughed
aloud at Dad's spellings, feeling sorry but
laughing anyway, and then my father's hopelessness overtook him and he turned back inside himself, breaking contact and losing my
mother's name.

He saw her in L.A. again after his discharge,
on the steps of a Bible-school dormitory at the
end of Hope Street, on an afternoon when he
had bought a frying pan and was carrying it
up the stairs, preparing to break the fire code
and make dinner in his room. He had not
known, when he enrolled at the college, that
Mom was a student there, too; he had thought
only of rest and of study and of kindlier people
around him; and to see "that girl" there, walking past with her friends, so startled him — my
mother glancing his way and then looking again
harder, waving — that he spoke the first words

in his head, saying, "I am cookink," grinning toward the skillet held aloft in his hand. Years later, that phrase, and his accentuation of it, and his ungainly stance and airbrushed rayon shirt would be a family joke, and my parents would choke on their dinner as they told it. "I am cookink," Dad would say, and Mom would laugh again, "Cookink, Cookink."

But for my mother back then, the days still were hungry and full of fear. In the years between the skating party and the meeting on the stairs, she had graduated from high school and enrolled in college, had learned of her mother's schizophrenia and broken off her wedding engagement because of it, had begun the hard years of looking backward, wanting to fathom all the harm that had come to her. She was living then in a hotel apartment with two women, working two jobs to pay for a degree in political science, eating nothing but water mixed with spoonfuls of brown sugar from a bag. At her first sight of Dad that day, she thought little else but "Oh no," and then he was gone from her head, having relinquished his place there to much darker thoughts.

Until he started leaving groceries at her door.

Somehow he learned that she and her roommates had no food, and he began sneaking up into the women's part of the hotel with bags overflowing his arms. Mom found this humiliating and asked him to stop; he did, but he continued to accost her on the red carpet of the lobby, speaking loud and barely coherent English as she edged away. He asked her for dates, he called out her name when he saw her, and my mother and her friends began pretending not to hear, walking evenly ahead and around the corners of buildings, then sprinting wildly away and ducking into doorways. When my father reached the corners, he stopped, looking both ways and wondering how they had disappeared so fast.

He followed her this way for months, and pestered her into going out a few times. He was sure he wanted to marry this woman — though she did not at first know this and would have been horrified to hear it — but he had to be sure of her vision, what sorts of worlds she could live in. He loved her, he said later, because she was not artificial, because she was the only genuine person he had met in this country; shy as she was, she was only shy and not coy, truly who she was in places where everyone else behaved however they had to to get ahead. In conversation, she and my father spoke, finally, the truth of their families and their lives — Mom's broken engagement, Dad's existence in war — and he told her then the hard parts: eating scraps of garbage, washing his face with urine so as to look less like an escaped prisoner. He told her of the family whistle, how in order to find his children even on dangerous nights his own father had taught them this code, warning them never to use it with others. Many times, my father had run out gladly toward the whistle, knowing definitely it was his lost father, or one of his brothers, for each of them sounded different when they whistled, just as each had a different spoken voice. He told her of another whistle which meant not "Where are you?" but "There's danger," and he spoke of the times they had used it, saving one another from death. If she was shocked, my mother did not show it, but asked him more questions instead, learning the whistle, hearing the talk and taking it in.

"If you got married," my father said once, testing her, "and you had to live in a hard place, what would you do to keep living? Could you do all you needed? Would you eat dogs or snakes?"

My mother thought, looking down at the table. It was a very hard question, she thought, but it was not a hard answer. "I suppose I would have to," she responded, looking up and straight at him. "I wouldn't like it, but yeah, I'd do it." Yes, Dad thought.

Yes, I knew that.

And they kept on like this, Mom avoiding Dad and finally getting caught, accepting a date and being drawn then in spite of herself into his stories. In public and in private he was inept, too direct, too untactful, but each loud opinion was a true one, spoken from a soul much larger, it seemed to her, than the rest of them there. I suppose it was this, in the end, that convinced her to marry him, this man of the serious self, this man with his simple standards, who demanded so much from the world.

Still, when he did ask her to marry him, she did all she could to sabotage the plan without offending; he was a friend, after all, albeit a peculiar one. Hearing the story myself many years later, I was amazed that in the end Dad prevailed. I know that when he asked, my mother hadn't the heart to give a direct no, but said instead that the college would never approve it; in those days, the students had to petition to be married, and the rule was strict that they must have been friends for at least a year, preferably two. But when my father submitted the request (saying blandly, "I've known her since a skating party three years ago," to which my mother said when she heard it, "LIES! I hardly knew you then"), it was approved — presumably, my mother said later, because they were thankful for any person willing to take on that very odd young man.

Mom felt nervous then, but still could not say no to my father. Instead, she set the wedding date for December 15 of that year, when school would still be in session, and because of which the college administration would most certainly bar the wedding. They did not, and thus broke both their own rule on appropriate dates for marriage, and apparently my mother's last bastion of resistance. At the wedding, her roommate said, "You can still get out of this, you know." And my mother put on her headpiece, saying, "Oh no, I can't." Years after, when people asked if she loved her husband more now than she had when she'd married him, she said, "Oh, a lot more. I didn't love him then." And this may be true. But I tend to think that if in the beginning my mother lacked what is known as romantic love, she was somehow overtaken by romance itself, of the sort I saw her embrace in my childhood, the sort which lived in Dad's songs, his histories, his uneven fit among middle Americans.

So my parents were married, and by the time they had me, and I had grown old enough to form memories, they had begun already to mold one another: my father had quieted a bit, and my mother become vivid, but still she left the iron too long on the glossy discotheque shirts Dad brought home with him.

But it was a great long time before children, with much overcoming to do. They attended school in the spring, but Mom quit after that to find work, and Dad transferred to Long Beach City College, abandoning his degree in foreign language and taking voice lessons instead. Mom followed suit with the lessons, and together they went to auditions and got parts in the Long Beach Civic Light Opera. But everything was hardship in those days; Dad could not keep a job, did poorly in school, felt scatterbrained and unkempt, and Mom kept asking him, "What is happening here."

"It's the world," my father said. "These people. Look at the light-opera crowd." He spoke of their fakeness, their careerism, their willingness to buy life at any expense. A woman in the chorus had even offered Mom cash for a two-line speaking part she had in a musical. "The talent scouts," she had said to my mother, "they'll be there. And you don't even care about this like I do."

They managed at most four hours' sleep per night between musicals, cast parties, work, and school, and they argued a great deal and ate very little. In time, my mother said, "This is enough," and they separated into different apartments, my father moving between jobs, my mother supporting only herself, still not easily, and still without peace. She filed divorce papers, which my father would not sign, and she took them home and threw them away. And still she continued to check on Dad, stopping in to see him, asking was he working, eating, sleeping at all.

It was one of those visits which turned it for them, or began to. After work, my mother drove to my father's apartment, walking down the basement steps, knocking and opening the door. Inside, there was shouting, and she saw there Dad and his brother Pietrek, hollering out in Polish, switching to Russian, throwing out German in between. They saw her and Pietrek pointed, saying *Twoja zona,* your wife, and they continued. My father's brother was obviously ridiculing Dad, waving around, raising his lips, and when Pietrek finally left, Mom said, "What was that?"

"He was making fun of me. Half a man, he says." Mom waited for more, and Dad looked around. He said, "We are married five years and no children." It was not the time for children, they had both said before, not like this, and not with Mom's fear of her own mother's madness, but even so, Pietrek's words had been mean; he had offered to "arrange" a child for Dad, if he could not produce any on his own.

"Do you think we can be together again," Dad asked, meaning, I think, did he have even her in the world.

Mom said, "The only way is somewhere else. Here, it's hard, all the old things around us."

The only other place my father knew was New York, that jumping-off place for immigrants: "New York," my mother yelled. "Are you kidding?" And Dad answered, "Well, where else, then." And because she had no better plan — at least, she said, one of them would find it familiar — she and my father packed up 750 pounds of books and took them on a bus. Mom showed Dad how to find apartments in the newspaper and they went searching, finding a third-floor walkup in Rockaway and hauling their books to it on the subway.

And there, too, they were strangers. The Polish community was vastly suspicious of them. "You're not a Pole," they said to my father. "You're a Protestant." On the sidewalk, as they drove by in the car, Mom and Dad saw two white boys pushing and shouting at a black boy on a bike. Adults stood around, watching, and my father said, "I'm pulling over." By the time he parked and he and Mom walked back, a policeman was handcuffing the black boy.

"Wait a minute," Dad said. "What did these guys tell you."

"This kid hit them. For no reason. He just started in." The man put his hand on the black boy, who was silent then and motionless and looking down at the pavement.

"They're lying," Dad said, and he told the whole story, waving his hands and shouting. "Yeah," the policeman said. "Okay, yeah." But he took the black boy into the car, ignoring my father's shouting.

My father turned to the grinning white boys. He lowered his voice and stood in their faces, raising his hands toward them, saying, "If your parents loved you, they wouldn't let you grow into pigs."

"Filth," my mother said. "Scum."

Another time it was a man with a wooden leg on the subway, and a street gang knocking at his crutches while a crowd sat around pretending not to watch. "Do you see that," my mother whispered. "Julius, do you see that."

"I see it," he said. "Let me put down these bags." He bent and stood up again, pushing out his muscles and shouting, "Okay, how about a guy with two legs." The gang looked his way and the man with the crutches lifted one up, ready to swing.

133

The boys began to disperse, backing away into shadows, but my father grabbed two of them by the hair and throttled them, shaking and shaking until their necks were wobbly and they began almost to cry. "Filth," my mother shouted again. "Punks. You should be killed, I'd do it myself." Picking up the groceries, looking around at the people there peeking over their newspapers, she demanded, "What are you looking at. You call yourselves humans?"

"Lady," a man said. "You could get killed yourself doing junk like that."

My parents were fully together by then, and fully apart still, it seemed, from the rest of the world. Dad went to computer school on the G.I. Bill, working part-time at a hot-dog stand on the boardwalk. They had a child their first year — me — and they stayed two more, my mother breast-feeding me for eighteen months because they could not afford baby food. When they had had enough of that place, when my mother said again, "This is enough," they drove back to California, where my father got work at an airline, having been trained in computers by then. It was 1964, and here began the construction of a family, the bearing of more children against Mom's better judgment, the house three blocks from Grandma's, the phone calls Mom dreaded in the evenings.

So I should not wonder about the black time, that it came on my mother with such force, or indeed that it came at all. When she had borne us, her three daughters and a son, she had been still watching, still looking warily into mirrors, searching her face for Grandmother's eyes. And in the early years while we were all small, she had watched us, too, for sadness, determining that at no time would she be the cause of it, or even be too far off to soothe it. Yet, when I was hurt, she had been across town, and gone too long to save me; this, I know, would have followed her, would have entered her sleep and smothered her, would have sent her certainly into black time. So what I find improbable is not the bare fact of her dread, but that she can have kept it in her hands, can have grabbed hold and put it away those times when it rose in her chest and threatened to unnerve her, to take her eyes away from all she must do those years to move us forward.

A time even came when I wished my mother would protect us more fervently, when for my sister's sake especially I pleaded for it, calling Mom feeble and uncaring as she watched her children misused and did not rise up in anger. We were in Spokane then at the house of Maureen and Martin, two friends from the California days when Mom and Dad had been light-opera actors, who had liked my parents and had them over on Saturdays, even after we children were born. They had moved later to Spokane and now, months after the accident, we were there visiting on a ten-day break from my new series of operations in Seattle. Leslie and Ian had been with them several weeks already; Mom had sent them along soon after we got to Seattle, rather than trail them behind her, duck-style, every day between my hospital and the rooming house where she stayed with Bethel. The hospital was a hard place in which to keep track of four children — one a toddler, one infirm, two loud and healthy — and the landlady at the rooming house viewed them as fearsome plagues, likely at any time to start a fire or bring down the walls. In the evenings she was clear about how little she enjoyed the company of my middle sister and brother.

So Mom packed Leslie and Ian a suitcase and bought small new things for their treasure chests. She called Spokane and planned train tickets, one for Maureen to Seattle, and a return one to Spokane for Maureen and the two children. At the station, she wrote a letter to my father, asking Leslie and Ian for things to tell him, and she said that they were going forward to a great fun time, that in Spokane they would see cows, and many birds, and deer walking on the pond behind Martin's house. She told them she would send notes through the mail, and that before long we would come to see them again, and when we did there would be games in their rooms and snowmen in the yard. Be good, she told them, and listen to the grownups. And then they were on the train, and Mom and Bethel were waving to them, blowing kisses down the tracks until they were out of sight.

The weeks in Seattle without Ian and Leslie were bleak ones for my mother; yet until I read her journal many years later I knew the bleakness only by how little she chose to say about it. Mostly it was her face that fell those first few days when Bethel crawled under my bed at night, calling for Leslie or Ian. When Mom had to speak of sadness, she did so quickly — and then never to other mothers on the ward, but solely to me, her family — before she turned on the television or suggested a game. With my father so far off and in the middle of his own loneliness, she would have thought it cruel to say too much to him of her troubles; instead, she wrote of hospital news: the state of my bone grafts, the drawbridge we watched go up and down outside the wide, shining window of my room.

Leslie's and Ian's treasure chests and luggage were lost by the train company, and

Maureen wrote that she was improvising clothes however she could. She said she was putting the children to bed earlier now, because when they got too tired they sat with their heads down and cried for their father. Leslie was taking it the hardest, Maureen said, although most of the time things seemed fine, and the children loved to watch her feed the cows. We could not tell from her letters that Leslie was crying from more than just homesickness.

When my ten-day break came, Mom had a doctor teach her to irrigate my wounds and to change dressings, then she packed up her things from the boardinghouse and took Bethel and me on the train. We were going to find Leslie and Ian, she said; they would be glad to see us.

Ian seemed just the same. He smiled with his big crooked teeth when he saw us, and he put his neck under my arm and held my finger, saying, "We get dessert after dinner." Leslie had grown chubby in those few weeks, and her shoulders had drawn forward over her chest. Under long bangs, her eyes were rounder, and she cried when she saw Mom, and then squeezed me around the neck. "Don't roughhouse, Leslie," Martin said. "You can't jiggle Natalie's head." When Leslie let go and watched up at him through her bangs, not smiling anymore, I was angry. With her head down, Leslie looked then the way Hobo had when tall people said his name.

I said, "Don't worry. She's my sister."

Martin stared at me with his foot in the air, mid-stride, and I put my treasure chest down, ready to run. Then Mom started talking, saying oh, wasn't it nice to be all together, and did we know that the snow here was as pretty as Alaska's. It was the first of many times when my mother would smile and chatter to avoid war, and by the end of those ten days I would hate that tactic and come close to believing it meant she cared nothing for what had become of her middle daughter.

I loathed Martin; this had always been so, even when he and Maureen had lived near us in Los Angeles and had been pinochle partners with my parents. In those days they had lived in an all-white house — white carpet, drapes, sofas, piano — and had kept a room in back where my brother and sisters and I slept on Saturday card nights. We brought toys from home so we would not be tempted to touch Martin's things; if we did, and if my mother and father were not in the room, Martin would pick us up by the shoulders and squeeze until our fingers went cold. "You belong in a cage," he would say. I am pleased now to remember that I usually wet the blankets I slept on, and that the urine soaked through them onto the white rug.

In Spokane, Martin seemed to believe that Alaska had made us more like animals than ever, and his constant comment was that "all the girls come out acting like boys." I was too weak and my head swung too heavily on my neck for me to be very rowdy, and Bethel was too small still for Martin to work much on, so he concentrated mostly on Leslie, aiming to teach her the appropriate differences between boys and girls. Leslie said later that things had been much worse with Martin before Mom and I came, that she alone was spanked for not finishing dinner, or when she and Ian both played tag in the house. Ian was Martin's darling, presumably because he acted naturally as a boy should, but Leslie was punished if she played in Ian's same way. My brother learned to click his tongue in his mouth and did it all day for three days, saying, "Watch, Leslie. You do it like this." When Leslie figured it out she was thrilled, and she and Ian sat on the bed clicking out rhythms more complicated than those Ian had formed alone; Martin heard from the next room and rushed in, grabbing Leslie up and swatting her behind. This was no way, he said, for a little girl to act.

By the time we arrived, Leslie had come

to find praise only at the dinner table, and I was sickened to see how hard she strove for it. There were no spankings now for unfinished supper, just long heavy stares and the verdict, "No dessert." Maureen dished out plates from a sideboard and carried them to us, handing around piles of spaghetti higher than any of us could finish. If one of us slowed down at all before our dish was empty, Maureen or Martin would look hard at us and say, "You know, someone worked hard to make this good food," or "In some houses you'd be in bed tomorrow with no supper at all." I was angry, especially when Leslie looked up at Martin and smiled, taking bigger mouthfuls.

Once I said, "If she can't finish, she can't finish," and Mom stepped on my foot under the table. I looked at my mother then and her fork was in her mouth and she moaned, "M-m-m. I love this sauce." Maureen was scooping out dessert — red Jell-O with marshmallows — and Leslie was looking at it with her eyebrows bent back, starting to cry.

"My stomach hurts," she said, and Martin looked up.

"But you still have food left. I guess there's no dessert." Martin took a bowl of Jell-O and set it down beside Ian, who had pushed his plate back with spaghetti still on it.

Mom fingered Leslie's bangs from her eyes

and told her, "Maybe you should lie down if your tummy hurts, baby."

"Can I have dessert later?" Leslie asked. "I ate almost everything."

Martin said, "Dessert is only for dinnertime. Tomorrow you might decide to finish your supper." Leslie's shoulders came forward, and tears came out her eyes, and she scooted her bottom off the chair. Mom put a hand between Leslie's shoulders and stood up to follow, telling her, "Let's go to the bedroom and read your new book."

Just then I could not breathe. Much later, when I was tall, I would take on my sister's bullies and fling myself at them fists first, just to see the blood come. But there in Martin's kitchen I was eight and skinny under my bandages, and my mother — the only real ally — had turned from this fight as if she were deaf to it. I simply could not breathe.

The first air I took choked me and I took more and screamed at Mom, "You're walking away. Tell him to leave her alone." And I lost reason then and ran at Martin, stopping short because I could no longer see him, and I called him a coward and a bully and half a man and every insulting thing I had gone to sleep repeating since we got to Spokane. In the bedroom, Leslie had stopped crying, and I slammed into my mother, wailing at her

142

now, asking how could she let Martin talk that way, Leslie was too little to stand up for herself, and no one here was standing for her. I shook when I talked, and she spoke quietly, saying this was Martin's house, we were guests, we had to go by his rules while we were here.

I hated Mom right then and thought she was weak. And for a very long time I despised that weakness, thinking she had stood still like that because she was afraid of Martin, or because she cared less for my sister than she should. My disrespect survived until years later when she seemed to change, and took on every enemy of ours as her own. She had raised peaceful children, and bullies came to view us as passive, or scared, and they picked on us, my brother especially, calling out "wimp" and "pansy." When I had swallowed this for too long, there were fistfights in the schoolyard, and my mother allowed me these, saying, "Yes, you have to stick up for your brother and sisters."

But that later attitude came from time and distance, I know, not basic change. I understood now that at Martin's house Mom was never indifferent, and not blind to all that was wrong. It must only have seemed to her a question of perspective; she hurt for Leslie and could offer her comfort, but she could not fight for her just then while she was fighting for so much else. And besides, Leslie was alive in spite of Martin. And although his offense was great sorrow, Mom had too recently known much greater sorrow — had chased after our very lives like cinders scudding away in the wind. So when she looked around her in those days at the harm Martin could do, at the trivial words he could say, she must have dipped her face a little and shut tight her eyes and, reaching a hand down inside herself, discovered that she hadn't the heart to withstand it.

CHILDREN'S HOSPITAL

I was always waking up, in those days, to the smell of gauze soaked with mucus and needing to be changed. Even when I cannot recall what parts of me were bandaged at what moment, I remember vividly that smell, a sort of fecund, salty, warm one like something shut up and kept alive too long in a dead space. Most of the details I remember from that time are smells, and the chancest whiff from the folds of surgical greens, or the faint scent of ether on cold fingers, can still drag me, reflexively, back to that life, to flux so familiar as to be a constant in itself. Years after Seattle Children's Hospital, when I took my own daughter in for stitches in her forehead, and two men unfolded surgical napkins directly under my nose, I embarrassed us all by growing too weak to stand, and had to sit aside by myself until all the work was over.

It seems odd that these smells have power to bring back such horror, when my memories of that time are not, on the whole, dark ones. Certainly I suffered pain, and I knew early a debilitating fear of surgery itself, but the life I measured as months inside and months outside the walls was good. There was a playroom in the children's wing, a wide room full of light, with colored walls and furniture, and carpets on the floor. A wooden kitchen held the corner alongside our infirmary, and my friends and I passed many hours as families, cooking pudding for our dolls before they were due in therapy. Most of the dolls had amputated arms and legs, or had lost their hair to chemotherapy, and when we put on our doctors' clothes, we taught them to walk with prostheses, changing their dressings with sterile gloves.

We had school tables, and many books, and an ant farm by the window so we could care for something alive. And overseeing us all was Janine, a pink woman, young even to seven-year-old eyes, with yellow, cloudy hair that I touched when I could. She kept it long, parted in the middle, or pulled back in a pony-tail like mine before the accident. My hair had been blond then, and I felt sensitive now about the coarse brown stubble under my bandages. Once, on a thinking day, I told Janine that if I had hair like hers I would braid it and loop the pigtails around my ears. She wore it like that the next day, and every day after for a month.

Within Janine's playroom, some of us were handicapped, but none disabled, and in time we were each taught to prove this for ourselves. While I poured the flour for new play dough, Janine said, "Did Mrs. Goodman make homemade clay?" Mrs. Goodman, she knew, had been my kindergarten teacher before we left California, before my accident, before all this, and she was the one to whom my mother had referred when my surgeons had first mentioned a glass eye; for Mrs. Goodman had lost one of her own through some illness, and missed many school days because of it, and between her trips to surgery she wore a glass eye, or an eyepatch very much like mine.

So Janine's question was not about play dough but about the ways people keep going on. What had Mrs. Goodman looked like, she said, with an eyepatch, and was she missing my same eye? What were the hard parts for a teacher like that? Did I think it was sad for her to miss school sometimes, and did she talk about the hospital? What color was her hair, which kind was her eyepatch, and did I remember if she was pretty? What would I be, Janine asked, when I was that age and these surgeries were past? Over the wet salt smell of green dough, I wished to be a doctor with one blue eye, who could talk like this to the sick, who could tell them they were still real. And with her feel for when to stop talking, Janine turned and left me, searching out volunteers to stir up new clay.

She asked a lot of questions, Janine did, and we answered her as we would have answered ourselves, slowly and with purpose. When called to, Janine would even reverse her words, teaching opposite lessons to clear the mist in between; this happened for Thomas and Nick in their wheelchairs, and I grew as much older from watching as they did from being taught. Both boys were eleven, and though I've forgotten their case histories, I do remember their natures, the differences that drew them together.

They were roommates, and best friends, and their dispositions reverberated within one another, the self-reliant and the needy. Thomas was the small one, the white one, with blue veins in his forehead, and pale hair falling forward on one side. He sat always leaning on his elbows, both shoulders pressing up around his ears, and he rested his head to the side when he talked. He depended on Nick, who was tight-shouldered and long, to take charge for him, and he asked for help with his eyes half open, breathing out words through his mouth. And Nick reached the far shelves, and brought Thomas books, and proved he could do for them both, never glancing for help at those who stood upright. His skin was darker than Thomas's, and his eyes much lighter, the blue from their centers washing out into the white.

When they played together, those boys, Thomas was the small center of things, the thin planet sunken into his wheelchair, pulling his friend in after him. It must not have seemed to Nick that he was being pulled, because he always went immediately to Thomas's aid, never expecting anyone else to notice. Janine, of course, did. When Thomas wanted the television switched, and Nick struggled up to do it, she called: "Nick, would you like me to do that?"

"I can do it," he said.

"But, so can I," Janine told him, and she strode easily to the television and turned the knob to "Sesame Street." "Sometimes," she said to Nick, "you have to let your friends be kind; it makes them feel good." She went back to sit beside Thomas, and she handed him the Erector set. How would he turn the channel, she asked, if no one else were here? What could he do by himself? And as the TV went unnoticed, Thomas imagined a machine with gears and little wheels, and Janine said she thought it could work. After that,

Thomas was always building, though he still asked for help, and he still got it. Nick never did ask, as long as I knew him, but in time he managed to accept what was offered, and even, in the end, to say thanks.

In this way and in others, Janine encouraged us to change. When we had new ideas, they were outstanding ones, and we could count almost always on her blessing. We planned wheelchair races, and she donated the trophy — bubble-gum ice cream all around. When she caught us blowing up surgical gloves we had found in the trash, she swiped a whole case of them, conjuring a helium bottle besides; that afternoon the playroom smelled of synthetic, powdery rubber, and we fought at the tables over colored markers, racing to decorate the brightest balloon. Janine's was the best — a cigar-smoking man with a four-fingered Mohawk — and she handed it down the table to someone's father.

She always welcomed our parents in, so long as they never interfered; and they respected the rule, acting consistently unsurprised. When Sheldon's mother arrived one day, she found her son — a four-year-old born with no hands — up to his elbows in orange fingerpaints. She stood for a moment, watching, then offered calmly to mix up a new color.

We children enjoyed many moments like

these, granted us by adults like Janine and our parents, and these instants of contentment were luxuries we savored, but on which, by necessity, we did not count. I've heard my father, and other immigrant survivors of World War II, speak of behavior peculiar to people under siege, of how they live in terms not of years but of moments, and this was certainly true of our lives. That time was fragmentary, allowing me to remember it now only as a series of flashes, with the most lyrical event likely at any moment to be interrupted. We children were each at the hospital for critical reasons, and a game we planned for one day was likely to be missing one or two players the next, because Charlie had hemorrhaged in the night, Sarah was in emergency surgery, or Candice's tubes had pulled out. I myself missed many outings on the lawn because my bone grafts rejected or because my eye grew so infected that I had to be quarantined. At these times, I would watch the others out the closed window, waiting for them to come stand beyond the sterile curtain and shout to me a summary of the afternoon.

In the same way that the future seemed, because it might never arrive, generally less important than the present, so, too, with the past. Although each of us children could have recited his own case history by heart, it was rare that any of us required more than a faint sketch of another child's past; we found it both interesting and difficult enough to keep current daily record of who had been examined, tested, or operated upon, and whether it had hurt, and if so, whether they had cried. This last question was always of interest, and tears we looked on as marks, not of cowards, but of heroes, playmates who had endured torture and lived to testify. The older a child was, the greater our reverence when her roommate reported back after an exam; we derived some perverse comfort from the fact that even twelve-year-olds cracked under pressure.

Those of us who did choose to abide vigorously in each instant were able to offer ourselves, during the day, to one another, to uphold that child or parent who began to weaken. If her need was to laugh, we laughed together; if to talk, we listened; and once, I remember, I stood a whole morning by the chair of a fifteen-year-old friend, combing her hair with my fingers, handing her Kleenex and lemon drops, saying nothing. At night, then, we withdrew, became quietly separate, spoke unrestrainedly with our families. We spent these evening hours regrouping, placing the days in perspective, each of us using our own methods of self-healing. My mother would read to me from the Book of Job, telling of that other day long past when a man's great sorrow came, not to punish him, but to prove him holy. Or she would sit with me and write letters to our scattered family — my father at work in Alaska, Leslie and Ian in Spokane. Of the letters that still exist from that time, all are full of sustenance, of words like *courage* and *honor*. It should have sounded ludicrous to hear a seven-year-old speaking such words, but I uttered them without embarrassment, and my parents did not laugh.

For most of us, it became clear that horror can last only a little while, and then it becomes commonplace. When one cannot be sure that there are many days left, each single day becomes as important as a year, and one does not waste an hour in wishing that that hour were longer, but simply fills it, like a smaller cup, as high as it will go without spilling over. Each moment, to the very ill, seems somehow slowed down, and more dense with importance, in the same way that a poem is more compressed than a page of prose, each word carrying more weight than a sentence. And though it is true we learned gentleness, and the shortness of time, this was not the case for everyone there, and in fact there were some who never embraced their mortality.

I first saw Darcy by a window, looking down

into her lap, fingering glass beads the same leafy yellow as her skin. She was wearing blue, and her dress shifted under her chin as she looked up, asking me was I a boy, and why was my hair so short. Behind us, our mothers started talking, exchanging histories, imagining a future, and Darcy and I listened, both grown accustomed by now to all this talk of ourselves. Darcy was ten, and she was here for her second attempted kidney transplant, this time with her father as donor. The first try had failed through fault, her mother said, of the surgeons, and Washington State's best lawyer would handle the suit if anything went wrong this time. This threat was spoken loudly and often as long as I knew Darcy, and it was many years before I realized that her parents were afraid, and that they displayed their fear in anger, and in those thousand sideways glances at their daughter.

As a playmate, Darcy was pleasant, and she and I made ourselves jewelry from glitter and paste, and dressed up as movie stars, or as rich women in France. We played out the future as children do, as if it were sure to come and as if, when it did, we would be there. It was a game we all played on the ward, even those sure to die, and it was some time before I knew that to Darcy it was not a game, that she believed it all. We were holding school, and Nick was the teacher, and Darcy was answering that when she grew up she would own a plane, and would give us free rides on the weekends.

"What if," Nick said to her, "what if you die before then?"

Darcy breathed in and out once, hard, and then she said, "I'm telling my mother you said that." Then she stood and left the playroom, and did not come back that day. Later, her father complained to Nick's, called him foolish and uncaring, and demanded that such a thing not happen again.

After that, Darcy came to play less often, and when she did, her parents looked on, even on days when Janine took us outside to look at the bay. Darcy grew fretful, and cried a good deal, and took to feeling superior, even saying that my father didn't love me or he wouldn't be in Alaska. When I forgave her, it was too late to say so, because I was gone by then and didn't know how to tell her.

Darcy's absence was a loss, not just to her, but to us other children as well. Just as we had no chance to comfort her, to offer our hands when she was weak, we could not count on her during our worst times, for she and her family inhabited fear, suffering in that peculiar way which admits no fellowship. I don't remember, if I ever knew, what became of

Darcy, because I came down with chicken pox and was discharged so as not to jeopardize her transplant. I like to think she must have lived, it was so important to her, and as I think this, I hope she did survive, and that one day she grew, as we all did in some way, to be thankful.

One of my smallest teachers during this time was a leukemia patient, just three years old, who lived down the hall. Because of his treatments, Samuel had very little hair, and what he did have was too blond to see. There were always, as I remember, deep moons under his eyes, but somehow, even to us other children, he was quite beautiful. His teeth were very tiny in his mouth, and he chuckled rather than laugh out loud; when he cried, he only hummed, drawing air in and out his nose, with his eyes squeezed shut and tears forming in the cracks where there should have been lashes. Most children's wards have a few favorite patients, and Samuel was certainly among ours. Those few afternoons when his parents left the hospital together, they spent twenty minutes, on their return, visiting every room to find who had taken off with their son. More often than not, he was strapped to a lap in a wheelchair, his IV bottle dangling overhead like an antenna, getting Motocross rides from an amputee.

Samuel possessed, even for his age, and in spite of the fact that he was so vulnerable, an implicit feeling of security, and it was partly this sense of trust which lent him that dignity I have found in few grown people. His mother, I remember, was usually the one to draw him away from our games when it was time for treatments, and although he knew what was coming, he never ran from it; when he asked his mother, "Do I have to?" it was not a protest, but a question, and when she replied that yes, this was necessary, he would accept her hand and leave the playroom on his feet.

I have heard debate over whether terminally ill children know they are going to die, and I can't, even after knowing Samuel, answer this question. We all, to some extent, knew what death was, simply because each of us had been friends with someone who was gone, and we realized that at some point many of us were likely to die; this likelihood was enough certainty for us, and made the question of time and date too insignificant to ask. I remember the last day I spent with Samuel, how we all invited him for a picnic on the lawn, though he could not eat much. He had had treatments that morning which made him weak, made his smile very tired, but this was the same vulnerability we had always found disarming, and I can't recall anything about that afternoon which seemed unusual. The rest of us could not know that Samuel would die before we woke up next morning, and certainly some things might have been different if we had; but I tend to think we would still have had the picnic, would still have rubbed dandelion petals into our skin, would still have taught Samuel to play slap-jack. And, for his part, Samuel would, as he did every day, have bent down to my wrist and traced the moon-shaped scar behind my hand.

SURGERY

There is a certain sound in the ears, like the crashing of rapids between stone walls, and a certain aluminum taste in the throat — familiar spirits who enter the moment before one succumbs to anesthesia. For that long instant, all of the senses are heightened — voices in the air grow louder, lights overhead brighter — and it always seemed to me that the moment before death must be quite like this, that in the body's final second it must enlarge outside itself to capture as much as the senses can hold, enveloping and drawing them quickly within, before the spirit leaves, and with it all awareness. It was only after being anesthetized many times that I learned not to fight it, not to claw ineffectually against unconsciousness and wake convulsing on the other side, but instead to relax into it, to close my eyes and lean backward into the operating table, further and further, as if the earth would open and my body would tumble into it whole, shoulders first. In the middle of it all, I would twitch — like a dreamer falling from a cliff — but this was no great nuisance, and was small cost for the lung-deep relief of abandoning desperation, of relinquishing hold on that which I did not control in the first place.

I hated surgery from the start, dreading its slug-footed approach and my helplessness in the face of it. I asked after each one if this was the last, and each time heard, "Wait and see." Wait and see if this graft takes, if it gets infected, if this is the one that makes your face seem normal, that closes up the path to your brain. The morning after an operation, especially in those critical early Fairbanks days when I was seven, the team of surgeons would visit to have a look at their work. They stood all around watching, and Dr. Gottschalk, the plastic surgeon, lifted me out from sheets that smelled of mucus and old bandages, then carried me to a chair in the center. He sat me upright, and when I started to fall, too weak in those first months to hold myself up, he murmured soft German sounds, holding my shoulders straight, until the room came to rest on dry ground. While the others conferred in flat tones about medication and sutures and all they should watch my scars for, Dr. Gottschalk said nothing, but bent closer down, began unwinding yards of white gauze, the linen which held my features back.

The talk went on, and the unraveling, and each layer that came away offered up its own heavy smell, its own yellow mucus stain until, as he reached the center, we sat there together in the warm steam of Betadine, iodoform, and rubber gloves. The last strip removed, Dr. Gottschalk reached farther in, drawing packings like bed stuffing out from my face. Then, as the others moved closer in, he held his palms up under my cheeks and stared into me, saying nothing, a long time.

"It burns," I said once. "Not like a cut, like a burn."

Dr. Gottschalk looked over to my seeing eye and said, "After this it will itch, and that will be good. It will mean you are healing." He looked at the other men. "And after she is healing, we do some skin grafts, and some bone. You think?" The men all agreed, the internist, the ophthalmologists, and the others, and only much later would it be clear to me how brave an agreement this was; for the Fairbanks hospital was small and just basically equipped, and to have saved me at all this far was already a vast achievement.

In those first two years after I was hurt, my surgeons in Fairbanks and then in Seattle worked mostly to save my life — grafting over open wounds, treating major infections — and later, by the third grade, when surgery was for my looks more than for my health, I had only to be careful and not quite so much worried, to clean out the drainage with peroxide every day and to watch each new scar cautiously, reporting any sign that the stitches were "compromised" or the bone grafts rejecting. In fact, though, and against all medical precedent, my body did reject its own tissue and bone, heaving it back out through each new incision, leaving my doctors and me always to start over, strategizing new ways to landscape space for a glass eye.

Early on, the Fairbanks doctors tried everything they knew. With part of my jaw joint gone, having been ripped out with my cheekbone the night of the accident, bone grafts in my cheek were difficult, but the surgeons made several attempts. Into that cavity they stuffed pieces of my ribs, shavings of skull from behind my ear, other bones where they could find them, and sometimes these grafts would do well for weeks, healing into place, it seemed, with no problem. Then without warning my cheek would enlarge, dissolving itself from the inside into thick brown liquid, and the bone would be thrust back out, dividing the healed scar and making it raw again. And I would be headed into surgery once more, not for progress this time, but to undo what should have gone well in the first round.

They could not explain this among themselves, why a body would reject its own matter. The skin grafts took more easily, and some even stayed in place, but there was always this awkward waiting between grafts, holding me in bed for weeks to see what became of this one. Sometimes, if the graft itself went well, healing its edges to the cavity and staying pink, the place on my arm or belly or leg from which the skin had been taken would oppose the sutures there violently, festering and growing enlarged. Those times, Dr. Gottschalk would make a special trip in to remove the stitches in my room, and though I was hollering already from the hurt of infection, he would quiet me for a moment and say, "I can't give you pain medicine now, I just have to take these out right here. If you can be a little still, I'll try to make it quickly." But however many there were who held my arms, however mildly my mother spoke in my ear, I still struggled and screamed, for the skin there would have swollen up and enveloped the stitches, and Dr. Gottschalk would have to cut and dig for them. Years later, my mother and I would discuss those moments and wonder aloud what possessed a man to endure that for someone else's child.

After the first months, Dr. Gottschalk and the others sent me down to Seattle, speculating to my parents that perhaps a big hospital would have more success. But there, too, each bone graft failed, and even the skin the new doctors replaced died within a week or grew profoundly infected, having to be removed and thrown away. Moreover, it was the early days of plastic surgery, and all skin grafts were full-thickness, large squares cut out from my body like sod, leaving wide, sensitive scars in their places. These procedures required many steps each, many surgeries, and for each one I remained in bed motionless for many days, careful not to jiggle the incisions. The first procedure was an easy one: a piece of belly skin, perhaps, cut in a long strip and curled under like a round sausage, left attached at both ends so the blood could feed through. When the sausage healed, one end was severed and attached to my wrist, sewn there for weeks while I learned to eat with my left hand. After that, the other end was detached from my belly and sewn to my eye cavity, my wrist again strapped into place while I lay beneath it in bed. In the end, my arm came down, and I had forgotten how to walk, easing myself to the edge of the bed and collapsing forward over my legs.

After all this, these weeks in bed and multiple surgeries, the graft most often failed in the end without cause. And even when the accident's first trauma had been healed, the original wounds patched over with what skin finally took, each successive operation — which should have been a movement smoothly forward toward an average-looking face — brought with it new emergencies and festering troubles, and the fight my body staged against itself led to many more operations than any of us had counted upon. And hating the sight and sounds of surgical theaters, I kept on with them anyway, sure as I was of prevailing, of finding myself one day well and whole and in possession of another blue eye. Surgery, I thought, was a necessary evil, and I had no choice but to walk through it in the best way I had, holding close to those who went with me.

Preparations began with a woman who came during the small dark hours of the morning to ask me my choice of hot broth or Jell-O. She came for years, speaking in a gray, comfortable whisper, bending close to my face when she woke me. She turned on the night lamp slowly, to make the smallest click, then tucked my sheets up and fed me, holding the spoon and the cup in dark hands not much larger than my own. The spoon-feeding started during times when, to prepare a skin graft, my wrist was sewn to my face or my belly, and later, when I could have managed the eating myself, we kept to the old way, offering and accepting nourishment without words. Afterward, her hand pressed my eyes and I slept, never asking her name.

The Jell-O and the broth held me till morning, when surgery was closer and the lights less gentle. A nurse or an aide marked my temperature and pulse, and if I hadn't an IV already, she brought in the hardware for one. My veins grew tired early on of needles, and at seven and a half my arms carried tracks like a junkie's; it took the best "poker" in the wing to find a good spot in under five tries.

Forty-five minutes before the operation, then, came the injected relaxant which dried out my eyes and my tongue, made my hands lie heavily on the sheets. The mouths in the room sounded metallic and sluggish, and the goldfish swam through Jell-O in its bowl. My lips felt too warm, stuck like paste to my teeth. I asked for ice chips to suck on.

Metal rattled against itself when the gurney arrived, and with it the pre-op team. They came wearing surgical greens, and if my head was not shaven, they brought me a paper bonnet like theirs. Over time, I came to know their faces, but only as they appeared standing over me, all in green, seeming very much larger than I was. Years later when we met on the street they would be delighted to see me, would pull my hair away from my face and approve my surgeons' expert scars; but I would not know them there speaking to me face-on, in street clothes, their hair and their lips in plain view.

In the operating room I was transferred, by the lifting of many hands, to a narrow rubber table, and a hot blanket lay heavily on my body. Overhead, steel bowls distorted images of me, of the instrument tables alongside, of long gas cylinders above my head. It was long before I learned to "go out" gracefully, to suffer the gas mask without calling out. At the first count, my words reverberated in my skull, bouncing from side to side like funhouse laughter. Adult whispers scratched enormously at my ears. An instant later, time had not passed, and I woke up feeble in the recovery room, sounds of struggle still pooling around my head.

So surgery was terror for me, a day of mad battle with no certainty of success, and years after it was over, when my father sprayed ether into his carburetor, I found myself flashing back, staring hard for a shaken time at the snow falling down. Yet in all this it was only the surgery I feared, and never the hospital itself, for in that place more than anywhere else I fit smoothly in, was only one of many other sick people, and amputees, and folks whose bandages were hardly unusual. I remember that a teacher from my school came once to visit, and before she left she stood in the hall with my mother, saying, "She seems almost to like it here." And this was true, in a way perhaps that my teacher did not realize, for a stay in the hospital was for me not confinement but refuge. In this place, children did not ridicule shaven heads, did not tear at my bandages, did not care to know how many names I would swallow before I started to cry. The hospital was not filled with salesclerks, flight attendants, pedestrians all wanting to know what had happened to my eye, and the only questions the nurses had were, did I need another painkiller and what did I want for lunch. In Alaska especially, I was the darling of the ward, because there were not usually other children, and I had my own bed among the women. Between surgeries, when my arm was on my head or I was waiting for the next operation to come, I made friends, and they snuck in chocolate or marshmallows and ate them on my bed.

Janie was a kidney patient in the bed next to mine, maybe thirty years old, with long brown hair twisted up in a clip. She had large hands like a man's, and she made huge jokes with her doctors, saying, "Look, it's just a kidney. Natalie has a spare I can borrow." Once, I had just called for a bedpan and was sitting on it under the sheets, and the hospital preacher came in to visit me. Janie did not mention the bedpan, but she spent the whole half hour giggling in her chest, shooing away the nurse who came to check on me. "She'll be done in a minute," Janie said. "She's OC-CUPIED, if you know what I mean." The preacher seemed bewildered when he left, pausing at the door to say, "My, there's some good spirit in this room," and as soon as he was gone, Janie and I exploded into such a loud giggle that the nurse came back in to investigate. "Hoo-hoo," Janie said, choking into her hands. "This child was PRAYING ON THE BEDPAN, and she never let on to anyone." The night she left to go home, she brought in a giant red bull that I called Garrett, after Janie's last name.

Sometimes, Juanita came into my room. She had gray, teased hair and tiny hands that wavered with multiple sclerosis, and she taught me to play Old Maid with a new deck of cards. Juanita helped me name my goldfish, drawing names out of her hat, saying, "It should be a yellow sort of name, don't you think?" And when we christened the fish Sunny, she leaned down and spoke his name to him, waving her finger at the glass. Times when I could walk, Juanita followed me to the baby-room window, and we stood there together, nearly the same height, naming the babies through the glass. "You come up with such good names," Juanita said. "Tina. I never would have thought of that one."

Nurses, too, came to sit, bringing egg-salad sandwiches, my favorite. "I'm going to the lounge," one would say, leaning her head through the doorway. "What can I get from the machine?" And I would answer back, "The usual." When the nurse came again, she would have a sandwich, and milk as well, and sometimes grapes or an apple. We would sit on my bed and carve fruit with a scalpel, making faces on it and eating the shavings.

And when my parents came, they brought lots of mail. Church people in town or from the Lower 48 who had heard of me sent cards and presents — a tape player, a rag doll, chocolate-covered cherries. (When I first had been hurt, doctors had worried about my thinness, about the veins showing green through my skin. Now, however, that I was confined to bed for as long as twelve weeks at a time, I grew plump on egg salad and candy, and for years my mother and I associated our weight problems with chocolate-covered cherries; I have hated them ever since.)

I found the hospital a safe place, and pleasant, full of people more like me than any I had known away from here. Only a few people made me uncomfortable, and they were all visitors from the outside. I could not understand hospitalphobes, those who never entered my room face-on, but eased around the doorframe, one shoulder first and after it the head, who produced a gift of flowers or chocolate and held it at arm's length while the rest of their bodies arrived. These people stood at the foot of my bed, clutching their jackets, speaking a little too loudly, a little too brightly. Everything in their manners — every look, every gesture — said, "People die in this place," and by the time they left I felt as relieved as they did, and a little peevish, as if they had insulted my country.

"Mommy," I said one day, when a woman from town had just visited. "Why was that lady jumpy like that?"

"Nervous, I think," Mom said. She leaned back in her chair and put her feet on my bed rail. "Some people just get nervous when they come here."

I said, "Nervous of me?"

"Oh, probably not of you. She's surely seen bandages before." Mom looked at me waiting for more. She yawned my way and said,

"Well, maybe she's never been in a hospital and she thinks you're unhappy here. Maybe she just feels bad."

This did not seem quite correct to me, since the look on that woman's face — and on all the faces like that — was not soft like pity, but instead tense, as from fear. But I was just eight then and my vocabulary not quite up to this distinction; I knew only my own impatience with that visit, my sense of something in the room left unaddressed. I learned graciousness only much later, when I was an adult visiting a hospitalized friend, and the man who went with me began to look nauseated and excused himself from the room. He came back in five minutes a little better, but still unable to relax in a chair; and on the way out to the car, I said, "Are you okay? Should I drive you home?"

The man said, "I'm sorry, no, it's fine. I just hate hospitals. Even the smell makes me sick." And here, I thought, I had myself walked past the janitor's closet, sniffing and feeling suddenly at ease, as if someone nearby had worn an old perfume I remembered liking once. It was a small but astonishing moment, and I thought about it for several days. In the end, I understood a shred more clearly this fact: that hospitalphobes had no reason to come to this place as to shelter, because most of them hadn't cause to feel unsafe on the outside.

OTHER
WOUNDS

"What does it look like under there?"

It was always this question back then, always the same pattern of hello and what's your name, what happened to your eye and what's under there. Usually I told the brief truth to my playmates, that the missing eye's socket was filled in now with belly skin, and a useless lid and lashes hung over it; if they pressed further, and if I was in a forthright mood, I said, "They're fixing me up for a glass eye. It looks about the same as ever." Other times, tired of spieling the same thin answers, I played to the earnest, breathing fourth-grade mouths, imagining for their pleasure a giant bottomless hole in my face, dark on the inside and so deep that only with a strong flashlight could one observe the red and festering cavity walls — and beyond them, the slick, pulsing lobe of my brain. Listening to this story, my classmates crowded in close, whispering, "Really? The

173

dog tore it out, just tore it like that," and they looked, not at me, but at my eyepatch, staring at it and moving their fingers unconsciously, almost as if I were not there. I felt suffocated in those stares and in the eagerness of those moving hands, for I imagined clearly what lay behind them: an impassioned wish to see, to reach up and uncover that eye, to stare and stare; the children pleaded with me to take off my patch, pressing close and whispering, "Just for me. I won't tell anyone," and I backed away toward the schoolroom door, thinking fast for an answer to hold them off. I spoke grave prophecies of wild, spontaneous infection should I ever uncover my eye in public, even once. "It has to stay patched," I said. "I could die if germs got in."

"How long," a boy asked, "how long do you have to wear that thing?"

I said, "Forever. Forever until I get a glass eye."

The children kept looking at my bandage, and a girl named Kim looked briefly at me and then back to the patch. "But doesn't it get wet in the bathtub?" she asked. "What happens when you get dirty?"

"Oh," I said, "I change it in the morning. I don't wear the *same one* forever."

Kim — or if not she, then always someone

else — asked, "If I stayed the night, could I watch when you change it." And I would go back then to my talk of germs and elaborate precautions, saying, "Even my mom can't be there or I'd get infected. Nope, it has to be totally sterile." It was a bald lie, and though it worked to save me from showing my eye, it also increased the mystique which surrounded me, bringing the children around to this topic again and again.

The single time when I did relent and agreed to show someone my eye, I was standing at the drinking fountain with my best friend, Marcy Spears, who said, "If I had an eye gone, I'd want to show you so you'd know what it was like."

"I already told you what it's like," I answered. "It's just a covered-up hole, no big deal."

Marcy smiled wide and breathed hard and grabbed my elbows with her hands. "Come on, Natalie," she said. "I'm your best friend. Please." She pushed her face close and laughed into my eyes. "Please."

"What will you tell everyone else," I asked her, pulling my elbows away. "They'll all want to see, too."

"If it's no big deal, I'll say so, and they'll believe me." I believed her myself, and ten minutes later when we stood inside a fifth-grade bathroom stall and I peeled aside my patch, Marcy hollered into my face and ran; and until the door closed out her voice, I could hear her down the hall shouting, "I saw it. It's so ugly. Oh, my God."

So that was the only time. Before and after that day, I strove hard to be usual, to blend in, to pretend that my eyepatch was not there, and I worked meticulously every morning to fit a fresh dressing exactly over the outline of yesterday's, hoping that if the eyepatch looked the same as before, my friends would not recognize it as a new one, would not imagine for themselves a graphic moment when I had stood naked in front of the mirror, throwing the old patch away.

But it was not always possible to look the same every day, for the type of patch I wore depended entirely upon the current stage of my surgeries. In the very early days after the accident, my wounds had needed more air, and I had dressed them with voluminous white cotton pads, making sure to leave breathing spaces but using more tape than I needed, stringing it across my nose, down to my jaw, up to my forehead — anchoring down every spot where the cotton might gap and let someone see underneath.

Those first months, I had been seven, the accident had just happened, and my Alaska doctors — and then my Seattle ones — were still saving my life, speaking only vaguely about a glass eye until they were sure I would live to hope for one. In Seattle, quarantined in my room for infections or bone-graft problems, I had dreamed out loud to my mother about a far time when, in the period just before a glass eye, I could graduate to a black pirate patch, smaller and less obvious on my face. Let the surgeons take as long as they needed then, I thought; if I could be rid of the huge gauze dressings, I would wait in peace for my eye to come. Months later I was almost eight, and my doctors said I could have a black patch for a while, at least until the next operation; I wrote my father a happy letter from Seattle, saying, "I had my arm up on my head [for a skin graft]. And do you no what? I can were a patch now." In the margin, I drew a bald girl with a pirate patch saying, "Boo-hoo I miss you." In Spokane that week, Maureen took the black patch for a pattern and made me forty others in calico and bright colors so I could wear a different one every day. I thanked Maureen and took the patches home, but I wore only the black one pressing dark against my cheek, calling to itself less attention. There was no joy, I thought, in floral eye patches when most people wore none at all.

Still later, after third grade, I was allowed

khaki adhesive patches almost the same color as my skin. They felt sweaty, yes, and coming off at bedtime they tore at my scars, but they were marvels to me, and wonderful: small and light, completely anonymous, they had no elastic strings for schoolchildren to pull. And every morning the eyepatch I lifted out from its wrapper looked identical to the one from the day before. True, I still must revert to the white cotton pads after each major surgery — begging at those times to stay home from school — but that was not often, and never for very long. Beginning then, with my first adhesive patch, I could go for long periods between grafts looking the same every day, and I was sure that if I didn't mention my eyepatch, it was invisible — like the dragons in my sister's room, who were there but who could not get us unless we referred to them out loud. At slumber parties after we moved to Delta, I wore my patch all night, laying my head down so as not to rub it off on the pillow, and locking the bathroom door in the morning to change it before anyone else woke up. And in the seventh grade, when the pharmaceutical company reinvented their product, took to using lighter, glossy cloth, I wept with my teeth held together and sent my mother out to buy every existing eyepatch of the old style.

At home only, I uncovered my eye, allowing it to breathe, keeping my hands clean and being careful not to touch it, and my family knew to keep surprise visitors talking on the porch until I ran upstairs to the bathroom. If I had run out of patches, or had decided not to waste one on a short visit from strangers, I stayed in my room until Dad called me with the family whistle, telling me, "Tosha, come on down." It was a dangerous way to live. We were all so accustomed to my face that none of us noticed whether I was "covered" or not — and while it was restful for me to feel this unremarkable at home, there were several times when my father or mother forgot to delay the drop-ins, and I stood patchless in the kitchen as they brought our friends inside. By the time I was thirteen, I became greatly wary of this sort of accident and had developed many means of hiding my face. If I could, I bent into the oven, checking a cake, talking over my shoulder until the crowd was well past. Then I moved to the door and around the house, to crawl into the bathroom another way. My parents' faces were lost and quiet when I walked back in and looked at them, forcing them to realize what they had done.

I grew weary of listening so hard for cars driving up, of coming home from school, having dodged questions and strange looks all day, to find that even my home was not safe for me. It was logical, if not pleasant, to assume that in public I would be viewed as a glaring curiosity, that "out there" I would have to smile when I felt like shouting at the thousand strangers who asked the same kindly questions; at home, though, I should find rest among these, the family who had lived within sight of my missing eye for as many years as I had myself. There came times in my middle teen years when I rose up against this fact, that even here I must remain conscious of my eye, must have a patch always at hand, just in case a visitor came to the door; on those rebelling occasions, I chose not to run from select ones among my parents' closest friends — I sat barefaced, instead, on the couch, measuring faces as they entered, reading their thoughts from the ways in which they opened their mouths. The self-exposure was not healing for me, gave me no feeling of liberation or of sanity, and I never drew comfort from the fact that those with the largest souls could speak easily with me after that first small silence when they entered the room. My body was so tense, my knees held so tightly together, that I am not even sure why I did it, except perhaps to measure statistics: to see how many there were in the adult world who would feel toward me the way that people did at school.

I did not start out fighting, but in time I came to it — first for my brother and sisters, and later for myself. In elementary school especially, before we left Fairbanks, I was always coming back from the hospital with new bandages and new scars, and, judging from the time my classmates spent inventing new and monstrous names for me, my bandages and I must have seemed an intolerable curiosity. I remember a boy on the back of the Fairbanks school bus punching my nose to see what would happen to the aeration tube running out from there and to the left under my eyepatch. I had not yet learned to hit back — much less to hit first — so I sat still that time with the blood running down, feeling a slow, spreading kind of wonder that anyone would do that, when the adults I knew all held me with their fingertips, as if some thin piece of me were likely at any moment to fall off. It appeared to me that moment, as it had before, that a wide, uncrossable line had been marked out between the world of children and school, and that of grownups, hospitals, and home; it would not have occurred to me, even at ten, to tell my parents much about how classmates and school-bus children treated me, for once I walked into our cabin and laid my mittens out to dry, I became part of my family's larger pressures — money and jobs, the Italians through the woods who hated Polish Protestants, my next round of surgery and hospital bills — and to speak of my school troubles there would be to magnify and discuss them, to invite them inside the walls where I lived.

In the same way exactly, what existed at home stayed there among us, and I never spoke of it at school. Times in the fourth grade, for instance, when we had no car, or when it was fifty below and too cold to start the one we had, my mother would call my doctor — from our phone if we had one, or from the neighbors' if we didn't — and ask how essential it was that I keep my appointment that day. "Absolutely essential," he would say then. "We've got to irrigate that graft or she'll be back with an infection tomorrow."

Hanging up, Mom called me over from Dad's treasure hunt and said, "Okay, Natalie, it's cold. Let's get really bundled up for this trip." Half an hour later, wearing thick sweaters under army-surplus parkas, our legs hardly bendable under layers of long johns, trousers, and flight pants, we wound double scarves around our heads and pulled our hoods over them. Dad kissed us through the cloth, saying, "Call from a pay phone when you get there, and then again when you leave," and Mom and I walked a quarter mile through ice fog to the paved road, waiting for the Air Force bus, hoping the driver would let in two civilians, a mother and child no less. Days when the bus was not running, my father took me hitchhiking, giving thanks to the people who, hearing the purpose of our trip, took us a mile out of their way to drop us at a busier and more promising intersection of the highway.

This was, as I say, the life we lived at home, there in Fairbanks with our hand pump that spewed rust-colored water — Leslie thought it was Tang — and my family's abundant Polish phrases and all the other factors too difficult to explain to my classmates. It would have been disheartening to try, and would only have underscored my unlikeness to my peers. Thus, home and school remained for me entirely separate planets, with distinct geographies and modes of thought, and each time I returned to class after a stay at the hospital I required a good day or two to reacclimate myself, to remember, Ah, yes, this is the way people speak to me here.

At school, it was all bewilderment to me, and fear, an important riddle told to a roomful of people who all, save me, understood the answer. When the fourth-grade boys in Fairbanks called "pirate" and "cyclops" across the lunchroom, or stood laughing around me on the playground swings, singing, "She's a one-eyed, one-horned, flying purple people eater," I lifted my chin and looked closely at them, saw fun hanging shiny off their tongues, and then I smiled, too, and laughed in my throat. I need not understand, I supposed, to take part. As I spent more and more time in hospital beds, gaining weight steadily, there was double reason to tease me, and I became "Hindenberg" and "Cycle 3," after a dog food for overweight pets. It continued on like this even after we had moved a hundred miles to our land in Delta Junction, through junior high there and through high school, even after I learned anger and the power in my fists.

To be fair, possibly some did not know they were cruel, or they did not know, at least, the gnashing savagery of their words; certainly when I ran across these people as adults they never seemed embarrassed to meet me, and their grownup talk of the weather or of the grapevine was pleasant, as if we were for one another welcome mementos of a sweet and familiar past. The one time, years after healing had come, when I visited my closest friend from those days and our talk turned, as it should, to nostalgia, my friend sat blinking her eyes for a long, unseeing moment when I told her how many times I had cried back then. She said, "But, but you laughed at that stuff. You thought it was funny. When you got sick of it, you just beat them up." It was too much history for her to rethink, and too little good could come of it, so I moved our thoughts off then to the joy, and the fighting.

For there was in those days much of each: fistfights on the school bus or in back of the gym, and the exhilarating breath of vengeance, of curled palms and moving arms and faces pushed into the gravel and held there, still cursing. It began on the Fairbanks school bus in the days before anger, when the neighbor children much older than I was sat behind my sister and stretched back their lips, saying, "There's a pirate in your house. And you're a Polack. The stupidest Polack in your family." We had been taught not to fight, to turn our cheeks aside, and Leslie stared forward in her seat, ducking her nose down into the muffler there beneath her chin.

"Leave her alone," I said from across the aisle. "She's only eight." But her silence came as submission to them, and the thin lips moved closer, still speaking, and after them came hands that caught up the ends of her scarf and pulled until my sister's head stretched backward and she gagged out, "Don't. I'm choking. Natalie, they're choking me." I was not a practiced fighter, knew none of the tricks for coming against people twice my size, but I had my hands and my knees, and I was not afraid of blood. And though I cannot say truly that I won that fight, its fury stayed with me a great long time, so that finally even my parents allowed me violence, so long as it preserved their children.

For their children did most certainly require saving. Where I at least learned deception — to smile and bow to classmates whose voices grew uglier the moment I showed I was hurt — my brother's face and my sisters' were appallingly truthful, easily read, quiet and small and astonished. And we were all in some ways ill-acclimated to our peers. Our sense of humor was our father's — absurd puns and loud, ungainly laughter — and our quickness to befriend other misfits was Mom's, and neither of these qualities boded well at an age when popularity depended entirely on one's precise and self-conscious likeness to everyone else.

And of course my own accident, the central fact to all our lives, overshadowed even my siblings' characters in ways that were hardly clear for years afterward. By grade school, where Leslie and Ian and Bethel had their first real contact with utter strangers, they were accustomed more to behaving well in a hospital visiting room than to ingratiating themselves to people their own ages. Bethel's difficulty seemed to be least — from kindergarten on, she seemed comfortable inside her skin, and she always, I recall, had the usual number of friends — and I wonder if this was because she was least deprived, during the hospital years, of my parents' singular attention, and most removed because of her age from the myriad worries of the day. Having been still of nursing age when I was hurt, she had been easily entertained, and it had been convenient for Mom to carry her to and from the hospital then, packing along her bottles while the other children stayed at home or, during the Seattle days, went to visit Maureen and Martin. I remember that, in my room there at Children's Hospital, Bethel crawled under my bed, lifting aside the sheets, calling for Leslie and Ian. She wept at not finding them, and I often used to imagine that at those same moments Leslie and Ian — still just three and five then — were crying for us; but Bethel at least could be comforted, easing off her cries into chokes, and then into tiny shudders, and finally into forgetfulness as our mother carried her off to the playroom and to the fish tank Bethel loved to watch there.

Much later I would learn that Leslie and

Ian probably were crying those times, for Maureen said they wept a good deal at first. It was hardest of all for them, especially there in a place where only Ian was tolerated by the adults. I know that when we saw them again Leslie had grown afraid, had developed the turned-in shoulders and the timid, shrinking expression which never left her entirely, which brought upon her that bloody misuse by others all her life; and I know, too, that although Ian had always been called "our dreamer," had always fallen into thoughtful stupors where his mind meandered elsewhere to consider dinosaurs or spaceships, he returned home from Martin's house the same silent introspector, easily missed in a busy room, only a great deal more so than before. The adults Leslie and Ian became later were healed versions of the children they had been, Leslie extremely shy still and Ian huge, spacy, and rambling, but both known in the world as quick and funny, thoughtful and kind, prone to ridiculous humor and outbursts of songs sung in perfect foreign accents.

It was not, of course, as though even my siblings themselves perceived clearly their own developments, or the means or the reasons for these. In fact later, when each of us had pursued our own talents and found joy in them, it astonished us all to sit as an adult family reminiscing and to notice how disastrously modified we could have become — like bonsai trees pruned at the hand of a perverse and lunatic gardener, malformed, as we all indeed were in small ways, by the inexplicable meanness of outsiders; yet, though the world had often been unkind to us, there were people in it who along the way had asked us questions which, as we found that we had so few answers, began our fruitful looking inward at each other, small periods of asking which disturbed and made us glad, for we found that between us our memory confirmed things we each had not realized were well known already by the others.

Bethel was ten when she asked what happened to my eye. We had moved to Delta Junction and then, after three more years in the trailer, up the knoll into this house we were still finishing; now that we had rooms to separate into, we often went off to talk — two of us sometimes, or three — speaking privately as individuals, not so confined to the group. When Bethel asked, it was Thanksgiving — more precisely, midnight the day after — and my bed was full of our selves, covered in quilts and thick pillows pulled from both our rooms, kept company by moon shadows falling through the window and resting on plates of leftovers held balanced on our knees. It was tradition. Every holiday, the children of the family waited for this hour to go "raiding," heating up bits of cold turkey and ham, sweet potatoes and stuffing, gravy, corn, cranberry sauce, pumpkin pie and cheesecake, the flavor of which seemed ripe only when snuck into bed and eaten in secret with fingers and cold spoons. This year we two, youngest and oldest, had raided first, and we sat now covering the laughter with our hands, expecting the others to tumble in soon and demand a fair share.

The question astonished me. Turning my head to where Bethel lay back biting turkey from a drumstick bone, I said, "What?"

"I mean," she said, chewing, waving the bone, "I mean, I know dogs bit it, but that's all I know. The kids ask me at school, and I don't know what to say." She stuck the bone's end in her mouth and crunched off some gristle. "It's kind of like, I never even saw your scars till Lorinda asked me where they came from."

"But you were there . . ." I started, and Bethel broke in. "Give me a break, I was one. A baby."

And of course it was true. At the time of the accident, the other children were spread from one to five years old; now that I thought of it, I was probably the only one with any real memories of the early days.

So I began the story, calling forth the years, telling of dark windows after school, of neighbors through the woods and sled dogs in their yard and me, picking a path to the door and bending close, hoping to silence the anger in a hoarse and hunger-throated animal. The telling, by now, was just history, and Bethel took it as such, and by the time Leslie and Ian fell in on our raid, we were on to other things, the desserts on our laps nearly gone.

It was this way for them all, the young ones of our clan whose sister held court from her hospital bed, whose mother said don't talk to strange dogs, whose own lives were houses built around doctors, and infections, and someone else's healing. Our days early on were too present and full of things happening, for anyone to ask for a history. But to each child came, at some point, a moment of wonder, brought on by a stranger's query, when they marveled at questions unformed in themselves, at answers that lay outside their small plots of memory.

My brother remembers being four and solemn, walking in the Fairbanks slough with his eyes to the ground and his shoes untied, considering the multitude of things he did not know. He was the thoughtful one among us, the small middle child our words passed over, and he thought now of unfathomable things: water from a hand pump primed with just one cupful, spilling over with many. He met in the way a neighbor boy, taller than himself by a head, who entered his thoughts, calling, "Ian. Hey, Ian."

Rising as out of great sleep, my brother looked up.

"Hey, Ian," the boy said. "How come Natalie wears an eyepatch?" Another unfathomable thing.

My brother answered nothing, but turned and walked back the way he had come.

In the cabin, Dad was on the bed and our mother was working high up at the counter. Shy for a moment because Mom seemed very busy, Ian waited until she was still, when the milk powder was mixed in a pitcher and she leaned into the stove, stirring dinner with a wooden spoon. He said, "Mommy?"

"What, baby," Mom answered him, biting the cuticle from her little finger, turning the pot handles inward.

"What happened to Natalie's eye?"

"A dog bit it, son."

He considered. Mom bent her knees and looked in at him. He said, "And then what happened?"

"She had to go to the hospital and get it

fixed." My brother fell into his thoughts again, and when he said nothing else, Mom rose again and went back to her work.

I was startled later on to learn of this, the extent of my brother's and sisters' half knowledge of our past; but I must have realized something of its existence, for I did play upon it when it suited me. After I was eleven and we had settled into Delta Junction, had set up a trailer and built a one-room addition on the side to stack our bunk beds in, we children spent our days picking blueberries and marking out forts with scrap boards nailed into trees that belonged, as we said, to our very own selves. In my fort one day, Bethel leaned her body the wrong way into a wall, pushing the nails out and collapsing backward in the ruins. I knew it, I thought, I knew this would happen, and I yelled then and pushed her away, and Bethel bit me hard on the arm, shocking us both and leaving two perfect moons on my skin.

"You'd better not do that again," I said. "Look what you left me with the last time." I held up my wrist to show her a half-circle scar inscribed there years before as part of a skin-graft operation. Bethel was only five now, and she believed what I said, and she wept for the horror of what I said she had done.

"Oh, Mommy," she cried, stumbling down the knoll and into the trailer, "I did an awful thing. I bit Natalie a long time ago, and now she has a scar, and now I bit her again." She retched out great chesty sobs, and our mother caught her shoulders in and held them.

"What scar," she said. "What are you talking about?"

Bethel described it to her — the thick, ropy curve marked out just behind my hand, and again the weeping overtook her.

"Bethel," Mom told her, "hush now. That scar is from surgery. You weren't even there when that happened."

"No, not that one. I did that one. Natalie told me. I bit her on the wrist and those are my teeth marks, and they'll always stay there forever." And Leslie and Ian came in then from the room alongside, and they were crying, too, both at once, saying, "No, it was me, it was me. Those are my teeth there. Poor Natalie. I bit her. I bit her." And what had been for some time a great extortionary scheme of mine ended just then in a way I preferred never to mention anymore.

Yet, while each of us children had gaps in the memory — gaps, as I say, of which we became aware only when they were pointed out by other people — what pieces we collected between us amounted to more than a whole, for when seen through all our eyes, our history took on a sense of convergences, of forces appealed to and moving in. Where I remembered clearly the events of my accident — my thoughts in the darkness, the steam of hot saliva on my face — these were all I could know, and only after we children sat cross-legged down and recalled aloud for one another our own stories did I have a full mind, a true knowledge of the feel of those years to my family.

Leslie, the second oldest, recalled farthest back to the beginning, to those very early days of our first Fairbanks winter, when Dad was working up north, and Mom stayed home hauling water, melting snow, lighting kerosene lamps with matches she kept dry in a box. Mornings, when our mother walked with me out the door toward the bus stop, Leslie sat with the two younger children at the trailer's kitchen table, spooning oatmeal into her mouth from a plastic bowl. When they finished eating, she and Ian pressed handprints into the frost shag on the window until Mom stepped back in and cleared the table off. Those mornings and days were filled, Leslie said, with yellow light from a flame, with darkness crowding in from the corners. The sun kept short hours, and when it did rise, its light hardly showed through the ice fog, barely reached in through the trailer's single window. All the lighting in those days was like that, the vague, darkened color of old bruises going yellow, and even after many years Leslie would still feel uncomfortable in rooms where the lamp bulbs were dim instead of white. On the coldest days there in the cabin, they wore their coats indoors, reaching for their toys with fingers grown pink and wrinkled from the chill.

Once a week, Mom took them all to the laundromat, and twice a week to get water. It was a long drive into town, and an even longer drive past town to the wellsprings; by the time the truck pulled up to the watering place, Bethel was sucking air from an empty bottle, and Leslie and Ian had sung all the songs they knew between them — road songs they remembered from the drive up the Alcan. Usually, after Mom had filled the water jugs and heaved them into the truck, Leslie and Ian took turns putting their tongues under the stream, chilling their teeth; but on that particular day, Mom kept them all in the truck while she worked. "We have to get home for Natalie's bus," she said. "There isn't time to fool around."

Mom drove away fast toward home, calling for silence as she leaned over the steering wheel, pointing her face at the ice fog over the road. The truck was full of the cold, and it burned through Leslie's boots, roughened the skin of her cheeks. When the wheels stopped on the driveway, Leslie climbed down, holding a mitten to her face, and followed Mom to the trailer; Mom was telling her to hurry, was carrying Bethel and hauling Ian by the hand. Inside, Leslie took off her snow clothes and laid them on the bottom bunk as she was told. Her stomach felt anxious at the sound of Mom's voice; Leslie wondered if Mom was angry, decided probably not. "Play with your toys, and share with Bethel and Ian," Mom said to her. "I'm going to get Natalie from Brian and Jeff's. Don't touch anything, baby, till I get back, all right?"

It was a long wait, with Mom opening the door only once to ask, "Is Natalie here yet," and quickly closing it once more when Leslie said no. The woodstove was barely warm, but even so Leslie's cheeks felt expanded as they began to lose their chill. The lamp flame wavered high up on a shelf, turning the room yellow and brown. She began, just a little, to feel afraid.

Brian's mother came into the cabin, pulling off her gloves, saying, "Hi, kids. Your mommy sent me over to get you. Let's get your things on." She spoke very fast, zipping their coats, grabbing a bottle for Bethel, and as Leslie followed her out the door, holding a doll to her chest, she knew nothing then of any accident, or where our mother was, or why I had not come home; her largest thought that moment, or perhaps her largest inarticulated feeling, was that she was going to someone's house without me along, and she wondered who, in my stead, would do the talking. She followed Kathy down the rabbit trail and beyond, past the Quonset hut, past the night sounds of dogs wailing and chains dragging on snow.

She remembered all this, Leslie did, the accident itself, and the months intervening, an amassing of faces and scenes buried back in her brain, but what she remembered most, and what broke all our hearts when she spoke of it — simply and slow, with not a shred of self-pity — was the feel more than the facts of those days, the pushing of herself aside to make room for my dying, that first night of many others when she lay awake afraid and wondering at the fuss, because in the hurry of the hour all the rest of them had forgotten to tell her what was happening.

And it was this way for years: those of our family whose age enabled them to sit apart from the rest must do so, so the others could concentrate on the one among us least likely, for the moment, to survive. Growing up, the younger children had learned to play quietly together, singing to themselves, and Bethel had sucked on her bottle until she was four years old because no one had had time enough or energy to wean her. To find some attention, the young ones had sometimes pretended to be like me, stealing my eyepatches and putting them on, coming out to the kitchen to say, "Look, Mommy, a dog bit my eye, too." My father said it was like having a runt in a litter; each puppy was loved equally, and each cleaned and fed, but the others were tragically and necessarily nosed aside so that at mealtime the runt could have its own teat. Perhaps this, or perhaps a thousand other things, were what formed on my siblings' skin that scent which forever invited predation; but I did not speculate on any of this until a great long time had passed. Growing up in those days at the center of my siblings' later-told stories, I saw only the circumstance and not the reasons, only the vicious circles of boys — their home-cut hair, their jeans signed with the flowery autographs of girls, their thin arms reaching out, tossing a hat — and my brother or sister in the midst of them. I lost all fear at those moments, all impotence and reserve, and as I broke in and upon those boys and felt them struggling beneath me, I was for a scarce instant glad of my size, and of the fact that, however I explained this to Mom and Dad afterward, I had in this hour become potent, had expanded my soul.

In the end, I think, my parents' own righteous anger was what caused them to sanction my fighting. In the main hallway of our cabin, Dad taught me self-defense — gut shots and neck chops and leading with the left — pausing as Mom walked by to say, "Do you think I should be teaching her this?"

"I suppose," Mom said, considering, balancing the berry bucket against her hipbone, "I suppose this is not vengeance, but defense. Just teach her how not to kill." Even this qualified permission must have seemed to my mother a sorrowful compromise, a giving in to what she least believed in: war, and the act of surviving on terms other than our own. But Dad continued my lessons now, reciting the list of moves to use only in situations of impending death, until a day when he himself fell on the floor and got up, rubbing his neck, saying, "I think that's it. Those kids don't stand a chance." A week later, I turned eleven, and not long after that we moved to our land in Delta Junction, my parents hoping, I think, that the schoolchildren there would be kinder to us.

This was not the case, of course, for though

we had changed cities, the world was the same and so was our difference from it, and the peculiar sociology of that new place made its pecking order more caustic, if that were possible, than even Fairbanks's had been. Delta proper consisted of two motels, a grocery-and-dime-store, three or four gas stations, and a good number of churches and bars. The fact was, though, that almost no people lived in the town itself — residing as many as fifteen miles away on barley farms or homesteads. Our idea of "neighbors" there were the four families who lived a quarter mile away down a dirt trail, and what socializing any of us did was accomplished by a drive into town or out to the Fort Greely army post eight miles away.

In some ways, the populations of Delta and Fort Greely were interchangeable, given that their number of residents was about equal. On any day, any ten people one met at the gas station would be about half civilian and half military, and we attended the same churches, some in town and some on post, made the same trips to Fairbanks's department stores, knew the same people. Civilians went "out on post" to Fort Greely's movie theater, and the school district encompassed and shared both schools, sending all high-school students — civilian or not — to Delta school, and all junior-high children out on post.

But the similarities did not compensate for the differences. The army post's geography was much like a middle-American neighborhood, with sidewalks and curbs, and neighbors next door, and dependable electricity, plumbing, and maintenance workers. The army families' incomes were monthly and not seasonal, and they afforded, in general, much higher-quality clothes and groceries, for they shopped at the lower-priced Post Exchange and commissary.

Most important, the average army family had not immigrated to Alaska by choice, and certainly intended not to stay. Among my military-school friends' parents, there was a high degree of dissatisfaction with this place, its cold winters and "mangy-looking" people, the high price and poor selection of commodities. Resentment among them grew that civilian people were allowed easily on post to attend the movie theater, and that those who worked non-military jobs there were given permission to shop at the PX. "If they want what we have," one woman said, "let them enlist."

And this attitude filtered down through those families, until their children took it on as well, securing a place at the top of the local social ladder simply by convincing the rest of us they belonged there. For town children such as ourselves who lived entirely without modern conveniences — without even a legitimate house, but a trailer — and who even among the civilian population represented the closest thing to the have-nots, there was little hope for popular approval.

Of course, we ourselves were not proudly satisfied with our trailer and wanigan, and were in fact still measuring out summers, hoping every spring that this year we would afford a real house up there on the hill on our land. Even before we moved to Delta, Mom and Dad had chosen that knoll, had cleared away trees and paced out the house site, tapping down stakes in the dirt. They threaded long strings to the corners and whistled for us children, telling us, "This is the size of our house." But those years we were poor, and building was costly, and each fall which came meant another year gone, another building season squandered and diminished. Those white evenings we watched the fireweed urgently, looking across the fields, for the native myth said that these flowers predicted first frost, let you measure how long until winter. Fireweed grew in tall stalks of pink-topped green, its flowers blooming early at the bottom, opening farther up all summer until, six weeks before frost, the last flowers opened at the top and then died, waving out cottony seeds on the wind.

After that the geese flew, and we watched them go over, despairing in ourselves for a house; but we spoke of this to few people there, for they would have believed they had shamed us into seeing our trailer and honey-bucket for what they really were: symbols of primitive squalor, small proofs that our lives were as yet less than theirs.

Thus, where in Fairbanks our ethnicity and my eyepatch had marked us as prey, here our way of life undermined us, and my continued stays at the hospital only added to our sep-arateness. Having been taught how to fight, I found now as much cause as ever to defend my brother and sisters, hitting out at groups of children who stopped casually on the school grounds to call them names.

But the large difference in these fights was that my opponents most often were army chil-dren, those who had grown up around talk of war games and enemies killed in battle. For them, even more than for me, adversaries were exhilarating things, to be sought after aggressively, not merely defended against; and whereas I knew mostly defensive moves — those to use once my brother was already set upon — the children I fought with knew the offensive ones, and turned them on me violently and often until I learned them, through experience, for myself.

My parents knew little of all this, only that I generally "stuck up for" Leslie and Ian and Bethel, and not that I carelessly risked my bone grafts fighting in their defense. By the time sixth grade ended for me and I transferred to junior high at Fort Greely, I was fighting more and more offensively and less defensively, simply because, being at a school separate from my siblings, I heard about their confrontations only after the fact, and had to hunt up their enemies after school. My mother, I think, must have known something of the violence, for it was she, once or twice, who informed me of Ian's bad day or Leslie's, and it was she, too, who picked me up in the car when I "missed the bus" after school the next day. It was a little startling, her tolerance of my fights, for when we were younger she had been the one most often to say, "We believe in peace, not vengeance." I am sure she continued to feel this way, even when she allowed me revenge, yet it must have seemed to her that if war was the only solution, then at least just one of us would wage it, and only in the names of the others.

Once, after I had changed back to Delta school for ninth grade, and my sisters came home telling how Ian had fallen to a girls' gang in the Fort Greely schoolyard, my mother and I ran to our separate cars, falling against each other, and she turned back on me, pushing a white hand to my chest. "Give me ten minutes," she said. "A ten-minute lead. And if they're still around when you come, you can have them." It was a shocking moment — my mother standing there like that, breathing, consuming us both — and I stayed. When Mom reached the school, she told me later, the gang was still in it, and they threw down their coats when she shouted, "Who's Yolanda."

Yolanda stretched herself out above her shoulders, and Mom stood chest to chest with her, grinding her teeth, saying, "Ian has a sister this tall and this wide, and she's on her way here. If she finds you, now or ever, or hears that you even looked at her brother, you won't make it to fourteen." Yolanda wasn't there for me that day, but she was the next, and though my mother had told me, "I think it's okay now, she won't bother Ian again," I had craved vengeance and I found it, keeping it secret from my family.

It was natural then, after learning violence, that I came to use it for myself, and somewhere in those high-school or junior-high years I found fighting to be the first real thing I could do that would impress people, that could make them, somehow, like me; or if not like me, exactly, then avoid me — or even find something different to ridicule. After a particularly bruising scrap between me and a boy, his friends would hand him toilet paper and spit out at me, "You're not even a girl; you're a guy." Yet this to me seemed a preferable jeer, less savage or harmful than a comment on my face or my size. And if children my own age found cause to ridicule me, there were also my brother's and my sisters' friends, who felt for my age and my eyepatch and my toughness something amounting to admiration. So I kept on. And most of my friends turned out to be boys — other boys than the ones who teased me — and they taught me basketball and woodwork, and when we were older I taught them to drive and helped them find girlfriends among the young women I knew.

In these ways I learned to be similar, to behave like the others — only more so. My movement forward in adolescence, from fights in my family's defense to those in my own name, appeared to me not as delinquency but as a claiming of ground, a shouting of my voice above the others. It seemed a righteous anger then, and perhaps at first it was, but in time I lost reason and I ran full-tilt at rough strife, no longer to improve, but to embrace it. In high school, around the time of my brother's confrontation with Yolanda, I fought many more fights, but mostly now without cause, just to be as good at it as all the others were, just so they would say my name. Besides fights behind the school gym, there were also amphetamines and alcohol, taught to me by these new and violent buddies and snuck into school in empty cassette cases; and again after that there was sex, for I believed more than anything that if a boy would sleep with me it meant I was less ugly than everyone said. It wouldn't do, either, I was sure, to seem to be smarter than my classmates — and certainly not to like school — so in class I pretended stupidity and forced my grades down, though often I did homework for other students in order to make them my friends.

It was, on reflection, a terrible life. I grew so accustomed to the racing fear in my belly that in time I almost did not notice it. I hid every vestige of delinquency from my parents, going so far as to have two sets of friends: the ones I brought home — clear of eye and tender of heart, who believed, as my parents did, that I was a wholesome and clean-living teenager — and the ones I went out with to parties, whose own parents bought us liquor and sat with us at midnight to drink it. Mom and Dad were busy with family matters, for the trailer had long since become too small and now, poor or not, my parents had begun to build us a house. We were living in it unfinished, the insulation still exposed, the interior walls framed in but standing open, and between working their jobs and building on weekends, Mom and Dad were too tired to look at me closely, or to wonder what I was doing when I spent the night with friends. The rare times when Mom found cause to mistrust me those days, I convinced her otherwise with genuine weeping — genuine, because when her eyes tightened down like that she looked small and swallowed up and betrayed and I thought, unrepentant as I was, that still I could not bear it.

This I cannot explain, the fact that I was less afraid *of* my parents than I was *for* them, should they ever discover what I was about. I was certainly concerned that my brother and sisters never find out, impatient as I was with them at that age; they were old in a great many ways, due mostly to the circumstances of our lives, and the esteem in which they had traditionally held me must not, I thought, be taken away from them; or, for that matter, from me. Even so, it was primarily my mother and father for whom I worried — although this worry was not large enough to deter me. Perhaps I felt this shred of protectiveness because I knew in some unconscious way — from all the words my parents and I spoke about college, and real futures, and about me being a doctor — that I was making a mere field trip into the depraved and the alone, while my friends really existed there; and in fact on occasion one of them admitted that he or she wanted out. Marcy Spears, who in the fifth grade had seen my uncovered bad eye and screamed, asked me around my fourteenth birthday why I never had her to my house. I was in a straightforward mood that day, or I would never have told the truth, but I did explain my parents and their standards and the fact that they knew nothing of my life away from home.

"What would they do," Marcy said, "if they found out? Would they kill you? I mean, how come they care if you party?"

No, I said, they probably wouldn't kill me. They'd be mad, and I'd never leave the house again till I was forty, but mostly they'd go on and on forever about trust and betrayal, and how a family is supposed to be all one fortress, no spies or traitors.

"You mean," Marcy said, and looked down at her narrow legs swinging there off the fencepost, "you mean your mom and dad LIKE YOU?"

Yeah, I said. They're my folks.

Marcy jumped to the ground and looked up at me, confusion wrinkling her face, making her sullen. "Jeez, Nat," she said and swore, kicking the dirt. She threw out her arms. "Jeez," she said again. "If your parents LIKE you, I don't see why you're HERE and not THERE." Two years later, when Marcy wrote me from reform school, her letter said, "I thought if I ended up here my mom at least has to visit me. Jeez, I don't even know where she lives now."

It was inevitable that at some point my parents would find incontrovertible proof of my goings-on, and when, just a few weeks after my talk with Marcy, they found marijuana and cheap liquor behind the Sheetrock in my room, they did indeed speak, at the top of their lungs, of trust and betrayal and sound fortresses. I think I meant it then when I promised them I would quit, but perhaps it was just their faces again, and not any genuine resolve. Did I think it would help, Mom said, if I went far away from the friends I knew here? It was deep winter by this time, and the snow was making us all feverish; and with the unfinished house and the lack of privacy, and the kerosene lights reflecting darkly off the fiberglass, the thought of getting away from it, from my family, from everyone, sounded delicious to me, and I said yes, I thought that would help. So after Christmas my parents put away the year's expensive building plans, sending me off to a private school in California, making it sound, to Leslie and Ian and Bethel, as though I were only off for adventure; and for a while I was perfectly sane, astonishing the school counselor with my change in grade-point average.

But as it turned out, the students at that school had heard beforehand from the principal's son that I was being sent there for delinquency and, having never met a live delinquent before, they each in turn had slumber parties so they could quiz me as a group. Eventually, they asked me to show them drugs and I found I was perfectly willing — this was the most popularity I had ever encountered in my life. I organized parties with booze and much dope, and before I was expelled from that place, the school counselor had me in to his office, where he offered to split a soda with me. Thanks, I said, and took the can in my hand, setting it down to make a wet circle on my knee.

"Natalie," the man said, "you could be a leader. You have all the makings, but instead you're an instigator. This is very hard to understand." I could not explain it and I didn't care to try, and my body filled then with the huge, intolerable wish that I had not accepted his Coke. Outside in the hall, I gathered back self-confidence for a brief moment, and as a last word to him, I had thirty friends set their watches and flush every toilet in school simultaneously, overflowing the sewer into the commons.

Back home, my parents' hurt was tangible, and my sisters and brother visibly confused — why all the tight faces, I imagine they thought, if Natalie has finally come home? — and this time I am sure I meant my apology; my father had been ill now for some time, his heart vessels growing clogged in his chest, and with a jolt I came back to true reason. I remained steadfast for over a year, and to lessen the chance of meeting up with old friends, I chose to have no friends at all. My high school enrolled me in college courses nearby, and arranged that these grades be credited to my transcripts at both schools. I hurled myself full-force at my studies, leery as I was of the threat of too many unfilled hours. I passed, thus, a great deal of time on schoolwork and on thinking, and formed now my first articulate thoughts of myself. My father was ill, and we were back to building, and it seemed reprehensible that I had ignored these in favor of friends who must be bought like commodities. I continued on like this, as I say, for over a year, resigned to the patterns I saw in the world, yet not so greatly distressed by them that I noticed myself pining.

Then, when I was sixteen, I fell in love — a sudden, violent, caustic first love, burning through my chest like an acid and consuming me there, shutting my eyes in the pain of it. For a few months I was both very alive and barely living, so aflame in my own joy that, had I stopped to take stock of my condition, I could have mistaken it for suffering. Mine was the terrible, exhilarating angst of a human body lurching forward at light speed, impelled so quickly through all those molecules of air that the skin begins to shed and becomes raw, and the breath cannot exit the lungs. The boy went to my high school and must have seemed, to the adult eye, just an average and listless young man with bad teeth; his attraction for me, I suppose, was the voice of the stories he told when we were alone, of all the people he had known, of the death very young of his father, of all he had seen Outside: rock concerts, drive-in movies, tailgate parties at the beach. He was not such a great stylist in his telling, but what mattered most to me, and to most young people like me, who had grown up apart in this far country, was that he spoke what he had seen of Things Out There, and his words became epic in their own right. The boy and I spent all our hours together and abandoned all the rest of the world, rolling cigarettes, telling stories, imagining. I would have sworn then, had anyone asked, that this, finally, was that most important and enduring thing in the earth, something greater than brothers or sisters or parents or self, and that all of those must hunker down to make room for it.

My mother suspected many times that my involvement with the boy was physical, and she confronted me often with questions and hard looks and references to my behavior of the past. As always, I was able to put her off with indignant and convincing tears, but for the first time I was protecting, not her and not even myself, but this thing, this state of being, which seemed hardly to do with either of us. "Mother," I would say. "Mother. You have a filthy mind. I believe you must be crazy." And this last statement punched out her breath, sent her off alone into fear, for insanity passed down from her own mother was what she dreaded always most of all, and any hint of it must be prodded and dissected and examined.

In the end, when I thought I had flu and vomited every meal into the toilet, Mom stopped me one day on the way out to school. Her eyes were tight behind her glasses, but this was more common now than not, and I managed not to feel bad for her. "Are you still getting sick," she asked and then, hardly stopping, "Is it because you're pregnant?"

I was outraged, partly at her, but mostly because this thought had not occurred to me before and I knew quite instantaneously that it was true. "Of course not, Mom," I said, turning away, looking back. "Honestly, that is disgusting."

It was the first of many terrible days. At school, I found the boy in the library looking through magazines, and grabbing his hand I told him — told him, too, that I must be four or five months along by now.

"What," he said, very loud, and everyone looked at us, interested in anything uncommon to see. "What," he said again, quieter this time. "How come you didn't tell me?" I hadn't known before today, I said, until my mother had asked me, and it occurred to me she was right.

I could not explain this absurdity, that a girl could miss four menstrual periods and not understand she was pregnant; even long afterward, when I was grown and could speak of the story to new friends, the idea seemed shocking and unlikely. I know that I had never kept a monthly record, had never planned ahead for cramps or for tampons, had merely dealt with the blood when it arrived, and used the misery as an excuse for missing school. And I remember thinking absently those months that it had been quite some time since the last one, and perhaps it was safe to fake cramps today, since the boy and I had fought and I did not feel much like school anyway. But that was the extent of the thought, as it was in those days the extent of the cosmos: circumstance required thought only insofar as it influenced that hour's dose of true love, and whatever continued along afterward could be pondered about tomorrow. It was the way I had shut myself out during alcohol parties, having known on some level that I might hurt my family but preferring not to imagine that, and now what I had preferred not to think of had forced the issue on its own.

At noon that day, my mother came to school, and in the wind under the flagpole she said, "It's true, isn't it?" I had spent the morning in a fever, grabbing after all possible means to hide this truth, all possible ways out, and had ended up here, holding nothing in my hands. I said, "Yes," expecting a great and violent cataclysm of the earth, but the wind continued blowing against my back, and the flag went on snapping open and shut again, darting above us like a fish.

My mother straightened up and her arms fell more loosely at her sides. "Don't you dare run away," she said. A hair blew across her glasses and she tugged it down. "I'm mad and I'll probably stay mad, but don't you dare run away." This sentiment, or more precisely this dread, informed my parents' whole response those next months, all their thoughts and all their actions, and all the ways they carried me along.

MAKING
AMENDS

It was a vast and horrible power I possessed then, however accidentally I had come by it, though I did not understand this for years; for everything our family had cultivated in itself and everything we thought we had owned was now unquestionably called to account, sacrificed by one at the center of all the others' lives — and scrambled after like spilled pennies by all. Here began a shouting time full of uncovered lies, when my mother and father faced what they had feared all along: family become strangers unawares. Their fear now was not that the earth would destroy us — not city living nor sled dogs nor cruel and contemptible people — but that we would destroy each other. Yet here, too, began a minute shifting of ground, a refocusing as it were, as my parents worked to conquer anger in themselves, and to remain loyal to the one among us who had betrayed our safest refuge. The power I had was to affirm our union or to give it the lie, to protect my family's belief in itself as a sure and impenetrable force, or instead to collapse it from within and abandon it, leaving us each to find our way.

In short, I could choose the boy over my family and walk away from that place; and certainly I might have done this, as removed as I was then from reasonable thought. But the choice, as it happened, was not offered me, for the boy I loved ran away to Texas the same week. He did it with tears, telling me beforehand that he was going, saying to me, Remember that story, and that one, and that one; saying he would write and that I should, too, that he would send me his address and someday I could move down with him, and on and on. I did get a letter several months afterward, and he said he was eating cheesecake and had almost found a job. But that was the last time, and to the stress of an uncertain hour was added a terrible morbid grief which I would not see as the least of all worries until a great many months had passed.

I could still have left, of course, as other girls had done before me. But in my grief over the boy and my fear of this pregnancy, I lacked the energy to go, even had I wanted to. I chose to stay, and my parents worked every hour to see that I did not change my mind, making me once again the one who held focus, while my brother and sisters took their places to the side. My father of the loud and rough-mannered immigrant soul never shouted at me after Mom told him my news, but called me in with his hand and stood talking. "It's a terrible grownup thing you have to decide about this baby," he said, "and Mom and I can't tell you how to do it." He looked at me a moment more, then away toward the wall just when I was sure I could not bear it. "Marriage would have been a bad idea so young, and anyway you don't need to do it. We're your family here." We had our home together, he said, and we had our God; I had a lot of thinking to do about the baby, and I might as well do it in a quiet and familiar place, around people whom I knew I could trust.

Mom and Dad's relative calm might have been hard to understand, had it not been for my father's Old Testament tale of King David. "You remember he had that baby," Dad said, "with that woman he wasn't supposed to be with. And God said, 'For punishment, your son is going to die.'" The king, my father said, lay fasting in the street the whole seven days his son was ill, and on the day the child died and David heard of it, he got up and washed his face and went in to eat dinner. His servants said, What is this behavior, crying and fasting when your son was alive, and then, when he is dead, going in to eat. And David told them, "While the child was yet alive, I fasted and wept; for I said, Who can tell whether God will be gracious to me, that the child may live? But now he is dead, wherefore should I fast? Can I bring him back again?" What the servants failed to see, my father told me, was that once a thing is done we cannot sit hating it; we gather ourselves back and proceed, asking for strength to prevail.

So, with my parents' promises in hand ("We will neither coerce you into keeping or not keeping this baby, nor will we ever express regret at what you decide"), I set about living in haste, imagining that if I found enough to do I could put off thinking a bit longer. This didn't, of course, work, but I accomplished some useful things. I kept on with college courses, adding more and more, and adding still to them a double load of high-school correspondence studies so that I could graduate early. This, my mother said, was a wise decision, because if I kept the baby I could take it off to college, and if I had it adopted, I would probably want to get away from here anyway. She spoke of other things, too, of all the time beyond this present time, when I would study to be a doctor as I had always intended, as we had always said as I grew up, there in the hospital with Mom near my bed and me dreaming out loud, imagining stitches like these sewn by my own hand, and children on the brink brought miraculously back. The thought had not seemed romantic then, only necessary, a tradition begun and meant to be carried on and fulfilled. And it seemed just as necessary now, for what my mother offered me in these dreaming moments was the hope for a day when all this thinking would be done with, my decision made and the baby kept or not, when our days would be normal again, and sleep much easier to come by.

My family agreed that we should keep this pregnancy a secret, "not out of shame," Mom said, "but so, if you decide to adopt, you won't have a bunch of nosies asking you miserable questions." I stipulated that even my brother and sisters not be told until I could face them myself, until I was stronger. Over the summer, while my belly was still small, I greeted company in the living room, and as the number and variety of visitors increased until virtual strangers were walking in and asking to see me, we realized that somewhere a rumor had been born.

Then my mother, who in earlier days had sanctioned my fighting in defense of her other children, became in an instant my own protector, fierce in her ways and so devious that

I knew then for certain that we bore the same genes. "Oh, heavens," she would say when anyone asked. "Natalie's upstairs, and we can't disturb her." And in a whisper: "She's studying for college, you know. We're very proud of her." I heard all this through the floorboards — carpeted by now, but still thin enough to hear through — and when everyone had left — grumbling, I imagined, that they had not gotten a look at my belly — I would go downstairs, where Mom and I would collapse into one another, laughing outrageously at the gall of "some people." At school, my brother and sisters, knowing nothing, believed they were telling the truth when they said, "No, nothing's wrong with Natalie."

But there were moments, too, when my mother's betrayed heart overcame her, and she flew at me, screaming, "How could I have trusted in you then, and how can I trust you now." I sometimes hollered back, and sometimes was mute, knowing, as I did, her right to rage. And in the middle of it all she would turn away and back again, and speak in a new voice, "No matter what I say to you, don't run away somewhere. It would be an easy and vengeful thing to do, but it would be very, very cruel to us." It went like this for a great long time, trust and distrust and my proving myself again, until long after, in college, my mother would come to town, worried at my avoidance of men — indeed, of society in general — and offer with a hopeful face to type my term paper in case I might have a date or a party to attend. For I was losing a good deal of social finesse those months in seclusion, and, as it turned out, a good deal of patience as well. In my family's circle of friends, we used the term *bushy* to name that condition of women and men who, after long periods alone in wilderness cabins, came townward to shop, scarcely remembering this society by then, fully incapable of pitter-patter or small talk. Now I was growing bushy, though I would not know it until I returned to the world, standing silent then and opening my eye at all this talk of the weather, all this hanging around and saying nothing. When that time came, my mother would laugh and understand, calling me "former butterfly," saying, "You'll remember it all pretty soon. You've always kept a party going." I know I can do it, I would tell her, but it seems absurd, a lot of work for no reason.

And a lot would seem absurd by then, a lot which before I had taken so seriously. School would come again, much too soon, and it would be interesting for me to note how much was the same there, and how much different. The news of my baby would be official, everyone told, and what indeed I did find when that time came were classmates, even old friends, grown distant, opening and shutting their mouths, saying nothing; for I was now even less like them than before. When my mother came for me at lunch, taking me off to eat away from the others, people watched at windows, and once on a dare a boy blushed and laughed loudly and said, "So how did you like it, having a baby come out down there."

Just fine, I said then and put my hands in my pockets. The group there giggled — very much like girls, I thought — and I said in haughty embarrassment, "What a lot of little boys you are," feeling a little sad in myself that I was not a little girl.

And it seemed that way in the end — after all the months of thinking, and of worry, and of deciding this large thing about motherhood — that here were boys and girls, and here was I, neither child anymore nor yet adult, quiet and removed among them. It seemed hardly likely that, once, these same children had made me cry, had appeared so large in the earth that any small thing they spoke could tear through my bones like gunfire. Yet had I been asked, even then, what had driven me toward that sort of youth, I could scarcely have articulated an answer; I knew only that I had done what I could to make friends out of enemies both potential and real, and I knew also the breathless relief that came from looking hard at a classmate's face and seeing in it no teeth. And in my own calm sense of nostalgia I continued to believe for a very long time that the chums I had made in those ways had truly been friends.

But all this was a long way off, past a great effort toward making amends, past a huge quantity of thinking. It was my parents' concern that no choice I made be based on a lack of alternatives, and during the months of my pregnancy — and afterward, too — they employed themselves providing my life with more than enough of these. Together, they led the whole family to a remote and private corner of our land and surveyed off a parcel there for me, and then, as we had when we first made a site for the family house, we all — parents and children alike — began clearing land, hauling away brush, planning a landscape. They hired a man to drill a well, and another to put down a septic system. They had gravel brought in for a house foundation, and Mom drew floor plans, many different ones, asking my opinion. Through all this, my mother and my father's constant refrain: "No woman should get married just to have someone to support her." A year later, when I went away to college, my parents would do all this again, would run again here, and there, searching out household things, for my school apartment this time, because my college would be a hundred miles off, a two-hour drive on a good day; my place, Mom would say then, should have enough in it to make it easy to live there, easy to study. We would grin then and have a laugh at some of their "necessary" purchases, for besides pots and pans and brooms and towels, Mom and Dad would bring home straw flowers, an Art Deco mirror, a beaded curtain for the door. "Oh THIS is special," Leslie would say. "What decade is it," and Mom would look my way and tip her head, and we would all laugh, suddenly and loud, at the pleasure we were having at stepping back two decades to the time of my parents' own schooling. The day I left for college, then, Mom would stand at the door and wave, all the rest of them behind her, crying a little at the change of things. We would have spent the summer turned inward, complete once again in ourselves and ignoring the world, disregarding it for as long as possible before we were thrust again into it, not at all needy, yet certainly more removed.

But for now, during my pregnancy, we were sufficient in ourselves, and my parents said so often, and proved it in all their assistance of me. To add to my alternatives about the baby, Mom brought home pamphlets: Boothe Memorial Home for unwed mothers, private adoption agencies, lists of welfare plans for women who kept their babies. She told me of a couple in church who were looking for a baby — a military couple who, should I choose to offer them mine, would soon be transferred elsewhere and out of my line of sight. Nights, while my father brought *latke* to the room where I studied, Mom put together a photo album for the baby, each page a collage of family history — both sides, mine and the boy's, and for this she must have done some monstrous research. "Come see," she said, when she heard me moving upstairs, and she showed me all her work, spreading it out on the floor: the family tree in photos, each with a handwritten caption, explaining. And scraps of memorabilia from my growing up — tickets to Europe, snapshots of tiny, one-year-old me with a German zoo gorilla, a copy of my kindergarten class photo. "Whatever you decide," she told me, "the baby will want to know where it came from."

They were sweet and hideous months, and on late nights when I took out the car to go crying, to grieve my loss of the boy and to think out a decision on this baby, I wondered at the self who could have abandoned this family, these parents who so earnestly tried to be kind. The past winter, during my days with the boy, my parents had finally finished us a house on the knoll, one with electricity and plumbing and carpets on the floor; but back then I had been gone too often, for too many hours apart, to relax fully into the place, and now in my seclusion and my breathless return to familiar things, I took to enjoying it with purpose, taking long, clean baths full of foam.

They were new joys, these bubble baths, for in the days of our slapdash cabins a bath had been a Saturday ritual before bedtime, and Mom would help us children pump ten gallons of water into a pot, heating it on the stove and pouring it into a round galvanized tub on the kitchen floor. We had taken turns in the water, the cleaner children first and then the dirty ones. Mom would size us up beforehand, inspecting our knees and muddy feet. "You," she would point. "You first, then you and you, and you last. Get a towel and be ready for your turn." The order of our washing ran roughly youngest to oldest, the baby being usually the cleanest of us all. Mom lowered her into five inches of water, and I was always a little jealous of Bethel's small size, her ability to stretch all the way out in that tiny round space.

When it had come my chance, Mom had

scooped the dirty water over my head and squirted on shampoo, scrubbing hard with her fingers and rinsing with clean water from the stove. On the bottom of the tub, my buttocks had grated against the sand. Afterward, as I had stood drying in my towel and handing her the soap, Mom had taken the last bath, squatting over her knees and washing her body in the gray-and-white silt of her entire family.

Those years, Mom and Dad had shopped with us in hardware stores, saving change and dollar bills to buy "conveniences," and I remember Mom's particular joy the day she had produced from the pickup a new galvanized tub, not round this time, but a three-and-a-half-foot oval, long enough, as she said, "to wash behind my knees for a change." She had hauled that tub to the top of the knoll, and that day we had taken our baths outside, splashing out soap on the ground.

Now, to save thinking, I took a thousand baths — four a day, sometimes — and Mom came in to visit, sitting on the toilet and talking. She brought cereal and milk in two bowls, and we ate there together, resting my bowl on my belly, speaking of building me a house. Some days, we did the old things by ourselves, going out in rain to pick wild mushrooms, taking our favorite knives to cut off the dirt.

In Fairbanks our first years, we had gone every summer to the city fair, to visit the stall of the "mushroom lady," a woman who knew all the varieties, and who got up at three in the morning to find samples for her display. We had learned those years of boletuses — three kinds that Dad remembered from Poland — and shaggy manes, puffballs and gingerbread mushrooms, and several poisonous kinds. As a family we had taken great buckets out to the army base, for, in all the area, the golf courses there had the best meadow mushrooms. We had waited until rain — the fungi grew fast then, springing up whole before worms could get at them — and then, carrying a pocketknife each, we had gone out picking, taking our buckets home full. For several lean winters we had lived entirely on mushrooms and egg noodles, taking Baggies out from the freezer where we had stored the fried mushrooms in summer.

So I came back to these familiar things, and both of my parents came with me. The land we had was reduced now to about one hundred acres from the original 258, for early on we had deeded small pieces to friends — Oscar and Vic, and Dick and Esther, all the people who had carried us forward over time — and still other pieces we had sold for the money, those years we had lived eating mushrooms. Still, a hundred acres was plenty, and it was ours, and as a family we wandered out over it, finding injured baby bunnies lying so quietly we had stepped on them, taking them home and feeding them, crying when they died. This had happened repeatedly over years, our taking the hurt animals home and trying to revive them, and Mom wept the loudest of us all, burying the things in the woods. We picked berries and lay in the fields, whistling the family whistle to call ourselves together, irritated when a small plane invaded our privacy, flying loudly overhead, through the air. These months, we were once again an alliance, once again defensible from the world.

The greatest shelter provided me at home — the one none of us could have foreseen needing — was from childless couples studying the rumor mill. In a town as small as ours, one would not have imagined the number of people — all races, all levels of income — desperately interested in buying a baby. Few of them asked directly — or if they did, they posed the question to close family friends — but on repeated days, as I struggled up the stairs to hide, not my patchless eye this time, but my belly, Mom or Dad would stand on the porch, delaying some young man and woman dropping by with a "present for Natalie" — crocheted slippers, chocolates, flowers, and once, in a daring gesture, a hand-painted poster of the words to Brahms's Lullaby. Some of these people were old acquaintances, some we hardly knew, but all would come in for tea and stay hours, asking was I at home, could they go up and see me, what did my parents think about the population explosion. One day a woman even ran past my mother up the stairs, pounded on the door — which, fortunately, I had locked when I heard her coming — and, when I said I was not decent, said, "Are you sure? I've seen naked girls before. Okay, well, I made you something, and I'm putting it right here by the doorstop." Mother said the woman peeked around the stairs a good long time before she went down, hoping, I suppose, to observe me in the act of finding her gift, a ceramic Byzantine-style clock painted in opal colors. In all, we probably had six or seven such visitors, but with the number of visits each made, and with the great number of other people stopping in just to ogle, it seemed impossibly more. It was also impossibly comic, impossibly infuriating. But it gave my mother and me a great deal more to conspire about, and promoted to a large extent the healing which must occur between us.

For I had exited childhood still fighting, though never again with my hands. My mother said, and she was mostly right, that the struggle now would be an effort of spirit, a consistent inward prevailing against all that lay, first within, and then outside us. I was sixteen, and we were tending now, she said, to our own internal strife, but after this was over and my baby delivered, there would still be the world to consider, and in my nine months' seclusion the familiar world would not have changed, would have become no more kindly, no less fearsome than before. But it was not as though, my mother said, we must any of us fight to uproot the earth, nor yet submit to its tyranny; it was enough in those days to abide there, fortified and in peace, as citizens of a place to whose wisdom we were silent and conscientious objectors.

In the end, it was the night before my due date before I decided I would keep the baby, and in spite of my parents' "no advice" policy, it was their influence which confirmed the thing in me. I had laughed a little in myself those months that Mom and Dad believed their opinions to be so inscrutably hidden; but my father, who said nothing out loud, was quite obviously sure I should retain custody. His face became too gentle, too unusually grandfather-like when a baby rolled by us in the market, for one not to have guessed his true thoughts. And Mom, whose history included babysitting for three of her sisters who had had children very young, was careful enough also in her language, but brought home, in her stack of pamphlets, a slightly larger number of those having to do with adoption.

I didn't mind their ideas; it would have been naïve to expect them to have none, and it made my mind a great deal easier to know both that they had opposite wishes, and that each was ready to stifle his or her own the moment when I expressed mine. Still, the situation was so amusing that one day, not long before I was due to deliver, I had called them on it in a discussion. "What," my father said, as though he thought I was lying. "How did you know?" And Mom laughed and punched him, saying, "You always think you're so subtle." It relieved the air in an elaborate, excellent way, and we all had a chuckle, and they both rushed in to claim that, all personal thoughts aside, it was and always would be up to me.

On the evening I finally decided, then, Dad and I were in the kitchen, telling Polish jokes and behaving like fools, and Mom walked in, her finger keeping her place in her Bible. "For the record," she said, "I think I've changed my opinion on the BIG MATTER. I keep reading all this stuff about 'suffer the children' and 'help for the needy.' It makes me feel lots more secure about keeping it."

That, for me, settled it, for at that hour, finding both parents suddenly on the same side, each of them confident in me as a mother and in themselves as grandparents, I realized that somewhere these months — in my mother's handmade album and my own close study of reputable adoption — this baby had already become kin, had taken its place at the table there where we sat all together, feeding on loyalty like bread. I knew, and felt I had known all along, that yes, I could manage this, that a family the nature of ours could sustain an addition quite comfortably. It was nearly Thanksgiving now, and finally I felt able to enjoy the season; we would have all Christmas to play, to learn our new places together, before January came and I returned to public school, the last semester to finish before I was through. My brother and sisters would try on their new names — Aunt and Uncle, that's my niece over there — and, though I did not know it yet, I would wake up through the night, lifting my daughter from her crib, crying with her, sometimes in exhaustion, more often out of dread for the fact that I had so nearly abandoned this comfort, this small companion in the way.

But before all this there was the question

of my siblings. Early on, I had asked that they not be told of my pregnancy until the baby decision was made and over with, so they could take their place in the result but not in the horrible uncertainty beforehand. Thus I had faced none of them in real conversation for months now, though I knew both Leslie and Bethel had found out earlier that I was pregnant, each by accident, and each without ever speaking of it to me. From Mom, I knew that Leslie had been asked at school and said no absolutely, her sister was not expecting, what a thought, and coming home spoke of this to our mother, aching and crying at the truth she heard then. "I told her," Mom said to me later, "that the secret was important because you might choose adoption, and she began to cry then and say no, you couldn't, she would keep it herself." I perceived these words as thoughtless and irreparable, and would not know for ten years how viciously and immediately Leslie had hated herself for speaking them; for the present, I saw only injustice — that, and the terrible aloneness it brought between us there, forgetting, as we did, that we were on the same side.

Bethel's discovery, too, had brought damage, both through her means of finding out and through her consequent handling of the knowledge. Watching me one day at the typewriter, she had seen me cover the paper as she passed by, and after I was finished and had thrown the backing sheet away, she took it from the garbage and ran a light pencil over the imprint of the keys. She said long afterward, and I believed her, that it was not curiosity so much as dread that made her do it, the feeling that forces were present she could not see, that she must at all costs uncloak them, discover how strong and how many. The paper she read was a letter, written to a pastor I knew far away, clear in detail and descriptive of my problems, and when she spoke, as Leslie had, to my mother, hers, too, was a voice of sorrow, of deep regret at finding the truth by accident. My rage then was unspeakable, but later grew to near-hatred, for, as it happened, Bethel — whose sorrow and unreasoning terror must closely have approximated Leslie's — had confided with weeping to her closest friend, who had then told her own mother, who had in turn begun the rumor which had brought all those childless couples to our door.

It had been difficult to understand, how I could have come after so long to understand the intrinsic value of good faith and yet find, as it seemed, others of our clan hardly thinking as they knocked aside the new walls, letting the world inside. In my room I had raged at Mom, saying, "I never want to see them again, or speak to them either. If they can't respect what's private, they're not my family at all."

"They're younger than you," my mother had said. "And yes, it was wrong. Just don't let's fall to bits now, when we're finally forgiving ourselves the big things." Don't talk to them now, she said, until I was over this anger; whatever I said out of hurt would likely be unfair, would certainly diminish all hope of coming together in the end.

And after time I understood she was right, that what I refused to forgive would also be refused me, and rightly. Bethel's infidelity, or Leslie's, I knew, had arrived here only as a result of one much greater, the one I had owned all myself. Now that in tremendous relief I had decided about my baby, about myself, what had passed behind us seemed almost trivial, hardly deserving of the effort to remember it. The present issue was that I still had spoken nothing to my siblings — had confided nothing, had neither accepted nor offered strong comfort. And I found inexplicably, even on this day of forgiving, that I still was afraid to meet up with them, afraid of those faces and whatever new and frightening thing I would find there. I could not do it, I said to my father, I did not even know if Ian had found out, and if he had not, I simply couldn't say it to him.

Dad put down his cup and tapped his finger — two taps, one-two — and then a closed hand pounded down, the way he always had done to stress a point. "You don't have to," he said. "Just get your things in order and I'll tell them."

At any rate, I would not have had the time. In the morning I was scheduled for that week's hundred-mile trip to the obstetrician, and with the slippery narrow roads and the ice fog, Mom and I had to allow four hours. We drove the highway singing as we always had, discussing baby names and finding none suitable, wondering about the sex of this person. I took the wheel as I insisted every time, for we had had a bad car accident once with a friend of ours in control, and now I was phobic about riding. Mom made belly jokes and laughed, for mine rubbed the steering wheel even with the seat pushed far back, and I had to reach for the pedals with my toes. In the parking lot to the doctor's office, Mom shut her door and, speaking across the car roof, said, "I hope she says it'll be soon. Then you can stop throwing up, and I can stop itching for my grandchild." A while later, the doctor pronounced me full-term, ready for labor any time, induced if I wanted, or natural. I chose to induce, that day if possible, thinking not so much of a frantic rushed trip in the snow, but more of impatience, of a hundred long hours of waiting, shaking my foot up and down, ready, now that I had decided, to get on with it.

But it turned out that, however ready I was to end this, my body was not; at the hospital, after thirty-six hours of induced labor spent primarily in choosing a name between contractions, I snatched out my IV tube and demanded a Caesarean. I was sure, I told my mother, I was dying — take this down in ink, I said, I'm making a will — and still more sure after I woke up, when I found that great shark's teeth had somehow plunged into my belly, shredding it from the inside like meat. Mom stood there then, leaning into my face, coming close enough for me to see without glasses. "A girl," she said. "Can you hear me? She's a girl and she's really pretty." I faded under again, but in the morning I held the baby, amazed at how tightly her legs folded up to her chest.

For the week I was there, attempting a walk every hour to the nursery, my parents were rummaging through the town, searching for the baby things we had so long avoided considering. A crib, they announced, and described it to me — dark wooden frame, bars close together — and a carrier. And after that cotton blankets, and diapers and T-shirts and socks.

My father called a family conference at home, sitting the others around him and speaking of me, my baby, the whole story. When my mother told me of it, she said, "Dad had a talk with the others last night. Ian never knew." Dear Lord, I thought, how could he have missed it? I had felt — indeed, had looked — so enormous. But Ian was the dreamer, half conscious in the world; or conscious, perhaps, of far more ethereal things.

"What did he say," I asked.

"Nothing, as far as I gather. He never says much." Mom reached over and moved a hair off my face. "Don't worry," she said. "They're all doing fine. Just wait till they see her." I could not tell then, and could not manage to ask, if she meant the others had revolted but would surely come around, or if instead they were truly fine and waiting for me. With Leslie and Bethel it would be hard, I knew, for it already had been; still, they had each had, since their first startled discoveries, a month or more now of thinking, re-forming, settling back in. And whatever small hurts they had come through before had always been used up in language, modeled into words, described and dissipated like elaborate and temporal sand sculptures built up on the tide line and abandoned. Whoever they were now, one could hope, both were still verbal beings, ready with words that would, in the end, sustain us.

But Ian. Here, I had not a clue. Having found out only yesterday, I thought, what possibly could he be thinking now. All these months, he had seemed pleased that I was so constantly at home, looking hard into me when I tickled him, wondering, I supposed, at this new attention. I had been grateful those moments, for they were dear in the way that an old house becomes dear in the short, intense weeks just before it is sold and moved out of. I had wanted to use them up, use Ian up, before the end — before today — in case, within all the re-visioning he would do inside himself, he should come to view those minutes as a lovely, dishonest time we would never both make it back to.

The trip home was a long one, exhilarating at first — Mom attending the wheel and I tending my baby, laughing insanely at old jokes, singing our favorite road songs — and then in stages more solemn, as I worried in myself over Ian — the others, too, but him most of all — and what kind of mood I would walk into at home. Mom guessed at my thinking and said, "It's hard to believe he didn't know, isn't it."

"Yeah," I said. "I mean, I've been so HUGE."

"Well, Ian always was a bit vacant." Mom looked at me and grinned. "You know what he said when Dad told him? He said, 'Shoot, I just thought she was fat.' " And that saved me suddenly from brooding, for we were off then into huge giggles, covering our mouths while the baby slept, choking and coughing on our own hilarity, and a mile later we were home, swinging the car in close to the door. I was exhausted from the hospital, and stumbled a little on the porch steps, grabbing tighter to the baby. "Hang on," Mom said and caught hold of my arm. "Everyone's inside. They'll wait just fine till you get there."

Mom went first, opening the door, and then people were out and spilling upon us — Dad and Leslie and Bethel, two family friends farther back, Ian behind them, holding his head above all the shoulders. We passed, unwinding the baby's blankets, through the kitchen, beside a pot roast on the stove and into the living room; in all the noise and yellow of the kitchen, in all the words and shouted welcome, we were a whitewater rapids of people, loud and caught up and splashing down at random. Leslie was saying, "Hurry, I want to see," and Bethel and Ian fell back, losing their view to the taller ones, and someone had hung a crayon banner — "Welcome home, Natalie and Charity" — and still I lifted more blankets aside with my hand. I sat on a sofa, grinning and self-conscious and listening to the furor, and each person took a turn holding Charity: Leslie first, shown how by my mother, glad but shy and looking at me; then a couple of friends, and then Bethel, clutching in with her arms and getting her first good view, starting for a moment and looking closer; Ian stepping up when Charity opened her eyes, both of them staring and thoughtful and solemn.

Then Dad said, "Time to eat," and we amassed in the kitchen, stood around loading plates, everyone still talking while the baby slept in her carrier, over behind us on the coffee table. In the jumble, one person was easily lost, and I saw Ian's plate still unclaimed on the counter, his cup and fork still unused. After a while, the circle divided and Dad told a joke while Mom stood speaking to someone else, leaving me silent and listening. I turned and looked back and saw through the doorway Ian, bending close there at the baby carrier, lifting aside a blanket and looking in.

"Hey Ian," I said, and he jumped, drawing in his shoulders and looking my way. I said, "Hey there, Uncle boy," fluttering my fingers at him, and Ian grinned and rolled his eyes;

when I turned back to the talk, he had resumed watching Charity, his face slack in its old dreaming shape, his eyes distant and alive.

EARTH
SONGS

So it was as my mother had said: the world continued on, and we in it, and things were not so greatly different at all. I finished high school in the spring and took college-entrance exams, and my brother and sisters held the baby, putting their eyes up close to hers, singing her all of our songs. Nights, that last summer before college, we went out late and had barbecues, eating leftovers in the hammock and swinging our legs. It was our first languid year, for our house was complete and we needed not rush now, needed only mow the fields, cut the firewood, and pick mushrooms, watching the fireweed bloom toward the top, knowing that when frost came we'd be ready. "Someday," Mom told her daughters, "someday some guy will say to you, 'Let's run away to the wilderness and live like pioneers, with just a hand pump and some candles.' And you'll look back at that man and tell him, 'Get lost, buddy, I've done my time.'" We laughed when Mom said this, for we knew she was right, that we could live hard lives again by necessity, but never at all from romanticism.

Then it was fall. I registered at the university and Charity attended welfare-paid day care, we drove home most weekends to see the family, and Mom typed my papers while Dad cooked potato pancakes, calling us all to come eat. At the table, my parents asked about my classes and I described them, the best lecture that week — in freshman biology, where we learned the chemical nature of bodies — and the worst one, also in biology, where the man had said, "We're too worried about feelings in nature; when we say a fish is afraid when it's hunted, we invest it with emotion it doesn't have." My mother leaned over her plate, asking, "Did you agree or disagree. When he said that, I mean."

"Neither, really," I said, thinking how long it was since she had been in school. "I hate to think that's true, but I don't know enough to say."

My mother waved her fork. "Maybe they don't expect you to *have* an opinion, just *form* one." She reached for the salt. "I don't know. I think you have ideas, and now you learn to justify them."

"Maybe," I said. "Actually, when he first said that, I thought . . ." And we were off, rehashing my class lectures, picking them apart, and on Monday I spoke in class — but only in the very small ones — saying, "I was thinking this weekend, and I wonder . . ." It was awkward at first, for I was seventeen in a college where the median age was about thirty, but I didn't look quite so young as I was and found that, as long as I was articulate, my teachers indulged this child in their classrooms, some even coming to like me.

And I in turn came to like school a bit more, nearly as much as Mom enjoyed it for me. Toward the end of that term, I had her read my mass-communications research paper, asking her how to write one. We sat on the couch or in her study and she read over my handwritten notes, saying, "Well, look here, for instance. It seems to me your point is this." She analyzed my topic, an amorphous and diffuse study of the advertising media, honing and focusing it, bringing it well into view. We discussed ideas I had considered only vaguely, paging through books from our shelves, finding some experts to comment upon. I tired of this long before Mom did, growing exasperated, saying, "This is just a term paper. I only want it good enough to hand in."

Mom looked up from a book, holding the place with her hand. "But don't you care what it says," she asked. "What you can say proves what you can think."

"Look," I said. "Mom. This is an intro-level course. No one expects me to think."

"I do," she told me, turning back to her page. I gave up then, said I was too tired for this, and went to bed upstairs while she was still reading. In the morning, she had relevant sources spread all over the table, looking up when I came down for coffee, telling me, "I know, I know, you're sick of writing this stuff. That's okay, finish this draft and I'll type it." In the afternoon, when I handed her my pages, written in ink, with words scratched out all over, she said, "It's ridiculous you don't think this is fun."

More than "fun," I think, my mother meant to say "worthwhile," for she herself had long been insecure at her jobs, doing fine work — substantially better than she had to, usually — proving herself against those far more educated. Most of the jobs she had had, in fact, were ones she was not technically trained for, and she had qualified for them by proving on tests that she could do them. She had worked a computer at Fort Greely and then, having grown sick of showing her I.D. at the gate, had moved to one at the school district office in town; when they had promoted her to business manager, she had come home insecure, saying to us all, "I can do the job, yeah, but everyone there has finished their degrees. I feel like I have to do twice as well as the rest of them." That year, when I was home for Thanksgiving, the vice superintendent completed his doctorate, and I watched my mother congratulate him, effusively but with some degree of reserve.

It surprised none of us, then, or at least not me and not Dad, when Mom said that Christmas, "What would you all think if I went to school next year?"

We were in the living room drinking milk and playing with the baby, and my dad put his legs up on a stool. "About time," he said. "You should have finished years ago."

"No, I mean," Mom said, "I mean, I'd have to quit work. And be gone part of the week."

I said, "You hate your job anyway. Get a student loan and we'll put an extra bed at my place."

"Yeah," Dad said, dropping his head back, finishing his milk. He brought it down and looked at my mother, her uncertain, almost guilty face. "Oh, what," he said. "You're worried about the house? Everyone around here is old enough to learn to do things. All along I've said it, you carry more than your share."

"And it's not fair, really," I said. "No one but you knows how to take care of themselves."

We meant to be kind, to support Mom's desire by showing how her pursuit of it would not inconvenience us; but that, I think, was precisely her fear, that things could go on without her, that her absence could become usual, nothing the rest of us would notice. This, she should have known, was impossible, for in our growing-up years she had made herself invaluable, managing money and schedules and even housekeeping, never supposing the rest of us would need to learn these. I think the younger children were to be surprised, in the end, at the hardship of her absence. For them, the year of Mom's schooling would be a precarious one, more quiet during the week and more unsettled, the floors piling up with debris that none of them had been taught to notice, much less to pick up. My father would yell at them, and I would, too, saying over the phone, "Don't wait for someone to clean up after you. Do it yourself, or don't mess stuff up in the first place." Shaking themselves awake as out of some long sleep, my sisters and brother would look around at the house and arrange a few things, waiting for Mom to come home so they could talk about school.

So it was my second year of college, and Mom enrolled along with me — "Journalism," she said. "I'm going to write; all my journals about coming to Alaska should go into a book." She drove to Fairbanks during the week for Tuesday and Thursday classes, and then back home again weekends. Nights at my apartment, we sat in the living room with our homework, and she called the family to check on things. "Are you sure this is okay," she asked then. "Did I leave enough for dinner." She spent the weekends at home preparing a whole week's meals and doing laundry, forbidding anyone to help her. Where before she had used to holler at Ian, "Look at these clothes on the floor; you just leave them because you know I'll pick them up," now she said none of these things, intent on doing even more of the others' share — viewing it, I suppose, as her penance.

She hardly slept at my house, completing all her studies there so she would not have to take them home. In the morning, when I carried Charity downstairs, she would have been up for hours, drinking coffee and taking notes. "Hey, Mom," I said, wondering if she had ever gone to bed. "What about some breakfast. You look hungry."

She said, "Okay, let me make it," and laid aside her books, stacking them on the floor.

"Ahem," I said. "I believe it's my turn?" I held Charity out toward her, turning my face aside. "But if you're taking a break any-

way, you might have a look at this diaper."
We laughed and Mom took the baby, calling
her by her nickname, saying, "Do you hear
that, Cheer? Your mommy thinks breakfast
smells better than you."

On the whole, we had a marvelous time.
We ate ice cream on my bed and invented
malicious and uproarious gossip about everyone we knew, sitting Charity on our bellies
and sharing with her from our own two
spoons. Or we went to late movies, sneaking
in our own hot dogs and chocolate, carrying
gigantic, conspicuous purses full of food. Some
nights, in the middle of a study session, Mom
would slam her book down and say, "Let's
go out for a celebration dinner. Someplace really expensive."

"What's the occasion," I would ask.

And Mom said, "Wednesday."

But gradually, my mother's eyes grew
darker, her body less erect, and when she
pushed out from her chair to help me at the
stove, she was abnormally quick with her
limbs, as if she had to propel her arms force-
fully to make them move at all. She moved
with great flourishes of activity, imagining, I
think, that if she just finished these — her
homework, the dishes, driving for milk at the
store — the day would be over, complete until
tomorrow, and she could lie back then on the

couch, watching TV until bedtime. But the lying-back moments never came, for there was always something else, some chore to relieve me of, or some piece of schoolwork due the next day. She was taking twenty-one credit hours at a time, hoping to finish up earlier that way, and she studied in odd, snatched moments at my apartment, between the thousand other things she found to do for my benefit. When I grew tired and tearful after too many days of stress, she met me outside my classes and said to go home, she would pick up Charity from day care. I was often too exhausted to see her own shadowed eyes, or if I did see them, I was too grateful to protest her offer. I merely went home and slept in a chair, looking up and reaching for my daughter when they arrived, watching my mother make dinner at the stove.

More and more Tuesdays, Mom arrived for school looking drained already, her week not even begun. Having spent the weekend "catching up" with the family, she would be in my living room vacuuming when I got there after class. "Hey," I called. "Don't you have homework?"

Mom switched off the sweeper and leaned backward, stretching her spine. She answered, "I thought I'd take a break and get this done."

"Some break," I said, grinning. I unplugged

the electrical cord and started winding it. "Now go sit down; you shouldn't be doing this."

"Neither should you," she told me, hefting the vacuum cleaner, taking it to the closet. "If I chip in with housework, you can spend more time with Cheer."

"Look," I said then, "it's my house. I should be taking care of it." Mom would sit down then in a chair and I would know I had hurt her feelings; I wondered what I could have said that would have been kinder.

It became increasingly obvious that year that Mom was functioning almost entirely on adrenaline and not on rested energy. Yet even so we were all tired in some way, and chose mostly to believe her when she said, "Go to bed now. You'll just be in the way while I'm mopping." At my apartment, I felt guilty sometimes for Mom's attention to my housework, but between my studies and driving Charity to day care, I could not often find the energy to protest. With more relief than regret, I merely said, "I know you're doing my share, Mom, but really I'm glad for it."

My father was the one in those days who brought the rest of us to account, who saw our mother's failing health and demanded the rest of us see it as well. He called family conferences secretly at home, telling the others,

"We have to each help where we can. Take some load off your mother, kids, even if she doesn't like it; she can't keep doing what she's doing." He called me at my apartment to say, "Encourage Mom and get her to rest. And encourage the other kids. They need you to suggest what to do." On the phone, when I knew Mom was still on the road back to Delta, I talked to Leslie about doing the dishes. "You should just have time if you start now," I said. "And maybe get someone to sort the laundry. Mom will get mad if you wash it, but it'll be easier for her if you put it in piles."

My sisters and brother and father began sneaking to do dishes behind Mom's back, or vacuuming furiously before she arrived home and caught them. "Did you have enough to eat this week," Mom asked first thing in the door. "Hey, what's that smell? DID SOMEONE MOP THIS FLOOR?" Coming inside after her, those weekends when I went along, I began to laugh, saying, "Mom, will you relax? Everyone lives here, everyone should work at it. Besides, you have homework to do." But this was the wrong thing to say, and I should have known that. For my mother's great wish was that, during the week when she "abandoned" her children still at home, everything else in their lives could remain constant; my mention of schoolwork indicated some change that had come, and made her perform more zealously at home, washing sheets and even blankets far more often than she ever had in the past.

"Verna," my father would say, finding her at midnight on Monday still filling dishes with lasagna for the family's dinner that week. "Honey, this is ridiculous. Here we've got all of us to run a house, and you're killing yourself to try it alone. The kids are growing up, even Bethel's twelve; let them do some chores." But Mom was adamant and threatened to quit school if anyone disrupted their schedule for her, if they, as she said, had to pay dues for something she was doing for herself. "I mean it," she said. "That was the rule before I even started, and you said okay." She worked this way at night, I think, so the rest of us would not see and feel guilty; for she had grown up with a mother who functioned on the guilt of others, and to have martyred herself that way in our eyes would have seemed to her an appalling throwback, something she had striven all her life to avoid. She was merely working, as she always had, to insulate us from the hard things, and only much later would the rest of us see this fact and regret what it cost.

It wasn't, of course, all heaviness in those days — not all, and not indeed even mostly.

Mom and I became terrific buddies, griping loudly about homework, even taking a dreaded required course at the same time so we could take turns skipping it. When we weren't together, we referred to one another in conversation, so much so that once when we were driving to a movie she told me, "You know, the women in Delta are really jealous of us. How much fun we have, and all."

"Jealous," I said. "How do you know."

"Sometimes one of them says so. But mostly, when I see them in church or whatever, they just ask what we did this week. Almost like, 'Come on, Verna, don't tell me you had another good time.' " Our apartment was loud and chaotic, and we had friends in sometimes from campus, watching TV movies or playing Scrabble, making up unlikely words and convincing the others they were real. Mom taught Charity to jump on the bed, or posed her in chairs for photography-class assignments, lying on the floor and shooting pictures from there, calling, "Hey, Cheer, what's that on the wall."

Still too, Mom and I had terrible, bloodthirsty fights, for it was awkward sometimes to manage the question of who between us was in charge, and who taking care of whom. After Dad said to take Mom's mind away from housework, I tried often to tell her to leave it, it didn't matter, we had no time to clean house. "There's plenty of time," Mom said, "at least for me. My classes aren't as hard as yours." This last was not true, or what was more true was that in school, as with her earlier jobs, Mom was insecure as to her place in things, and worked doubly hard on her studies, prevailing against who she thought she was: an old lady of forty-four among bright young classmates in their thirties. "Mother," I said, "that's baloney. Just let the apartment alone. I'll clean it really well when school's out, and we'll just pick up the little stuff until then."

But she would not agree to this, though she took to managing the place in secret, while I was upstairs in bed. Having begun my protests in concern for her health, I grew now to be angry, suspecting my mother of "mothering," of robbing my adulthood away. "What are you doing," I yelled once, when I found my mother feeding coffee cake to Charity. "I told you she's not to eat junk food."

Mom put down the fork, slowly and without shouting back. "It was the fastest thing," she said. "I didn't feel like cooking real breakfast." She handed me the plate and went to pour coffee.

"Then don't do it at all," I threw out, following her. "Who said it's your job?"

261

Mom's answering voice was reasonable and tight. "It seems to me," she said, "that you could use the help."

Standing there with my coffee cup, I knew we were both right, Mom surely more than I, and I grew more irritated knowing this, grabbing around for more words. "It's only help," I told her, "if you do something for me that I'd do myself. And I wouldn't feed her cake."

"Coffee cake."

"JUNK FOOD." And on and on. I told her she was doing us all a disservice, that she had raised children who were dysfunctional, who knew nothing of the world and would never be self-sufficient. In anger I turned cruel, and my mother was shocked and enraged, standing up and hollering back, saying this kind of talk was beneath me.

"Okay, fine," Mom shouted, "I'm staying somewhere else — a hotel or something — and you can have your own life."

"Oh, good," I hollered. "You just do that." On occasion, she would call my father, tell him she was coming home for good, quitting school, and he would drive the hundred miles to my place, ready to deliver a lecture. Once there, he would find us sitting in different parts of the house, sulking and nursing our wounds, watching Charity play between us;

and when we saw him, we both began talking over one another: "She said I was interfering," and "Do you think she's being fair," and "She hates me and I hate her back."

My father would listen a moment to all this, and gradually, from his eyes and then on to the rest of his face, a great laugh would build inside him until, just when my mother and I were at the edge of hysteria, he would erupt, squeezing his nose and laughing, wiping his eyes on his sleeve.

"THIS IS NOT FUNNY," Mom and I would shout, and he would say, "Oh, it is, it is. You two sound like sisters, and you act like them. Oh, ho-ho." By the end, we all would be laughing, Dad having embarrassed the two of us as we sat there feeling, by that point, foolish and absurd. Waving at the window later as Dad drove away, Mom would stare out at his taillights and say, "It's just that sometimes I forget you're eighteen. I forget what to expect from you." It seemed to be a compliment, and I had no answer to give it.

For in some respects we were becoming more and more alike, liking the same people, respecting the same sorts of humor. We had a lot of jokes between ourselves, and our favorite was, "No problem, I can handle rejection." "I'm off to class," Mom said one day, picking up her books. "I'll see you at home."

I turned down my lips and pretended at brave tears. "No problem," I said. "Really, no problem. I've taken rejection before, I can take it again. You just go ahead. No problem." The joke grew from there just like the old Rodney one had, until we were saying it at the most inappropriate times: over dinner ("No problem, if you want chicken I can do without hamburgers. Really, no problem, I can handle rejection"), outside the library, before Mom's trips back home to the family. At the table in the student union, I pushed back my chair and said to Mom and the friend who sat with us, "Be right back."

The woman said, "If you're going to the bathroom, I need to come, too." She said to my mother, "Watch my stuff?"

"No problem," Mom said. "I can handle rejection. I'll just sit here alone and bite my nails." Our friend seemed bewildered at the joke, looking at us both uncertainly and acting very polite when she returned to sit next to Mom.

That last time, just before finals week of spring semester, Mom pulled her car close to the apartment, loading her things inside and running back to poke Charity's belly. "I'll call when I get home," she said. "See you Tuesday."

In the pitiful voice of our joke, I said, "That's fine, no problem. I can handle rejection. We both can, right, Charity?" Mom laughed, and started to shut the door. "No, really, no need to feel bad," I called. "Really. No problem."

Mom said, "Yeah, yeah. Okay, see you."

"No, REALLY. I mean it. You just go on your way, don't worry, we'll be fine."

"Oh, WILL you cut it out," Mom said, beginning to look sad, as if she thought I meant it. Perhaps I did, in a way, for I had grown increasingly used to her company, increasingly sorry when she was gone.

I called home on Saturday, and Mom answered, breathless. "We were out shooting pictures for my photography final," she said. She said it had been a wonderful, fast weekend, for my brother and sisters were on a school trip until Sunday, and she and Dad were having, as she said, "something like a second honeymoon." How was my weekend going, she asked, and I said it was fine, a little boring, but I was taking a study break just then and making a quilted book bag from scraps.

"I impress myself," I bragged. "When you see this bag, you'll steal it right off me."

"Get it done by Tuesday," Mom said. "I'll check it out then. I can watch Charity, and you can get all studied for finals." Okay, I said, no problem. I can manage till Tuesday all alone, no problem. My mother laughed.

The next afternoon, Charity was stacking blocks and I was rewriting some biology notes, trying to memorize an incomprehensible diagram about the human circulatory system. The phone rang, and I thought, Good, I'll talk to Mom instead.

But it was Leslie, crying so hard over her words that I had to say, "Leslie, stop. Okay, now say it slow so I can understand."

"Mom's had a heart attack, I think. She's on the floor of the garage and Dad's giving her CPR. Natalie, I think she's dying."

It was one of those familiar, unspeakable moments, the ones that had always brought on this feeling, this sense that everything now must be done at full attention, deliberately, with an absolutely conscious mind. "Who have you called," I asked. "Did you call an ambulance." Every word enunciated, every thought considered through.

"I can't get through. The medic at the clinic is out of town. I want to go help Dad."

"Leslie, you have to do the phoning so I can drive down. Call Fort Greely, get the main number and tell them it's an emergency. Be sure you give them good directions, and tell them the whole thing."

Leslie said, "Okay, I'm writing this down. Okay. I'm okay now. What else?"

"After that, start calling the churches. Call them all. And Les?"

"What."

"Get Bethel and Ian. Be sure to tell them what's happening. I'll be there in two hours, maybe less."

"Hurry, Nat."

And still everything was quick, conscious, and studied. I took down a suitcase from the shelf and wadded clothes into it, some of Charity's and some of mine, and extra diapers and T-shirts. I checked my daughter's diaper in case it was dirty. I picked up two books for her to look at, and when we were in the car — not four minutes since the phone call — I was aware of many things: the sticky spot on the gearshift lever, the crack in the windshield above eye level, Charity's untied laces. I tied the shoe and took off. Twice on the way I stopped at churches, the same ones, I suppose, that my mother had phoned the night of my accident, standing there with her handful of quarters, letting our request be made known to the world. "It's my mom," I said to the people. "They think she might be dying."

The pastor at the missionary station went out with me to my car, telling me, "I'll call some more people. Tell your dad. Tell him everyone's praying Verna will live."

I stopped and turned on the man. "No," I told him. "That's not what I said. Ask for the right thing to happen, and that, whatever it is, we can take it."

"Okay," he said. "That's what we'll say." He shut the door after me, then leaned his head through the window. "You did the right thing," he told me. "It's good you stopped here."

I was careful on the road, talking out loud to myself, to God, avoiding the potholes as I drove, reasoning aloud about a friend's recent funeral, about old conversations with Mom, about my own ability to bear this new thing, should I arrive home and find my mother gone. A few miles from home, a horse ran into the road, and after her a foal, and still I was studied and firm, slowing down and passing near them, speeding up and shifting again into second. To remain steady was all I had, I thought, for fear could only claim us if we allowed ourselves to tremble in its face.

This same thought had occurred to me just that Tuesday; I had discussed it then with Mom, and the coincidence seemed unthinkable now. That day, we had attended the funeral of a high-school classmate who had died in a fire, and we both had cried and driven home speaking of death.

"I don't know when it started," I said, turning the car into the road, "but I've gotten to feeling superior, like we've seen so much tragedy and here we are, afraid of nothing, leaping tall buildings at a single bound."

Mom agreed. "It is a fact," she said, "that we know crisis best of anything. It's more familiar, I think, so we trust the way we've learned to behave in it."

There was more to my thought, and I spoke it. "Wait, no, I meant something else. I meant I've gotten proud of it. Like, heck, we've been through every single possible ordeal, and now we know we can manage anything." I took my eyes off the wheel and saw Mom looking at me. "But not death. We haven't seen a death. We're spared there, maybe because we couldn't manage that one."

"Probably so," Mom had said. "My gosh, though, we've come close enough." Now, driving home, I thought, Please don't let that have been an omen.

I drove into Delta past the Baptist church, and a man walked into the road there, waving both arms and shouting something I could not hear. "What," I thought, "is he crazy," and I swerved, slowing down and stopping. It was Mr. Toth, my social-studies teacher from seventh grade, and he came around to my window, saying, "Your daddy is in there, in the church. He wanted me to flag you down."

I looked and my hands were almost still, but to me it felt they were jerking on the wheel, rhythmically and fast, with every great surge of my heartbeat. Already turning the car around, I was suddenly profoundly grateful, and I said to Mr. Toth, "Thanks. I mean really, thanks so much, it was good of you to watch for me." He waved and I was gone again, driving the other way and into the parking lot at the church.

I left Charity in the car, handing her a book and saying, "I'll be right back, baby. Stay here a minute." Inside, I heard the church service going on and people singing — that's right, I thought, it's Sunday — and in the small hallway were my father and his best friend, John, huddled inward and talking, my father standing a bit too straight, moving his hands with the same large energy my mother used when she was tired and trying to finish the last few things before bed. Coming up from the side, I said, "I'm here, how's Mom."

John and my father turned to me with their red watery eyes, and Dad said, "Listen, Tosh, the others are still home and we need to get there." He looked at John, said, "Well, thanks very much," and John grabbed his arm. "Let us know what you need," he said.

My father passed in front and toward the door, saying, "Come on, Tochka."

I would not think now, would interpret none of these red eyes or cracking voices, would believe nothing at all until I heard it spoken out loud. "Dad," I said, catching up. "What happened with Mom. Is she okay."

My father reached the door and stood opening it. "She's doing the best of any of us; let's get home to the others." I looked back and saw John listening after us, and he turned away then, back to the sanctuary door.

I would concentrate on the physical, the small necessary things for now. "Wait," I called to my father. "I have to stop for gas. I'll follow you after that."

My father was hurrying to his car, but stopped now. "I want to get home," he said. "Get gas in the morning."

"They won't be open," I told him, pushing the point. "I have to leave at seven to make class."

"Okay," Dad said. "But I won't go ahead. I'll come and pay the guy."

So at the station a man filled the tank and my father got out of his truck to stand watching, pulling out bills from his wallet before the attendant was even through. I tightened Charity's seat harness and felt the pulse still

271

jerking in my arms, but I would think only on gasoline and on thanking my father, saying to him, "I feel better with a full tank."

"Yeah," Dad said. "It's better to have it. Now let's go." I followed him the three miles toward home, considering only the road and my daughter beside me, closing off my inward mind.

At home, I climbed the porch steps with Charity and went after my father into the living room, smiling around, ignoring the expressions on faces, saying into the air, "Hi, I'm here." Someone said hello, but after that, nothing. My brother and sisters were sitting down, and all around were friends my father had called: pastors and old co-workers, a man from down the road, every praying person we knew. I was careful still to think nothing, to take my place among the faces and wait to hear what was spoken there. My father's face was old, unshaven, the same gray color as his hair. He put a hand on my back, hardly touching, sitting me down, and he stood in the center of the room. "Kids," he said. He breathed in, gathering enough air to form words. "Kids, your mother is with the Lord." He turned to me, touching my hair, apologizing. "You had to be able to drive," he said. "I couldn't say it before."

There was no thunderclap, no eruption of

lava from beneath us, only my own shrinking face, its blood melting down from it like wax.

Everyone went to school the next day, myself included. Outside the family, no one in town understood this, but we had spoken about it the night before, after the praying people had gone home. "It's the way we know to do things," Dad had said then. "We continue on and don't stop." Turning to each of us, he went on, "You don't have to go if you can't manage it, we're not looking for heroes." And we all knew what he meant, that this was a question, not of doing battle, but merely of remaining erect — standing upright on our feet, however hard the river ran around us. When we spoke that evening of our choices — to attend school or to stay home and catch up later — we spoke also of those accident years when I had moved in and out of hospitals, sometimes urgently in the night, and when one of the parents had always stayed home in the stable center, making breakfast, packing lunches, sending the children to school. We had learned it then and it was in our minds now, and here we were this time, as Leslie said, "sending our own selves to school."

But, of course, other people found this extremely odd. The school counselor had each of my siblings into his office, telling them,

"Name how you feel. Are you sad? It's all right, you can cry if you'd like." None of them did, not there, and not out of carelessness or some absurd pride; rather, it was because this huge a grief must be dealt with like joy, privately and with passion, out of earshot — like a honeymoon — from those who did not share it.

I spent Monday, in fact the week, on the business part of dying. I collected mother's grades — straight A's and, as she would have said, "from a forty-five-year-old matron" — and withdrew her from school, went through and made sense of the finances — always, before, her domain — and wrote out a sheet instructing Dad on how to pay the monthly bills. This behavior, too, no one understood. I heard visitors say to my father, "Oh, your daughter is brave. You must be very grateful." But they were wrong, for not a shred of this was courage. It was, instead, a fragile leaning into the familiar, into my mother's own lessons on coping: gather back energy while you do the calm things, hurl yourself at the details, at every last procedure of which you are fully in control.

The funeral was as we all discussed it, neither morbid nor somber. After Dad's heart surgery a few years before, we had examined death minutely, named it as something not to shrink from, as something preferable, in some cases, to life. We read scriptures on heaven, began to call it "home," half as a joke, half in earnest. As a family, we made a deal that, should any of us die, the others would feel glad for us, have a simple funeral at little cost, wear something other than black. "But you can grieve," my mother had said then. "You should not deny that. Just realize that you grieve only for yourselves, for a kind of homesickness and not at all for the one who has died." Now we discussed those thoughts among ourselves, how indeed this felt like homesickness, a regretful and tearing nostalgia for some sustaining thing now having moved out of reach.

And it was again as my mother had said. We bought a plain coffin, and asked that she not be embalmed. Because it was May and the ground was still frozen at the cemetery, we hired a man with a hydraulic drill, had him break the ground so we would not, as was usually done, need to wait until summer for the burial.

I wore lavender to the funeral, and the others the same sorts of colors. I had found one of Mom's class assignments, a brief history of herself in twenty minutes of class, and our friend David read it there, describing in my mother's words her understanding of life, of the world, of marriage and family. Her story began: "I am middle-aged, female, devoted to husband and offspring, otherwise a loner, foremost a child of the Creator, in a youth-oriented, male, hedonistic, secular-minded world." She continued for pages, speaking of her mother and schizophrenia, of herself growing up among cities, of meeting my father and wanting children, of bearing them finally and bringing them to live in this place. In the end, she said, after houses and land and a thousand hard moments of prevailing, she had named her final desire: a degree in journalism, a minor in philosophy, each brought together to form a new creature, a writer of words who could know the human mind. When David finished reading, he folded the paper and looked over my way, and I held up my thumb, meaning, "Good show."

We smiled and shook hands with the town, driving before them to the cemetery, and at the grave, when people were dispersing and the coffin was about to be lowered, my father took a breath and began to hum. Lined up as we were close together, the family heard him and looked his way. It was one of the old road songs from before, from our very early migration to Alaska, and we began then to follow after him, opening our mouths wide around the words. Behind us, people hesitated

in the leaves, shuffling back and stopping —
not sure, I suppose, at the etiquette here. None
of them, as I remember, sang with us, though
the song was probably familiar. It was an old
classic hymn about faith in the earth and
peace, about living in the world and then leaving it, happy to be gone.

The things of earth
Will dim and lose their value
If we recall they're borrowed for a while.
And things of earth
That cause the heart to tremble,
Remembered there will only bring a smile.
But until then, my heart will go on singing.
Until then, with joy I'll carry on
Until the day my eyes behold that city.
Until the day God calls me home.

We sang a full verse and the chorus, all melody
now but harmonious just the same, and afterward, while other people filled in the grave,
we continued the song in the car, shouting
our voices raw, rolling down our windows and
letting in the wind.

MOVING

OUT

If we had learned now, as a family, anything from the world, anything of the rhythm of lifetimes, what we had fathomed was this: that a life proceeded upward as a series of eras, like layers of the forest floor, built higher and settling in and covering one another, over and over, growth and sudden decay and new growth, world without end. When we had been new in Delta Junction and the summer fires had come to our woods — or rather to the woods on the edge of the town — all the animals in them fled or died, the trees burned, the permafrost melted and caved in. The tundra soil, formed of roots and dead moss and the decay of a hundred generations, kept burning long after the trees were all ashes; my father, and the other firefighters with him, cut the tundra into foot-deep squares and turned them over, exposing the underside of clay or frozen earth — the same earth once buried, perhaps, beneath these same charred trees, now brought suddenly to light again.

Sometimes, too, a fire burned straight down, smoldering for years and widening out, undetectable on the surface. After time — who knew how long — this pit of embers prevailed, and a whole acre collapsed in on itself, sagging downward and burning away, leaving under the sun a new and primordial earth.

So it was again now a time of new ashes, a smoldering and watchful time like those early years after my accident. My mother's death had come as a searing great fire, and as a family we had fought it as such, pulling on boots and wide hats and gathering up hatchets, chopping at flames and carrying in water, until in the end we had stood there as survivors on the bare, smoking surface of the world. Yet even after those first consuming days — after Mom's funeral, after her bills were dispersed into files, her clothes packed into boxes or passed down among the family — even then there was still a great hurry among us, a pressing on and turning over of the sod; for my parents had sold our house just a day before Mom died, leaving us two weeks after the funeral to pack all our things and move out.

It had been a necessary but difficult thing to sell it, and my mother had placed the idea before us two years previously, during the hard, scattered time of my pregnancy, the days when we were finally becoming whole in ourselves, when Mom had brought cereal to the bathroom, eating and talking as I floated my belly in a real tub. Nights at the table, Mom had spoken increasingly of our debts, the two mortgages and all the others, saying finally to us all, "It's a terrible thing to leave this place, but I don't know what else we can do."

We protested, of course, and for as long as possible — until we all agreed it was hopeless — Mom had listened, had paid half the bills one month and half the next, hearing us say, "We can't do it again; finally we're in a house, and we can't go back to the trailer."

For it was among our most feared things, then, the thought of "going back" to that time, that hard and claustrophobic condition of living. After moving to Delta, we had lived in the original trailer for three more years before building the house, hauling water downhill from the hand pump, pouring Pine Sol into a honeybucket to cover the smell, driving to Fairbanks for movies or dinner, just to get out of that small enclosed space. A drive would begin after breakfast when Mom cleared away the paper plates, shoved them into trash bags, and announced, "We're going to Fairbanks. Get your coats." We rode all the way singing, scraping our names into frosted car windows, and the day in the city was a rushed one, for we had to pass home through the hills before dark. The roads were narrow, with few guard-rails, and we could look out and down over hundred-foot cliffs, skidding sometimes too close on the ice. When we were halfway home, "Mystery Theater" came on the radio, and our mother turned it up for us and copied the announcer: "Good e-e-evening."

It was the era of the Alaska pipeline boom, when people like my father made larger pay-checks than they had ever imagined in their lives, and when statewide inflation had risen with the frenzy, making us nearly as poor as ever. What money people did have was spent most often on travel, for to remain too long in Alaska with no break made one forget the outside world, become expatriated from the planet; for few "real world" interests made the way up to this country: baseball and foot-ball were distant and disconnected events one watched only on TV, musical groups on tour sent their records up instead of appearing themselves, even mundane things one read of in books — ice cream trucks, fireflies, back-yard trees growing apples — seemed somehow mythic, belonging to a land far removed from this one. In 1976, the summer before I went to school in California, my parents sent Leslie and me on a tour of Europe while Mom and the other children went to Hawaii, visiting California family on the way; through all this, my father stayed home working, turning his pay into traveler's checks.

And as the money went like this into perishables, we had spoken every day of a house, of building one with windows and toilets and bedrooms for us all. We children shopped through catalogues, sitting on our bunks and circling pictures, decorating bedrooms in our heads; and Mom drew floor plans, hundreds of them, holding them up for us to look at. Each was two stories and a basement, two baths and a laundry space, with balconies over every snow porch with a view. We made plans, as I say, yet believed in them just vaguely, for we could afford only to build the house ourselves, and the three-month summer season was too short a space, even with twenty-four hours of daylight, to include time both for building and for earning the money to do it.

Gradually, as the furor of the pipeline peaked and money flowed with greater gusto, my father began to grow weak, short of breath and dizzy, saying to my mother, "I don't know what's happening. My energy is all going." At the work camps, he was known for his strength, his ability to lift three, sometimes four hundred pounds, into a truck, and the other men thought he worried about nothing when he found average loads to be all he could do. That fall when I was twelve, my parents were in the meadow clearing away the brush, and my father said, "Honey, I have to go in."

My mother squatted down, gathering an armload of sticks. She said, "Okay, you go on, I'll just do a little more." Frost slicked the dead leaves, and she skidded a little getting up. My father said, "No, don't stay alone out here. Come on inside. I'm really feeling sick."

"Julius," Mom said, "just a little more. Let me finish what's started, and I'll come." My father said okay, he'd help clean up this last bit, and half an hour later they made it back to the trailer. The next morning, my father had vomited all night, saying, "No air is getting to my head," and Mom went to the neighbors' to call an ambulance. In Fairbanks, the hospital said, "Pericarditis, take it easy," meaning that Dad had been burning the brush piles, asphyxiating on the fumes, that he had no lasting heart problem at all.

There followed a year of this, my father saying, "I'm weak, I have no air, something is wrong," and of the rest of us looking at all he managed to carry, thinking he should be happy to be so strong. In January 1976, after I turned thirteen, my father crossed a street in Fairbanks, leaving a union call with two of our friends, and he found himself suddenly unable to walk. "Look at this nice car," he said to Nick, stopping to rest with his hand on it.

Nick looked at it. "Uh, yes," he responded. "What's nice about it." The thing was dented and a little rusty, nothing at all to mention.

"Oh," my father said, "I just liked the look of it," and he tried to walk again, following his friends, finding that still he could not do it. "Would you mind," Dad asked, "you know, while we're in town anyway, would you mind taking me to a doctor." Sure, the men said, let's go, and when Dr. Grauman examined Dad, he told him, "We won't chance a treadmill test. I'm putting you in the hospital."

Mom got a call at her job in Delta, and my father told her then, "They're sending me to Seattle. Triple bypass. They won't let me come home to get my things."

"Okay," Mom said, "I'm going with you. Just give me a day to get the money." She began quickly to sell things, pawning, as she had in the days of my accident, all our instruments, and she phoned the churches again, ones in California and ones closer by. She picked me up after school, pulling me back off the school bus. I wondered at first if Mom had found drugs in my room, but before I could form an appropriate defense, she told me about Dad, enlisting my help. "I have to find places for you kids to stay," she said and, my own separate life forgotten, we made up a plan, a friend's house for me, another for Ian, a schoolteacher near town for Leslie and Bethel. In the rush, we forgot once more to tell the others what was happening, why they were staying with friends, and Bethel didn't know until school the next day, when someone sympathized, "I heard about your dad. Is he going to be okay." She phoned me then where I was, saying, "What's this about Dad? Gosh, Natalie, no one ever tells me *anything*." It was not, she meant, the first time the young ones had been left out. "Bethel," I told her, "I know. It's just everything was fast, and Mom knew she could trust you to do what she said, and she forgot to tell you the reason."

It was the early days of bypasses then, and my father's didn't go easily on him. When he came home, he squeezed my finger, and his hardest clutch was like a child's — light, and with the palm almost smooth. He told of skin staples and machines, of nurses who shoved respirator tubes down into his stomach rather than his lungs and almost killed him. He told of coughing in the night and of the splitting open of bones inside his chest. Had he known, he said, what the surgery would

285

be, he would much rather have died and left a good insurance policy. "Baloney," Mom said. "Just think what you'd miss." When he had left the hospital the surgeon had said, "No driving cars, and no sex," and at his first check-up afterward, Mom had grinned, reporting, "Well, he didn't drive a car."

So those months were difficult, my father so uncomfortable with his new weakness, and so apologetic in his complaints, that thereafter his "condition" became part of our humor. Squatting with us to pick blueberries into a bucket, he would grunt and stand slowly up, sweating from his forehead and breathing; and when the rest of us looked at him, he pulled his mouth into a smile and, tapping his chest with his thumb, said, "It's my condition." Later, when we were all stiff and bent from the picking, Mom would sag sideways into a bush, lying stretched out and groaning, "Oy vey, my condition." Dad was never to be truly well again, never again satisfied in his body, for where he had felt stupid in this country because he struggled with the English language, he had always been somehow vindicated by his physical strength, his ability to do greater things than his peers; now he was merely average, and sometimes not even that, and he cursed his hands, looking down at them and saying, "I can't even manage like I should." My parents spoke with us openly after this about death, about their wills, about who would take care of us in case they were gone. We pondered for years on my father's death, never quite believing in it, yet so deeply resigned that we were stunned in the end when our mother inexplicably preceded him.

For now, though, there were other concerns alongside health and illness, for with Dad having stopped earning pipeline wages, a house was seeming less and less possible. Spring came and Bethel turned seven, and Mom wiped the trailer walls with a rag, cleaning off soot that leaked out from the woodstove. The honeybucket stood open in a corner, covered with a cloth, and the smell of Pine Sol leaked out from it, filling the trailer. I continued, with Mom's employee health insurance, to make trips to Fairbanks, to the plastic surgeon who "revised" the worst scars on my face. Driving me those hundred miles, Mom would slow down as we passed her favorite houses, and we would remodel them in our heads, speaking out balconies and storm windows. The best, my mother thought, was the log cabin by the river, small and neat, with the bark still on, the porch roof held up by log pillars. "I'd put a round window," she said, "just above it, and a deck over the porch with railing. Then a garden in the sun over there, and a greenhouse on the bank near the water." Years later, when she was in school, she would take pictures of the place, saying, "I'm going to write a story about the best old houses, and maybe ask some people for the history."

In April, three months after Dad's surgery, the snow began melting, and we spent as much time as possible outside the trailer, looking out at the woods. At the cable-spool picnic table, my mother drank tea with us and fed the camp robbers dry dog food from her hand, saying, "It's getting too hard, this trailer. If I knew how to swing it, I'd say let's build the house."

A bird flew down for more dog food, landing nearly in my father's cup. Dad pulled a hand over his hair. "Then let's do it," he demanded. "It will be tough, but we have to. We can't live here with teenagers."

We children began shouting. I asked, "What, are you serious," and Bethel knocked over her tea, saying, "We're going to have a house?"

"Yeah," Mom told us, "I hope so," and that night after dinner we ignored the camp robbers, sorting through floor plans together, choosing in the end my mother's own favorite, the one with a laundry chute dropping down to the basement. "Electricity will come someday," Mom went on. "But for now a house is the thing." We'd been with kerosene lamps for so long they hardly were bothers, she said, but to have drains instead of buckets under the sink — *that* would make us Rodneys.

The site itself had been chosen for years, a knoll covered with birches overlooking a meadow, and the well there was already drilled, the hand pump installed with a pail underneath. All along we had climbed the hill every week with our jerry cans, lining them up on the ground. The pump was tall and red, the height of a man, and we took turns working it — one adult or two children at a time, for to pull the water up 160 feet through the pipes took more than one child's strength. Water did not come immediately, it was too far down, so Dad would begin and the rest of us would count, "ONE, TWO, THREE," and at twenty or so pumpings we heard the last air sighing out of the spigot, and we rushed to catch the water in a jug. Our rhythm established, we switched off and kept going, standing aside when it was not our turn, looking around at the house stakes tapped down hopefully into the sand.

For all the work of pumping thirty gallons at a time, and for all of my father's loud breaths, the well was an improvement over hauling water in jugs from the laundromat.

We had collected, too, other "conveniences," all the things to get us by, to make the trailer more bearable. When our eyes had gone bad from kerosene lighting, Mom and Dad had discovered propane lamps, ones which hung on the wall and gave off white light, glaring at us from ash mantels. Our friends had taught us to hook a television to a car battery, and evenings we watched the black-and-white picture, sitting around at the table. After that, we found other 12-volt appliances — a hand mixer, a radio — and we spent many dollars at the gas station, paying a man to charge car batteries.

Now, perhaps, we would still manage with these things, but in a large house with real rooms. We could have a Christmas tree, Mom said, maybe even someday with lights; and years later, when I was long back from California and my tuition no longer took all the money, we would get electricity, those lights would indeed be our joy, and we would string them around windows in October. For now, my mother continued her computer job at Fort Greely, measuring out money to begin building, and in May my father started back on the pipeline, against all our protests about his health. "What," he said. "You see anybody standing in line to give us money?"

Construction began that month. A man with

a backhoe dug out the basement, another poured the concrete, and for a while the work load was lighter than we children had expected, easily managed around my parents' jobs in the daytime. Dad brought home huge ham sandwiches from his pipeline job, for the company let the people make their own lunches, spreading a buffet in the morning and sending the workers around. Dad made a sandwich like Dagwood's, with ham and cheese and tomatoes and onions, dabbing mayonnaise so thick that it soaked through the bread. Evenings, then, when we picked him up from work, we children checked through our father's lunchbox, passing around and eating big soggy bites of all that we knew he had saved.

And the house building went on, still easy at first. We laid our hands in the basement's wet cement, and my father scratched out our names with a nail, putting the date alongside. With a hatchet and saws, the family cleared brush away from the birch trees, curving a long driveway around them.

But once the basement was dry, the real construction began, and my parents stayed up every night after work, nailing floors, framing walls, measuring out space for the windows. I made dinner and carried it up the hill, and everyone took a break then, sitting on the floor and looking out between wall studs at the trees. My father's face was happy but sagging, and he seemed too small inside his body. In our trailer bunks at night, with the window shades lowered to keep out the sun, my brother and sisters and I listened to the hammering on the hill, making jokes and bouncing the mattress above us, poking at one another with our feet.

It was slow work, and exhausting for my parents, who built all night and on weekends, with the friends who dropped over to help. They lived between paychecks, buying rough lumber and plywood from the yard, straightening bent nails and using them again, breaking at dinner to sit on rolls of Visqueen, making jokes with the people. Dad stood walls on the chalk lines, grunting as he lifted, saying, "I just don't have it anymore." We children moved through the walls, getting splinters from the studs, and Mom took them out with her tweezers. The fireweed bloomed to the top, and geese and cranes passed by overhead, and Mom and Dad kept working, ignoring the calls of the birds. As fall came on and our breath clouded the air, the chalk lines we snapped rubbed off on the frost, and we swept the wood dry and chalked it again.

In October, only the bottom floor was enclosed, the top one merely framed in under the roof. Snow blew in from the ends there, and Mom and Dad swept it out every evening, shielding the kerosene lanterns from the wind. They stapled fiberglass insulation to the ground-floor walls, covering them with Visqueen and demanding that none of us puncture the seal. "We could winter in the basement," Dad said. "Plenty of people do it around here."

My mother shook her head, saying, "And plenty of people never make it back out. No, we put up with the trailer till the upstairs is livable." We had some Ukrainian friends, a family of carpenters, and they had envisioned a house of their own and had built it over years, working intricate wood cabinets and floors, laying careful stones, and for two decades they had lived below it in the basement, blowing cement dust off the chairs. In the end, they finished the house and moved upstairs, and though by then their sons were grown and only the parents remained, they decorated the boys' rooms with basketball trophies, laying out quilts on their beds. This sort of future, my mother meant, was not acceptable, she would not be lulled into slow action by living in a basement which was merely good enough for now.

But with the shorter days now, and a real house in view out the windows, the trailer became unbearable for all of us, and we grumbled and yelled at each other, squeezing past in the gangway. Though my parents knew nothing of them yet, my drug parties escalated, and I spent as many weekends with friends as I could. Northern lights waved around in the sky and at home we watched them change colors — red and green and yellow — but we could not truly enjoy them, for when the sky was clear enough to see the lights, it meant deep cold was coming on, and heat would fall up toward the air. Dad got out the weed burner, a sort of stovepipe with fuel which those of us without electricity used to start our frozen cars. He slid it under the engine and lit it twice a night, turning down the flames so the car would not catch fire. "The house garage," he said, shuddering back into bed. "I'll get some sleep when it's done."

At Halloween, our friend Margie asked to use the house to host a girls-club camp-out, and Mom said, "Well, go ahead, if you can survive the cold there."

"No sweat," Margie said. "The kids will see ghosts in the insulation foil. They'll end up sharing sleeping bags anyway."

So the party was on. The girls of my family slept over with the group, and Margie told stories, turning the lamp wicks low. We ate popcorn and chocolate and lit a fire in the barrel stove, and Dad covered the stairs to the top floor, conserving the heat down below. We thought about lighting fireworks — we saved them till winter because there was no nighttime on July 4 — but the outdoors was cold, and we decided not to brave it. Mom came up periodically from the trailer, looking around at the crowd, unbuttoning her coat. "It's not as cold as I thought," she said. "This is not half bad." To make the place more comfortable, she swept wood dust off the exposed studs, and pushed the fiberglass more evenly between them. The window spaces were framed but not cut out, and she and Dad lay insulation inside them, careful not to spread fibers through the air. "It's warmer all the time," Mom told Dad. "The barrel stove is heating the whole place."

On Sunday, the girls went home, and I sat in the trailer reading the comics. Mom went to the house to sweep up the popcorn; an hour later, she banged open the door and, looking around, said, "Julius."

"Uh-huh," Dad muttered, sitting up from his nap.

Mom's glasses had fogged up, but she didn't take them off. "The house is warm, and those kids made it the night. I'm not sleeping another one in the trailer."

"Me neither," Leslie yelled, and Bethel said,

"HOORAY," and then we were crowding into the wanigan, tearing the bunks down, taking them apart. "I get the big bedroom," I called.

Mom said, "We can only use the main floor. You girls have to share."

"Hah," Leslie prodded. "WE get the big bedroom."

"Stay off of my bed," I said.

So we were moved in five hours, hanging our hats on the studs, putting our beds singly on the floor. We slept on the main level, listening to the wind blow upstairs, and Ian filled the lamps while my father trimmed the wicks. Our sleeping bags collected wood dust, and our skin itched with fiberglass until we learned to stay away from the walls. "Natalie," Bethel said that night. "Can you get under my bed and bounce me up and down." No way, I told her; it's dirty down there.

So this was the house we had sold just before Mom died — leased, actually, with an option to buy — to a children's home in need of more space. "We'll have a loan to buy it in a year," the people told us. "This is just the place we've been looking for." We had lived in it two years unfinished, and when I had turned sixteen, just before I was pregnant, my parents had taken out huge loans to complete the house, saying, "It has to be done while the kids are still home. It's pointless to go this slow." Those debts had finished us off, had sent my mother into many months of paying only half the bills every month, putting off the others, digging them deeper, until she had said, "I hate the idea, but if we don't sell now for cash, we'll lose it anyway." The house was two years on the market, making my parents despair, and when they signed the lease papers before my mother died, there was both relief and sorrow, for the loss to us now was concrete, not merely dreaded and hoped for.

After the funeral, then, we began to clean house — or rather, I started off with a vengeance and took the family with me. First I went back to school for finals week, and nights in my apartment I cleaned it, cleaned until my hands turned wrinkled and my lungs grew congested from the fumes. In the kitchen, I emptied all the cupboards and washed them out, establishing new places for everything. Now the baking dishes would move by the refrigerator and the plates and glasses take their place, there on a shelf by the counter. Garbage bags had a drawer now, not a cabinet, and the broom went to a different area near the door. I cleaned the bathroom, too, and the closets, thinning out my wardrobe, washing the clean clothes, buying new shoes. Mom's bed got stacked over Charity's as a bunk, and her schoolbooks placed in my bookcase, or taken down home to the family. Outside the window, a woman walked by — dark, familiar hair, a blue backpack torn and repaired — and I knocked on the glass and shouted out, then waved stupidly at the stranger's face which turned to me. I could not bear, as I read from Faulkner one night, to think that someday it would no longer hurt me like this; yet neither could I bear the former arrangement of furniture, the familiar place I might walk into and forget myself for a moment, calling "I'm home" into the void.

I lived those days in a furor, seeing much to be done and no mother there to do it, and suddenly the protective covering she had imposed on us seemed the fault of the others, those in the family besides myself who had accepted her buffering and stood aside while she died of hard work. After finals I went back to the family, looking around at the house and shouting, "No one packed anything while I was gone."

"Relax," my father told me. "We've got ten days."

"Dad," I said, feeling angry, losing my breath. "Look at all this stuff. A year wouldn't do to sort through it, even if we were Mom."

Dad nodded. "Okay, you're right. It isn't much time." He took my elbow, drawing me to the stairs. "Kids," he hollered up, and when they came he said, "We have a lot of work left, and everyone has to help. Start with your rooms, and Tosh will tell you what to do."

It must have been madness, the way I bossed the family then, though it was madness born of grief, the same source I imagine from which rose the others' plodding slowness. I saw this time as a frantic throwback to the California days, when we had discarded all we owned and moved to Alaska, holding only our treasure chests on our laps. "Keep only what's essential," I said again and again. "If you can do without it, put it in this pile." I began packing books in a tall mountain of boxes, making excursions into Bethel's room or Ian's, holding up torn magazines or odd socks, shouting, "You call this essential? There's not enough boxes IN THE WORLD for all this stuff." My sisters began to cry, and Ian to withdraw to his bed, and as the progress seemed to slow, I hollered still more, telling them, "Look, I'm not Mom. You killed her, letting her do your own jobs."

"We didn't kill her," Leslie said. "Or if we did, we *all* did, you too." I wouldn't see myself clearly for a very long time, and when I did and remembered what I had said, I would be ashamed.

But not all the moments were like that, and sometimes I came back to reason, clutching around at the others. Nights, when everyone was tired, we sat on the floor and spoke of our mother, making new jokes and feeling guilty that she didn't know them. "I feel," Leslie said, and we all agreed, "like I don't want to experience anything new, or I'll wish too bad to tell it to Mom." We all wanted in this way to freeze our lives, to move not an inch forward to a place where our mother had not lived. The mornings were hard and we lay back on one another's bellies, eating sandwiches before I whipped us on again to go packing. Bethel came to my room crying after sleep, saying, "I woke up thinking my dream was real, and now she's not here after all." It was the same way for us all, and we took to our beds early, working hard in the day and imagining other things while we slept. We were older, we said sometimes, than we had ever expected to be.

And we could not tolerate music. The song at the funeral was the last for some time, and even canned grocery-store tunes brought us to choking, for, with us, strong feeling had always been tied into song; those days, emotion itself was an unbearable thing, something to be viewed only swiftly, only from the very brief corners of our eyes.

My father rented an apartment with two bedrooms in the basement, and on the first of June we put our last boxes in storage, going back to the house and handing our keys to a man there. He gave us the first rent check and we exchanged best wishes; then we were down the drive, looking hard at the gravel, keeping our faces in front of us.

The plan was now to build another house on some different corner of the land. We had gone through Mom's file of house plans, and the one we chose was something like the first, complete with laundry chute and two bathrooms. "I don't know how to start, exactly," Dad said at dinner. "We need the septic system and the well first thing, and we won't have that money for a while."

Ian stood up and reached for paper towels. He was fourteen and already taller than any of us, and he hunched over my plate, handing a towel to Charity. "Where is this house going to be," he said.

I said, "On my land," and I stopped, shocked at this new thought. It had only just occurred to me, and now that I'd said it I felt somehow profoundly relieved; for it was still, for me, the days of cleaning house, upending the earth and making it new. The sooner we got started, the better. "On my land," I said again. "Across from Leslie's piece."

No one spoke for a moment, looking at me; then Ian sputtered, "What, we're taking your land? No one tells me these things."

"Me neither," Bethel said, and Dad spoke over her, "What are you talking about. Mom and I set that place up for you."

"Yeah," I told him, "but this is for me. I want to get back on the land." My father shook his head, and I began to reason. It was wasteful, I said, to put in another well, another sewage system, when we had these already, in a place I might never use myself, or not for a very long time. "I'll be in school forever," I reasoned. "And we don't have a lot of time; summer's moving on, and we're living in an apartment with silverfish."

"Then what," Leslie said. "You trade for different land?"

I grinned at her. "Yeah, maybe yours, it's got better trees," and we laughed, poking our forks at each other. Leslie said, "I KNEW you weren't being a hero."

Dad called out, "Wait, let me think." He handed Charity a piece of bread, saying, "Okay, we do it, but only like this. We build a house there, but it's yours, and when we're all gone, you keep it."

I thought a moment, feeling a little weighed

down, and then a little glad. "Fair enough," I agreed. "More than fair." For in the end, I knew, the plan had always been to build us each a house, on each of the properties we were assigned, so that whether we lived there or not, or whether we moved away, there would always be a home base, an estate full of Kusz houses within reach of all the others. If I took the family place, it would only be the first of several, and the others would have one like it in time.

But still it seemed hard, this decision, for the real argument that day had not concerned nobility, nor offerings nor acceptances nor kindness; the hard thing here was the change itself, for we were altering plans which had been formed in our mother's own mind — erasing them, it seemed, much too easily.

Yet in truth this was not an erasure, and in time we would all understand this. That week of the funeral, when I had sat among Mom's papers and the stacks of our bills, sorting them, understanding their sense, my father had stepped in once, leaning on the door. "Your mom told me," he said then, "that it would be like this. She said, 'If I died, you'd get a lot of help from Natalie.' " My father brushed at his hair, pushing the cowlick under his cap. He said, "I didn't believe her then, but she knew." And this was our way: We were, as my parents had said, a small country, sufficient as far as possible in ourselves, each a necessary member, each holding on to the others, bearing them along. With one of us gone now, the others moved forward a place, filling that spot with our selves, adding our hands to the work. For me, there were papers: bills, tax returns, forms for our schooling and loans. Our mother had managed these — too privately, it seemed now — and to one of us must fall the job of learning her ways, writing them down and schooling the others. In truth, and somewhat to my discredit, I liked the control of my new position, the way I could hold all the levers, making sure our lives were just so, our movements calculated my way, our troubles seen from far off.

My father's place was new as well, and he moved to the center, becoming now another kind of teacher. Before, I had watched Mom for ways to raise a child, had listened when she said, "Hold a baby like this when you feed her: close to your chest and turned in. Let her know you won't drop her." These days, my father spoke such things, telling us all, "When you take her on a walk, explain things. Name the berries, tell her stories. She should know everything you know." Ian and Leslie proved highly patient in this, now that it was partly their job, and slowly I began to trust them with the child I had permitted only our mother to babysit. Ian taught Charity her tricycle — how the pedals worked, what made the wheels turn around. He led her outside and showed her spruce cones, picking out the seeds, showing how squirrels ate them in winter; when he brought his niece back inside, Leslie began to speak stories, what games we had played in these fields, which of the songs we had learned then. And Bethel moved between jobs, standing quickly up when one of us shrilled the family whistle, shouting, "Hey, I need some help over here."

And so we were back to familiar things: to building, to planning, to clearing land. The children of our family had grown up hearing of wall studs and floor joists, half-inch plywood and sixteen-penny nails, but mostly we had stood aside looking at these, occupied less with real building and more with sweeping aside the fresh sawdust. These, though, were the days of rearranging, re-forming, settling back in. Dad handed hammers around and we carried them with us, chalking out lines and sitting astride them, nailing down plywood for a floor. Ian the dreamer was Dad's special concern, for our new struggle was to remain intact — one of us missing, but the rest well installed — and we noticed now more than before all the times when Ian meandered vaguely off, walking and thinking and apart. I think this frightened my father, for he spent much time running along, calling and catching at Ian's arm.

"Son," Dad said, "come over here. We're going to nail up a wall. This is the fun part, it goes so quick; and I need you to help get it straight." He taught my brother the tools, to square the boards off on the ends, to saw on the right side of the pencil line. Leslie and Bethel worked, too, bringing in lumber, sawing or hammering what their arms had the strength for, and everyone watched out for Charity, taking turns as babysitter, keeping her off of the ladder.

For myself, I inherited Mom's job, deciding the height of the windows, drawing diagrams of walls, measuring boards and marking them, laying them out on the floor. I knew some things from having watched my mother do them, and the others my father taught me, paging through the clipboard, tapping the paper with his finger. "Yes," he would say, pointing to my picture of a wall. "You have a top plate here, but you also need a *top* top plate, one that runs along here, pulling the corners together." This was probably not the correct term, but we all loved its sound, and later Bethel would step up with her armload of boards, calling, "Hey, where does this go?

Is this the top plate or the *top* top plate?"

"Top top plate," I told her. "Over there."

Bethel said, "Top plate?"

"No, *top* top," I repeated. "What, are you deaf?"

"No," Bethel said. "I just wanted to hear you say it again."

But I continued to boss the others, making a discouraging and slow project worse, hollering when they seemed lethargic, telling them, "This is your job, too. How come you're just standing around?" I sulked when my father wanted a window in what I thought was an odd spot, and he said, "Okay it's your house, we'll put it where you want it." He gave in on every point I made, never seeming angry, for what he wanted, I think, was just peace — peace, and the promise that he was giving a future to one of us at least, offering her what she most asked for. The others backed away to the woods and came around again, and I wondered after time if they were cleansing themselves of me, approaching back in only when they were sure they were armored.

July passed and we were into August, and with school coming on — for me in Fairbanks, and for the others in Delta — it became clear that the house would not be livable by winter. Even with the friends who came sometimes to help, the bottom floor was just partly framed in, the walls still open to the air. Dad was still working days as a computer operator on Fort Greely, and the nights and weekends were running him down, making us watch his gray face. While he was at work, the rest of us could not build, for none of us could get the lines as straight, and we needed him to proceed; so I invented jobs for us, piling firewood, picking berries, anything to make us seem active, and I was angry when the others said, "Let's just rest till Dad comes home."

"Oh yeah," I shouted. "Let's just do nothing. Let's all sit around and die."

Bethel said, "Nat, this isn't fair. We're just tired, and we have to be quiet *some*time."

Of course she was right, and I was wearing down as well, wanting mostly to sit around talking with the others, planning out their high-school graduations, visiting our mother's grave. Our grief seemed less when we spoke it out loud, and together we did so, saying, "Remember how Mom got us ready for school." Ian did the best imitation of this, pantomiming our mother's bedroom door. He said, "Imagine me naked," and he threw open the invisible door, shouting out, "FIVE MINUTES," and slamming himself back inside. Then: "TWO MINUTES," slam, and "ONE MINUTE," and he pulled a housedress from the air and tugged it over his head, calling, "I'M IN THE CAR AND YOU'D BETTER BE THERE, TOO." It was among our funniest memories, and we made Ian act it again and again, laughing and convulsing as we watched.

So school arrived and the cold was much closer, the house nowhere near livable. The fireweed blossomed and died, and the wind filled with cotton floss, the seeds of the fireweed flowers. "Kids," Dad said, "I guess we'll spend winter in the apartment." It was a tough admission for him, for it meant a year more of displacement, of living from the few scattered boxes we had stacked among us in that small space. All summer, those bright evenings after work when we had driven cars out to the land, we had passed the drive to the old house and turned away our faces, speaking quickly then on small things, bouncing ahead over gravel. Once, when Ian and Bethel had walked in the woods, they had crossed the property line and met some boys from the children's home, standing with knives and peeling birchbark away from the trees. "They die when you peel them," Ian had protested. "It's like cutting off their skin." A boy had looked at them then and spit on the ground. He said, "Mind your own business; get lost. You don't live here anymore." Except for mention of that meeting, none of us spoke of the old house, for as our father said, "It's *not* ours now, it's theirs. Pay attention to what remains, and we won't use up energy wishing backward."

A lot did remain, Dad said, and though he still could not bear to make music himself, he encouraged us to return to it, bringing us books he unpacked from their boxes, settling us in to former things. I read the notes while the others looked on, and Bethel learned Mom's alto, sitting on the cleared ground and pronouncing the notes, saying, "Okay listen, tell me if this is right." Leslie took tenor and Ian baritone, and we learned each part together, breaking into four when we were through. Behind us, my father whistled our whistle, making us jump, and he called out, "Once more, with feeling," and we started in again then, watching him conduct us with his hammer.

RETURNING

And then it was September, schooltime, and I left to go back to Fairbanks. We had cleaned the construction site, putting away tools, sweeping the chalk dust, and the family had loaded my car and said goodbye, waving at Charity from the road. "It will be a hard year," my father had said. "You alone without help." In this he was certainly right, for the year was both lonely without Mom and filled with difficult studies, junior-level premedical courses designed, it seemed to me, to weed out the fainthearted. Yet in some ways the world itself seemed vastly easier, or vastly, perhaps, less significant. For it occurred to me now as it had before, that with the arrival of crisis sound reason returned, and I stood removed again, wondering how in the past it had frightened me. My first two years of college, I had stood aside, watching people, tired by then of their second glances at my eyepatch, their repetitive litany of questions, but interested, too, in the facts of the people

311

themselves. So I had watched from safe places — places, that is, from which they could not watch me back. There had been two boys who came afternoons to shoot baskets outside my apartment window, taking off their shirts and snapping them at each other. The black boy would pass to the white one, holding his knee up and bouncing the ball under, and the white boy would crouch and dribble and shoot, acting passive and shrugging if he made the basket. Sometimes, one of their younger brothers or sisters would come, too, and I watched the older boys defer to them, handing the ball to the smaller ones and lifting them closer to the basket. "Hey, look at that," the black boy would say. "You did it, not bad."

From the back row of a psychology class, I had watched a woman with very long hair and nails, and I watched everyone else watching her. She stood out there in a way that, at the time, had been somehow embarrassing for me, for in a college where half the population lived in cabins without water, scrubbing down once a week at a pay shower, this woman wore lipstick and high heels, and never the same outfit twice as long as I observed her. She seemed not at all uncomfortable at standing out in that way, and I had scarcely understood this and kept sitting where I could see her — her and all the other turning heads in front of me, following her to the front row as she entered.

But a lot seemed very different now, and I walked through open spaces of yard, caring much less when the faces turned toward me. Last year, when my mother had stayed in my apartment and we had spoken of futures, the two old themes were medical school and my glass eye, and we had gone in to my plastic surgeon again, ready to resume surgery now that I was fully recovered from pregnancy. The last effort, before my baby, had been a graft of Teflon bone, made to fit into my cheek and ingrain itself there, forming a bond with my tissues. "Rejection-proof," my surgeon had said. "But then, so are your own bones, theoretically," and months after we had applauded the graft as a "take," I had woken suddenly in the morning, feeling that my head had grown larger. At the mirror, I had leaned far forward to see, and the cheek had seemed to explode, spilling out brown liquefied fat on the dresser. After surgery to remove the prosthesis, I had been discouraged, had rebelled against this latest failure of my body to respond. To Dr. Wennen, I said, "What's next, was this the last chance?" Wennen had sat on my bed, looking at my face, then glancing away and speaking. "Let's wait a bit," he said, "and see what technology comes along."

"Okay," I told him, "but not for long. I've

been working on this a whole decade, and I want to finish up with this eye."

When my mother and I visited again then, after Charity was born, Dr. Wennen sat next to my chair, holding my chart in his lap. "Look," he said, "I've never seen such a file." He held it up, measuring its thickness in his fingers. He shook his head. "Ten years and two inches; young woman, this is quite an achievement for a kid."

"So how's technology," I urged. "When can I have an eye."

Dr. Wennen rolled his stool closer, bringing his face near to mine. "We've done fine work on some of these scars," he told me. "We took care of the worst ones, they've faded nicely, you don't even look like a casualty." He looked away, held my chart up, seemed to change the subject. "There's ten years in this file," he went on. "More than half your life. How much longer do we do this?"

"I don't know," I said. "How long will it take."

"That," he replied, turning back, "would depend on your body. And it's usually not real cooperative." He waited, and I waited longer, and he continued. Even if he was able, he said, to make space for an eye, to manage a bone graft which took, so many muscles and nerves were gone that the eye itself would never move,

314

never blink, always look artificial. He said there were ways now of setting an eye into latex skin, of pasting it to the face every day; but that, he said, would not be so greatly different from an eyepatch, and I agreed reluctantly, thinking that probably it would even be worse, a plastic and grotesque piece of costuming set in bloodless skin, staring out and intimidating all the people I would speak to.

Was it really so bad, Wennen said, to look this way? My wounds were old news; I was used to them. Maybe I should stay the way I was — blending a few more of the worst scars in, perhaps, but keeping this, the familiar face I had learned. He said I looked remarkable for what I had been: the night I was hurt, the skin hanging off in shreds had all been shaven, then pieced back on to cover my bones; no one had known then what piece went where, or if, when the hair grew back, I would have scalp on my chin and cheeks on my head. "It's turned out beautifully," he said, holding my hair up and looking. "Maybe it's time to like things this way. To be grateful, I mean, and stop struggling."

I had felt that I might choke; for here was one of few others in the world, others like myself, who had believed in medicine like strong magic, who had struggled all these years against failure, who had, I thought, been prepared to go on until we prevailed against this body. Now my champion was bowing out and leaving me — admitting, it seemed to me, defeat. I had not answered Wennen then, just listened and thanked him and gone home with my mother and slept, for sleep was always my escaping place, and I very much wanted escape now.

Wennen had spoken, as I say, what had seemed at the time difficult words, but in the months since, I had grown more conscious of myself, the habit of running my tongue inside dog-tooth marks left in my mouth, of putting my first finger inside the tooth hole in back of my neck. I noticed my impatience, at times, with strangers who saw only my eyepatch and not the faded scars, who assumed I had an easy illness and not a long struggle behind me. I began to feel, in a sense, that I had stopped just in time, before all traces of history had been smoothed from my face.

It was in keeping, too, with my history, that I was studying now to be a doctor. Growing up, I had been glad to know the difference between bandage and suture scissors, to take these home and to use them, cutting the tape for my eye pads. The act itself of applying a bandage fascinated me, and early in the accident years I took the job from my mother, learning with each new surgery how to care for this new wound, how to wind the gauze this time so it held my features in place. In Seattle, the surgeons taught me to irrigate the grafts, to mix saline from tablets and to baste my eye like a turkey, holding up a cloth to catch the flow. Later, when I was sixteen and the last bone graft rejected, I stood in front of mirrors and packed the hole with gauze, pushing in each strip with the forceps, enjoying the smell and the wincing burn of iodoform inside on the tissues.

And I still loved to do these things, to cut at a specimen and learn what was inside. I had made a friend at the medical school, a pathologist named Crick who taught in that place, and who came down the hill to the undergraduates, teaching us human anatomy. Our friendship began in that class, when he had discussed organ donors, how bodies tended to reject outside tissues, recognizing them somehow as alien. "What is the reason, then," I had said, "when a graft from the same body rejects?"

Dr. Crick had stopped and leaned into the chalkboard, looking hard at me and saying, "I've never known that to happen." He waited there, watching my face, and I answered, "Well, it always is that way with me."

After class, Crick had walked me out the door, asking me things, discussing my eye, and it happened he knew Dr. Wennen, the surgeon I had been with for years. In his next lecture, Crick drew wide pictures on the board, discussing graft rejection, saying, "I talked to Wennen this week, about that question of Natalie's. There are only theories, but this is how it may work." We knew, he said, that a rejection operated as an immune reaction, dissolving the grafted tissue into liquid as if it were some foreign germ, surrounding and attacking it with white blood cells, breaking it down. Perhaps in a case such as mine, where even my own tissue was eaten away, the body had become more specific, had mapped itself into regions, had decided it was not one country but several, and no immigration was allowed. Or perhaps it had fortified itself against so many germs that now it shot from the hip, not waiting to identify the alien tissue. It was a figurative way of speaking, Crick said, but sometimes figures were all we had, our only way of describing what we did not understand. Crick and I were great friends after that, and he seemed to like all I asked him, sitting in his office with a Coke, or in class discussions and lectures. "I enjoy your kind of questions," he said once, "because they're the same ones we ask ourselves." He met my mother before she died, and he shook her hand hard, pointing over at me, saying,

"This woman *should* be a doctor. She has just the background to like it."

Crick asked me in as an undergraduate to his classes on biochemistry, immunology, and infectious diseases, taking me off with him to autopsies and dissections when a particularly interesting case came to town. He watched me at first for signs of fainting, seeming glad that I was fascinated instead, and he pulled open a cadaver's face, laying it open to expose the inside, pointing with a probe, saying, "This is what your face is missing, this here, and this; and if they were to make you an orbit, they'd have to construct one like this." He poked at the pink planes of muscle, probing the smooth connections until they separated into groups, one for opening the lips, one for drawing them back. I pulled the white tendons, operating the face by hand, and when we looked at the nerves, I bent closer in, saying, "My mom saw cords hanging out of my eye. Maybe it was this one, or this group over here."

Coming home after these field trips, I would tell my mother what I had seen, and she listened and said, "Blech, that grosses me out." And then, more seriously, "But this is good for you; very good. He's explaining your self to you, and about time." She had, I knew, been as sad as I was to give up on surgery, to relinquish in the end a glass eye, for her great wish must have been to return me as closely as possible to a perfect seven-year-old body, and now I never would have one. But instead I had Crick, and I at least could learn what had gone on, could be fascinated by it rather than repulsed, poking around and learning my own history.

But my grades were falling now, this year after my mother had died, and the classes were grating on me. I still loved Crick's, all the ones dealing with humans, but I had to take other biology as well — plant form and function, invertebrate physiology — and I showed little interest in them, irrelevant as they felt to my life. I was turning down Crick's field trips to the pathology lab, going home instead weekends to the family, helping build on the house before snow came. It was what I preferred now: to remain in the close center, keeping track of things there, not a hundred miles away on the fringes. When Mom had just died and I told it to Crick, standing in line at the bank, his face had grown frail behind his glasses and he had reached for me; I had turned myself a little so the embrace was a spare one, and had said, "No, don't be nice or I'll cry." My friend had looked dismissed then, and very sad, but what I had to give him was not much, and what I did have I saved for the family.

Now in class Crick was carrying me, giving me extra points on exams if I answered him correctly in discussion. "You know this stuff," he said in his office. "You're just not thinking when you write it."

I looked up from my lap, trying to apologize. "I know," I said. "I know you're disappointed. I admire your help. Really. But I can't seem to memorize anymore." This, he must have known, was true, for in the past I had known a diagram after seeing it once, and now I had forgotten it by class the next day. "If it's any comfort," I told him, "I'm doing the best in your courses."

Crick laid the papers on his desk, reaching for coffee and pouring me some. "But you still want to go to med school," he asked.

"Yeah," I said, taking the cup. "There's nothing else I want to do."

Crick looked at his coffee, then back at me. "There's still the entrance exam," he assured me. "Do well on that, and your grades won't matter so much. I'll recommend you, and that should help some."

So for a time I was back to the lab on weekends, working painfully hard on even my most hated classes. Charity went with me now that Mom was gone, and she touched the dead birds while I memorized them, or played on the floor with her books. But my brain was not there, or my energy, and I went as often as I could back to Delta, seeing Crick only in classes, or in a scattered few moments in between. In Fairbanks I missed Delta's winds, the way they arrived in the fall, blowing hard and pounding my face, the way they expanded my chest and made me breathe wide breaths, buoying up my whole body. There at home, Leslie was looking into colleges, for she was graduating from high school this year, and I gathered together the forms, ordered her catalogues, spoke with her counselor at school. "She's doing quite well," he said, "but not as well as the tests say she should." We encouraged each other along, Leslie and I, and she turned down some very fine schools, deciding instead to go to mine, to live in rooms close to my own. "Just get through this year," she said, "and next year we'll do some fun things."

So Christmastime came, and I made ready to go home, planning to abandon the world. Before I left, I met up with Crick and he took me to dinner, toasting my health and saying, "To my favorite person around." He poked Charity's belly, looking up at my face. "Study hard for the MCAT," he said. "Pay attention to your classes in January, and do as well as you can." I will, I promised, and felt immediately tired. At home, I did as I had planned, attending to family and ignoring all else; had I the energy, I would have studied, but even after sleep, when I opened a book, I grew instantly weary and passive, and I closed the book and put it back under the bed. My school apartment lay empty a month and the plants all died, but I thought nothing of this while I was away, saying, "I'll deal with all that when I go back." There was little space for a tree in the Delta apartment, but we cut a small one anyway, visiting the storage garage and opening boxes, looking for ornaments inside. We put up the lights and sat looking at them, thanking heaven for electricity. Gradually over winter, more and more boxes had been brought to the apartment, sitting open and spilling on the floor. "It's like the days on the highway," my father said, "when we emptied the trailer every night to make a place to sleep."

Dad had four days off at Christmas, but for the rest he worked a computer desk job at Fort Greely, coming home in the evenings to play board games. Until the hard cold came, he had gone, after work at the office, to take care of the new house, tacking up tarps to cover it, and he spoke of the house all the time, worried that the exposed wood was rotting, the basement cracking or heaving, the squirrels making nests from the Visqueen. He looked weary now more and more, colorless in his face and hunched down, swinging his arms to propel his body forward; walking was difficult, and the rest of us worried for him, asking in light voices, "So Dad, how's the condition?"

"Still there," he would say, laughing back. "If I croak, you know how to run a funeral." When we spoke this way in public, people were shocked and turned aside; but this was our way and had been always, even the night of my accident, when our mother had joked with the neighbors, speaking of Rodneys with real plumbing while my surgeons spent hours on their craft.

The road to the new house was drifted high with snow, and we parked the car where we could and waded in, stopping for my father to breathe, then going on. Work on the house had halted because of the cold, but we came to look at it anyway, to assure ourselves, I suppose, that it was there. Charity asked for a snowman and Ian tried to help her, but the snow was too dry in the chill to stick together, and it powdered away on the ground. On the way back out, we were careful not to look at the children's home, and when Charity said, "Look, Grandma's house," we said yes there it was and brought her mind back to other things, turning our own faces away.

Before school again in January, Leslie got final acceptance at the university, and we made potato pancakes to celebrate, piling on the sour cream. I stole Bethel's pancakes when she got up for a drink, and my father leaned back on the couch, laughing. "One more semester," he reminded me. "And then you can steal Leslie's dinner in Fairbanks."

"Very funny," Bethel huffed. "She's probably ripping off Charity's already."

I said, "No, right now it's Ian's," and I reached toward his plate, getting my hand nearly stabbed with his fork.

Then it was back to school, putting Charity in day care, registering for classes. I worried about the studies, for it was increasingly difficult for me to study a mixture of fields, French one day and literature the next, and after that ecology, or vertebrate species or taxonomy. I called Crick at home and he did not answer, and the first day of classes a woman asked me, "Are you going to the funeral."

"What funeral," I said, and she told me that Crick had shot himself in the head, alone one night in his study, leaving no note behind. "No one understands it," she said. "He never mentioned a thing."

But he had, now that I thought of it. Twice in class we had discussed the brain, and he had spoken of other people's failed suicides, how they shot themselves here, or over here, missing the vital parts. "You'd think," he had said, "that they would do homework beforehand. If the guy wanted to die, *this* is where he should aim." If a man missed the right spot, he said, he was being irresponsible; for he would end up a live cripple, forcing other people to care for him.

Now I felt irresponsible myself in some ways, and utterly hopeless in others; for I owed Crick a great debt of emotion, and a great deal of time besides that, and with all I had seen of him I had apparently not known his true mind, had dwelt on my own weak spirit and never his. I called around to Crick's colleagues, asking their minds, and they said he had obviously planned this ahead, probably by many months. Gradually and alone Crick had readied his papers, cleaned out his files, set up the bookkeeping so it was easy to take over. He had written fine lecture notes and typed them, explaining what he was doing, how someone else might approach his courses. I knew myself that Crick had been through several marriages, that the last one had dissolved only recently, but none of this seemed large enough cause for one's dying, and I thought on this hard and grew tired. What I did know was that my friend was a pathologist, a careful student of death, and when he had spoken over bodies lying out on a table he had been clinical and exact, pointing out items with relish, unattendant to the soul that had left this place.

In all, it was a feeble semester, my worst by far since I'd started. Academically, I was less and less proficient, hardly there in my mind, and after French class one day the professor asked me, "What's happening with you? Your accent is there, but you're forgetting the words."

"Just laziness," I said. "A long Christmas break, and I forget how to study." Thérèse only looked at me, shaking her head, and after that she called on me more often in class, quizzing me in front of the others.

In the end, my grades were appalling, and I mentioned nothing of them to my family. I had a D in physiology and C's alongside, and the only courses which helped the average were those in the humanities, English especially, for I knew words and books and took to them easily, needing only to read and not memorize. It seemed bottomless, the hole I was in, and I tried hard not to think what I would do, now that my medical dreams were caving in around me.

But I need not think just yet anyway, for it was May, and school was out, and there were now other problems than grades. It was building time again, and the family was ready for it, ready for a house before winter; still, we had another thing to discuss first. Dad was forty-nine and still working computers at a desk out on post, but over winter he had gotten a letter from the laborers' union in Fairbanks. "They say," he told us, "when I'm fifty I can retire with a pension, but I have to get vested first." He had thirty days' work left to vestment, he said, and a year to get them in. "But my health," he said, "my health. In a year I won't be able to do the work anymore, so I think I should do it now."

"You mean," I responded, "take a leave from post." I looked at the others, all those faces of concern. Turning back to Dad, I said, "Laborer stuff is hard work. At least you have an office job now."

My father leaned back into his chair. His face was bright in the way my mother's had been, those nights in my apartment when she had pretended at energy she did not have. "Yeah," Dad agreed. "But it's just a thirty-day leave. They'd give it to me, no problem." He looked around at the others. "And we could still work on the house at night, just like usual."

Leslie sat up straighter. "If you think we're worried about the house," she said, and Bethel finished, "Oh, right, we'll bury two parents in two years, that's terrific."

I was still thinking, balancing the scales in my mind. "I suppose, though," I mused, "you should get vested. If you have to stop work altogether, you could use the pension."

"Okay," Dad said. "And it's only thirty days."

It seemed like more than a hundred. During the days while Dad worked, I planned out the walls and marked boards, and Ian or the others cut them. Some of the time, the cuts would be crooked, and Dad would arrive home and saw them again, saying, "Ian, I showed you how, it's like this." They were late nights and our father grew white, and the second week of his job a truss fell on him there, bouncing him onto the pipeline and then to the ground, breaking his shoulder and giving him a concussion. He put a finger to his ear and there was blood in it. He didn't report this to the management, and spoke lightly of it to the family, for he had two weeks until vestment, and he wanted to keep working. It would be years before we knew all of this, why he grew dizzy and nauseated those evenings when we lifted walls on the chalk lines, why he winced in his chair, why he held Charity now only on his right side. At the time, we were just worried and not panicked, and we pushed as hard as possible those nights as we built.

And still it was slow, too much to get done without help. Friends arrived, and more friends, most of whom had houses of their own going up, and who came by in groups to help us, putting up siding on the walls. The house was tall, and we were all afraid of heights, and our friends put the roof up with my father, just as we despaired of finishing it. Nick climbed a ladder and balanced the rafters, and Dad and others nailed them down, standing back to look when they were done. When Dad had finished with the union job, he went back to Fort Greely and worked, and the days to us children seemed slow, for there was little we could do without him.

The children's-home kids wandered sometimes through the woods, looking up at us working on the top floor, and we waved at them once and continued on, asking nothing about the old house, or what it now looked like inside. We were on a different corner of it, we told ourselves, but this was still the same land, still ours, and we were working hard to get back to it.

Besides building, we cut firewood, hoping to need it by winter. We put logs in the truck and drove them to the house, and my father cut them short with a chainsaw, stopping to rest it on his knee. We stacked them in piles away from the house, spraying for ants and pounding on wood beetles with our shoes. Dad's paychecks and the rent money we counted out on paper, a little for bills, a little for the apartment, and more for our tab at the lumberyard. My father's face was pale all the time and he worked his shoulder with his hand. When bill time came around, he handed me the papers, saying, "You write the checks and I'll sign them. All of this makes me too tired." Summer, he meant, was moving on, and there was too little hope to go around.

In the end, it was all too much. The Fort Greely job had been bad for years, for people there, as my mother used to say, "think the silliest things are important." Military people, my father said, were forgivable, for they must live their work. "But civil service," he said. "They're *civilians,* for goodness' sake. Those people should know better." The flag there went up and down the pole, and the people seemed to bow to it, stepping out from their cars and saluting. "It's not a god," Dad said. "And here I'm made to treat it like one." Driving home after work, passing the guards at the gate, my father said he felt unleashed and giddy, and in the mornings when he stopped to show his I.D., he was reminded too clearly of the war, all those places he had passed through, assumed by the people to be guilty of something yet unnamed. By the middle of that summer, then, he had had enough; he was vested now with the union and had a tiny pension, and with us working so hard on the land, trying to get free and back to our own things, the contrast with Fort Greely seemed too great to be ignored; he left the job there, saying, "I've had it," and the rest of us said, "About time, Dad. Mom told you to quit years ago."

But there was also the problem of money, for the children's-home rent must go farther now, and too many things were competing for it. In August, the landlord for the apartment raised the rent, and my father shook the letter at us, shouting, "All of this money for silverfish?" He sagged a moment into his shirt, then stood erect, putting on his cap. "This is ridiculous," he said. "We're getting that house ready by winter."

And it was ready, but only in a primitive way. By the time school started, the walls and roof were just covered, the studs still exposed to the room. There was little insulation yet, though it had not grown tremendously cold, and as Leslie and I got ready for the university and Ian and Bethel for high school, Dad spent his days feeding the woodstove, putting up fiberglass with a staple gun. The family was back to no electricity or water, and we broke out the kerosene lamps from the old days, putting in wicks and lighting them. We had a last cookout before schooltime, and Dad asked us children to sing, listening to the phrases and counting out time with his finger. When we were done, he sang some songs with us, some of the old ones from the highway. "Well," he said then, looking around at the land, "it's a house again, and land, and we're finally living on it again."

So it was 1983, my fourth year of college, and Leslie's first, and as we drove in my car to Fairbanks, I asked her, "Do you feel like you're headed to the real world?" I took my eyes from the road, looking at her.

"No," she said, looking back. "Not the real world, just the world."

It was good to have company again, good to have Leslie over from the dorm, to watch television or make dinner or sit up late, teasing Charity. We talked a great deal about Mom, and Leslie asked how it had been then, having our mother for a roommate, and I told her a lot of things, grinning when I talked of the fighting. We spoke, too, of our father, and drove back to Delta for weekends, discussing his health in the car, the very drawn look to his face. Leslie watched Charity when I had a late lab, and would have her books on the table when I arrived home. I already knew my grades were hopeless, but I said none of this to her, just walked to the stove and spooned up some dinner. "How's the pre-doctor," Leslie called, and I responded, "Overworked."

This was true. I had been embarrassed in the past by Dad's gratefulness for help, his soft face and voice when he said, "Thanks for doing the bills." I had even, I think, felt a little superior, not very patient with his intolerance for stress. "Dad," I would say. "It's just a little thing. Don't get so worried about it." I had not understood then that crisis accumulates, building up in the chest and filling it, until each small new pressure feels more like a thousand. That school year I was repeatedly ill, with head colds and flu and small unexplained fevers. When I was not legitimately sick, I just ached, drawing inward and flinching at Charity's cold hands. In class I felt dull, and cared nothing for knowledge, and on the phone my father asked, "Is everything okay there. You sound sort of feeble."

"Oh, yeah," I said, more broadly. "Leslie and I are getting along great."

"Let me talk to her," Dad demanded. "You're not telling me everything." When I handed the phone over, I glared at Leslie, whispering, "Don't you make him worry."

I stood close to Leslie's ear, listening. "Hi, Dad," she said.

My father told her, "Now I know you guys hate me to worry. But if there's something wrong there you should tell me. I'm the dad."

Leslie grinned at me. "Oh, no," she told our father. "Everybody's tired, but the weekend's coming. Just go stoke your old stove."

And Leslie became as much help to me as our mother had been, as reliable in her assistance, and as concerned. Charity was four and loved Leslie's company, and she came inside from the monkey bars one day, crying and saying, "I was hanging on the bar and a big kid pulled off my pants." Leslie and I were angry and asked Charity questions, frightening her with our loud voices. "Wait, Cheer," I said. "We're not mad at *you*," and Leslie told her, "Come on outside. Let's go find that brat." In the quad, Charity was afraid, probably thinking Leslie would kill the child enemy; standing a little behind, she pointed to the "big kid," a girl about seven years old, and Leslie stood over the girl, looking down and ranting. "Okay," she said. "Let's pull down your pants. Right here in front of everybody. Yeah, and then let's tell your parents how you've been acting." The girl nearly wept, and told Charity she was

sorry, and after that she was always very protective of my daughter, helping her onto the
monkey bars, keeping the other children from
bothering her.

On an evening when I had just come in from
school and was arranging my books and preparing to study, Leslie phoned, sounding apologetic. "Now don't be mad at me," she
pleaded. "Dad made me PROMISE not to call
till your lab was over."

I pulled my coat back on and reached for
Charity's boots. "So I take it he's alive," I
said.

"Yeah, but he broke his leg. He says it's
hanging off the kneebone and flopping, and
he wants you to drive down and get him."

"When did he break it?" I demanded. "And
how did he call you."

Leslie said, "Noon, and I guess he drove
himself to a pay phone, probably in first gear
and burning out the clutch."

Charity and I got to Delta at nine, and
I lectured Dad all the way to the car. He
had crutches, because after slipping on the
ice he had driven himself to the clinic. They
had wanted an ambulance, but Dad had said
no, his daughter would come, and then he
had driven to the high school in his linen
splint, laying his leg across the seat. When
Bethel and Ian had come, he had sounded

the horn, and Bethel had driven him home on her driver's permit. Dad had called friends for them to stay with, and waited for me at home, alone and not able to stoke the stove. "That's a ridiculous story," I said, shouting a little and helping Dad to my car. "Let me tell you about broken bones," and I spewed forth a lot of Crick's lectures, becoming furious and saying, "You wouldn't be in all this pain if you'd accepted an ambulance."

My father laughed a little, grunting and looking small. "Tosh," he said. "I'm not working. I don't have the money for ambulances." I had nothing to say to this, feeling tremendously sad, so I checked his leg instead, looking around the edge of the splint. The bone wasn't pushing through the skin, but it was seriously broken, and now I was worried but also interested, thinking back to my studies, to the cadavers in Crick's lab.

On the way to Fairbanks, Dad talked quite a lot at first, shouting from the back seat to keep me awake. Then the pain made him nauseous and he stopped speaking for a bit, and I reached over the seat to feel his skin. "Hands on the wheel," Dad ordered. "You trying to kill me?"

"Nope," I said. "You're doing fine on your own."

We got to Fairbanks at midnight, and Dad

said, "I want to sleep before the hospital. Let's go to your apartment and call them in the morning."

I felt he was being absurdly difficult, and I told him, "No way. What kind of an idea is that."

"I want to have my own doctor, not some intern on duty." He was loud in his opinion and I gave in, helping him to the apartment and grumbling. "Okay, fine," I said. "I'm going up to bed." In the morning, his doctor asked, "Just when did you break it," and Dad responded, "Yesterday." The doctor turned his face on me, looking angry, and I pointed back to Dad, saying, "Ask him. I'm just the driver."

"Oh sure," Dad said. "Miss Temperature-every-five-minutes."

In a way, it was a good time, for I was back to what Leslie called "real things," and not so embedded in school. Dad had surgery and we visited him, whistling our whistle at his door, taking pictures of his leg, his IV, his drugged smile in the bed. We called Bethel and Ian, telling them the news, and I drove Dad home from the hospital, bullying him about what not to do.

"I hope," Dad told me, "you're not missing school. I knew this was going to be a problem."

I said, "Oh brother, you worry about everything." I fidgeted at the wheel. "What would you think," I asked suddenly, "if I changed my degree plans?" I had not thought I could say this to my father, but now the real world had come again and the importance of small things had retreated.

Dad sat up. "What, quit school?"

"No, but if I changed my major, I mean. I'm doing awful in biology."

Dad thought a minute, tapping on his cast. "Tosh," he said. "Did we take you away from school?"

I objected, "No, no, not that at all. I'm just not good at this, or at least not up to the stress." I was convincing us both now, reasoning out loud. "I can't take twelve more years this way, not even one. It has nothing to do with the family; it's me." I looked back at him over the seat, watching his face. "I was thinking, though, about English, but there's really no jobs in that."

My father began laughing, holding his leg steady and bending over it. "That was your worry?" he said. "About a JOB? Who told you college was invented to get you employed?" He laughed some more and became quiet. "You do what you're good at," he told me, "or at least what you like. Your family expects that of you, but only that."

It was a great relief, and also a great hard thing. "Part of it is," I told the family later, "that I was considering the good parts, all the stuff I was interested in. I still love that, can't stand to leave it." Leslie looked at me then, waiting, and I went on, "I forgot about the dying, though. I'm just sick of all that stuff."

"What a pun," Ian giggled. " 'Sick of all that stuff,' ha-ha."

This was in the spring. I had given up, it seemed to me, something I had in a sense out-lived, and now I finished my courses more easily — a little depressed, but less tired — and I would go for a fifth year of studies next fall, moving to a "degree in books," as Bethel said. Leslie finished out her own year, and Bethel and Ian theirs, and in May 1984 we would begin again building, taking it more slowly this time, forcing our father to rest. Dad called me during finals week, speaking loudly into the phone, very worried or very glad, I could not tell which. "Tosh," he said, "I'm at the realtor's."

"What for," I asked him. "Are we selling some land."

"No," Dad answered. "It's the house, the old house. I mean, the children's-home one." He paused, sounding casual, as if someone were in the room. "They're closing down and giving up the lease, and Clara wants to know

340

if we still want it on the market."

"What," I shouted. "Are you insane. Tell her no way, no way . . . Oh, wait a minute. She loses a commission on this, right?"

Dad spoke lightly. "Something like that," he said.

"You don't really want to sell it again, I assume."

Dad answered, "Yeah, right. That's right."

"Then I say," I said, shouting again, "I say tell her no way politely and get out of there. I'll be down in two days and I'm moving in."

"Okay, Tosh," Dad spoke, still brightly. "I'll mention that to Clara. I thought I'd check what you thought."

"Oh, right, go ahead," I said. "Blame it on me."

So the children's home moved out, precisely two years after they'd moved in, and I went over our bills once more, calculating how many we had paid off, how many were left to consider; we would manage, I told the others, one way or another. The only sour thing happened when the children's-home staff were packing up boxes and Dad was at the other house pounding nails. He had nothing to eat there, not even coffee, and he grew dizzy and faint, and his "condition," as he said it, was coming on. He walked to the children's home and knocked on the door, poking his face in and calling. He sat on the steps with his head down, feeling worse, and he went into the house to call somebody. "Hello," he called out, "I've come to use the phone," and no one was there, and the phone was dead, and he saw a box marked "food." He opened it and took a can of stew, opening it and leaving a note saying "I.O.U." Later that day Dad went back to explain, and one of the men saw him and said, "So no one was home and you had to steal something. Like you couldn't call somebody and ask. You're getting this house back, what more do you want."

"I'm sorry," Dad told the man. "I tried to call. I was sick, and I didn't think I could drive. I'll buy you another can."

"No need," the man said. He opened another can like it and spooned it out pointedly for the dog. "No need," he repeated. "We've got plenty."

It was petty of us, but that day made the whole move more satisfying; as a group, we had felt both sorry for the children's home and glad for ourselves, a little guilty when the joy took us over. For we, too, had once lost this house and then mourned it, and though we could forgive those people their sadness-turned-to-anger, we were angry ourselves that they had directed it at our father. Now, on the drive home for the summer, Leslie said,

"All I feel now for those people is rage. They touched our dad, let's kill them," and I laughed with her and pointed to the back seat, whispering, "Don't joke like that in front of Charity."

"What," Leslie said, grinning, lowering her voice. "You thought I was joking?"

At any rate, the enthusiasm of the day was unqualified. The people moved and we never saw them, and in the house we each ran to our rooms, shouting out reports on the damage. "Graffiti," Leslie hollered. "They carved graffiti on my windowsill."

From downstairs, Ian called, "It's a little scraped in here, but nothing big." I heard my father say in the kitchen, "Right, son. It was a little scraped when you lived there."

"Dad," Ian breathed. "How could you?"

Bethel and I met in the place between our rooms. "There's a hole in Natalie's door," she shouted. "I can see it from here." She turned to me, and she was grinning. "This is sure fun, huh?" she said, and then we returned to loud voices, moving between rooms and conferring.

So we were back to the land, the original piece we had known, and we set up the furniture exactly as it had been, opening boxes we had packed and had in storage for two years. We tilled the garden again and tidied the greenhouse, and before long we were settled exactly as before. Bethel walked into Leslie's room, closing the door and waking her up. "What are you doing," Leslie asked, and Bethel said, "I thought there was a mirror behind this door."

"There used to be," Leslie said. "Now it's just a ghost mirror."

Bethel said, "We'll buy another tomorrow," and we did; for what we knew most surely was this thing about ghosts, that we would move forward in the world most easily if we carried the old things in our bags.

There followed a year of reprieve, when Leslie and Charity and I spent holidays with the others in the old house, decorating with paper and tinsel. The union job which broke his shoulder had broken also, it seemed, my father's whole body, and he stayed home now on the small union pension, making day trips to the unfinished house, doing small things to preserve it. He lit the stove there and spread ant killer, stopped leaks and hung Sheetrock, and in the evenings when Ian and Bethel were home from school, he cooked dinner at the big house and called me on the phone, breathing hard into the receiver. "I filled in Mom's grave again," he said. "The dirt keeps sinking in, I don't know why." Even lifting the shovel, he said, made him breathe like this, dizzying his head and turning him nauseous. He said, "The old condition, you know. I think I'll rest tomorrow." He was irritated when people at the cemetery interrupted him, stopping to ask about the grave marker. We had had it carved in wood with an old Jewish farewell. "Next year in Jerusalem," it said, and on the phone my father told me, "I don't want to explain it to everybody. They can look it up in a book."

Dad had made a new will after Mom died, leaving his things to his children. "I'll ask John," he had said then, "if he'll take care of the kids."

"Dad," I told him. "They're all in high school. You'll be around till they're out." We still had been building the second house, working toward midnight after Dad's job. He had spoken as little as he could of feeling sick, but about the will he said, "You never know. I'll put down John as godparent just in case."

"What about me," I asked him. "Why can't I take them."

My father looked up from his lap, opening his eyes and reasoning. "You have your own child," he answered. "You don't need three others."

"I do need," I had said, "my brother and sisters," and the will had been written that way, with our friend John, to whom Dad had gone the night my mother died, as second guardian in case something happened to me. We would preserve as much as possible this full circle of family, one gone now and perhaps another later, but always with the rest of us banded together. Signing the document, my father had pronounced, "This is good. The family taking care of the family," and he had seemed somehow eased in his mind, smiling and sealing the envelope.

We had a good year, as I say, though not a wealthy one, and the two children still home graduated from high school, Bethel a year early and Ian on time. They, too, chose the state university, and all winter I had brought them the forms, filling them out on the table. "Ian," I asked, or "Bethel. What's your social security number, your grade-point average, your date of birth." In the end, I knew theirs as completely as my own, and we mailed the forms together, discussing futures.

My father said again, "This is good," for when his children were all in the world he would not have to worry so much, to put off his dying with such a strong hand. The rest of us knew these thoughts of his, and spoke of them respectfully with fear, saying, "But we WON'T stop needing you. It will never be the right time." Perhaps not, our father said, but at least we all would be safe, all able to care for ourselves.

It was an odd sort of tension among us, my father's wish to stop struggling and ours to keep him with us. We considered his weariness, and likewise he considered our grief, and each of us moved back and forth in our minds, wanting not to "win" at the expense of the other. I took him to his internist that year, though Dad objected to going. "He won't say anything new to me," Dad said. "I'm an old guy falling to bits." And Dr. Grauman looked at him, ran all the tests, and said in the end, "Another bypass. The new vessels are all choked, and you need them replaced."

"No way," my father answered, putting up his hand. "The last one nearly killed me, and it was supposed to keep me alive." There was living and then there was living, he said; he was not going to go through that again.

Dr. Grauman sighed. "Well, tell me if you change your mind. Maybe you should talk to your kids."

It took many months of persuasion, and we children spoke to Dad respectfully, knowing he was tired, but wanting to keep him around. Bypasses were better these days, I told my father, and the surgeons had had more practice. He wouldn't even have to fly out of state this time; there was a good new guy in Anchorage.

"Tosh," my father had pleaded, "and you others. You have to understand. Living for its own sake is a stupid idea. Your mom's having a great time now, and I want to go see her."

Bethel had spoken up then, her face all serious and careful. She said, "We all do, Dad, but not one at a time. All together, when the world is over."

My father had laughed, drinking the rest of his coffee. "If anyone heard us talking, they would call in the suicide squad." He was glad suddenly and we all knew the reason, for our parents had spoken always to us of the second world, the new heaven and new earth where those of us still alive, who believed and watched, would not have to die and be separated, still waiting; Bethel had meant now that we still remembered all this, and counted out days in our heads, and my father smiled and was thoughtful, finally persuaded into surgery.

It was fall 1985 then, the beginning of school, and I told my father to fly to Anchorage, that I would follow him there. I went to Delta first to find something to pawn, some way to manage my ticket. I took out my jewelry and a violin, putting them into my car, and Charity and I drove to the churches, speaking there to our friends. I wondered distantly how many times between us my family had done these same things, made these same visits and calls. It was good to have something to follow, I decided, a routine set in place for the hard moments. Before we left Delta, my friend Emily ran to the car, sticking her hand in the window. "Look at this while you drive," she said. "Some people thought this might help you some." I took the envelope and thought it was a letter, and fifty miles away I opened it and found money, enough for my plane ticket and Charity's, even with a last-minute fare.

So we met my father in Anchorage the day before his surgery; I bought bus tokens and a map, and we went shopping all day, ate fish and chips, bought him slippers and a hat. Even with the plane fare paid, I had put off all my bills and brought the money with me, and we spent it everywhere, on trivia. It was like our very first road trips in California, when we packed the car full of hard rolls, took all our money and went away, squandering our nickels deliberately. Over lunch now, Dad made death jokes, saying, "This time tomorrow it'll be all over, and I do mean all over." I had to be back in school on Wednesday, I told him, "and you'd better not croak on the table tomorrow. It would ruin my schedule."

In the malls, I held Dad's first finger in my fist and Charity held another, and we laughed as we always had at the looks we drew from store clerks. "They think I'm a dirty old man," Dad said, "holding hands with some young thing." And it was true that we did not appear much like blood relatives, except that with age he had shrunk five inches to my same height. Where I walked cautiously with my toes pointed in, Dad moved forward with his shoulders, bringing up first one and then the other, but slower these days, like a man used to swinging stronger arms. His skin was paler than mine, too, the cheeks looser on his face, and his smile was much wider, full of many more teeth. Still, I thought the family blue eyes should have labeled us kin, even if he did have two to my one.

Between stores, we sat on wooden benches, telling Polish jokes, and my father slid tiny gray pills under his tongue. His cowlick fell white over his eye, and he laughed at it, pushing it back and putting his new cap on over it. He needed a haircut, he said, and asked if I had brought my good scissors. We crossed the street and he stood for a moment on the other side, pushing air out past his cheeks and fingering his top button. I bought myself a long book to read during the surgery, and late in the day my father left me looking in one more mall while he took another bus back to the hospital.

My father had been afraid to come for the surgery, afraid of all he remembered from the last time. The nurses, he said, had almost killed him then, blocking off his lungs in their clumsiness, and they had shouted at him when he was weak, as if he merely imagined he was in pain. The pain itself, I told him, was not in our control, but I had come to watch the nurses, ready to holler and to push them away. When I had told the others this plan, Leslie had laughed, saying, "Oh, I can see you hitting a nurse like it's grade school." She had been quiet for a moment, then told me, "But man, I hope you do it. Don't let them shove him around." In Anchorage, though, I found quiet people, nuns and medical staff as gentle as the best I had known growing up. I called Leslie from a pay phone and told her, and she said, "Good. I assume you won't need to hit a nun."

Still, my father was afraid; and with my mother gone, I was the next oldest, the next of us most responsible — for the family, for him — but what I could offer Dad now wasn't much, or wasn't, it seemed to me, sufficient. I could come here with him, buy him lunch, spend the day shopping, preparing later to bully his nurses at the first sign of trouble. I could say that surely in ten years the surgeons had learned more, that the operation had most certainly gotten easier. I could say that he was obliged to live a while longer, if only for his granddaughter, and for all of us here who would grieve. I could remind him that I, too, knew this dread: the sliding in of needles again and again; the taste of Pentothal rising in the throat; the falling backward and waking, dry-throated and sluggish, on the other side. I could say that I knew, too, of necessity, that cliff-edge path we endure only by thinking hard on other things, and that I knew this mostly because of him — from the stories he had told of himself all those years, sitting on my hospital sheets, speaking of adversity as the small, hard seed of courage.

My father was five when World War II came to the Polish town where he was born. He tells clear stories of prewar Zamość, of the life-sized chessboard in the square, and of tournaments between city mayors who came to play as king-pieces in their own games. My grandfather Peter would call, "Let's go, Dodek," and my father would sit watching the games, tall on Peter's shoulders, holding on with his knees. The knights on the board were real horses and real men; at the king's order, a knight flourished his sword and a pawn reeled in the square and fell, then was dragged off the battlefield by his shoulders. The games were clean and fair, and after each one a cheer went up, and everyone ate and drank until bedtime.

When real war came, it was Peter who knew most clearly what it would bring. He was a giant man, a war hero from the czar's army of the first great war, and he knew as Nazi troops occupied the town square that soon only survival would matter, that soon, as my father said afterward, "men would turn to dogs." And they did. Upstanding Polish people stopped the looting of their houses by embracing their captors, by turning with them against the Jews. In the symphony where Peter was violinist, musicians who had respected their partners for years turned vicious, spitting out slurs through their teeth, demanding that Jews no longer come to play. Polish Gentiles burned Jewish houses, hoping the Germans could see; Peter refused to go along, even to understand this madness, and his countrymen turned on him then, calling "Jew-lover," and "Fool." His own house, he knew, would go soon, and probably his family with it.

Peter led his wife and his four children into the night, away from the Nazis into Russian-occupied Poland, to the town where he had been born. There the pillage was of Soviet making: old landmarks were now rubble; huge buckboards carried Polish grain away to trains and on to Russia. My grandmother Julia believed that in Russia things must be better, that the authorities would let them in because she was Russian and had family there. Nothing, she told Peter, could be worse there; people could not be more afraid, children could not be hungrier.

And so Julia began making it clear she was Russian, began speaking Russian to the soldiers, asking the time, telling of her mother across the border. My father remembers his shock when he first heard her speaking words of another language; he was six, the youngest in his family, and this was his first realization that his mother had a past, that history went back to before he was born. After months, Julia's idea worked, and the authorities granted one freight car to refugees who wanted to cross over the line.

It was November, and the train ride was many days long. People began dying of cold and of hunger, and men again turned to dogs. Anyone in the boxcar who had food immediately lost it to the crowd, and was often beaten to death in the struggle. Peter crowded his family against the corner, and told them to eat what little they had only at night, and to bury it otherwise in their bundles. At train stops, he lowered himself and the oldest son, John, out the door and scavenged for hot water to drink, for a woodstove, for firewood. Among the rags his family had tied together were embroidered silks, and he traded them to stationmasters for the stove, for bread. Each time he and John brought something back to the boxcar, Peter shouted for people to come out and help. We must keep warm, he told them, you must come out while the train is stopped. But no one would. In the struggle the refugees had lost impulse, as children abandoned, and could no longer work for their lives. They tore instead at the bunks Peter built for his children, beating the boards into splinters for the stove. As the train reached the Russian work camp, most of the refugees inhabited their bodies, but not their reason.

The Russian situation was not better. No fewer people were dying or without hope, and Polish refugees there were looked at through the corners of Soviet eyes, as outsiders coming in. Peter and Julia were taken separately for questioning that lasted into days, and the questions did not change. Who were they, why had they come here, didn't they plan to undermine Russian intelligence? To the NKVD — what would later become the KGB — families were dangerous entities, and parents were likely to teach subversion to their children. When the middle son, Pietrek, got tuberculosis, Peter burned his hands in a wood fire so they could go to the sanatorium together and he would not lose his son.

It did not strike the NKVD as likely that Julia wanted only to go to the Ukraine, to the collective farm where her mother was. The questions continued, until finally Julia persuaded them to let John, sixteen by then, go to Moscow to find her brother Philip, who was an officer for the NKVD. In Moscow, it was John who was questioned, and slapped, and accused of spying, until finally he found that the man doing all this was the uncle he had come to see. By the time John got back to the work camp, Julia's mother had arrived to see her.

The family did make it out of the work camp, and before they left, Peter bribed the authorities with more silk, and got two sacks of bread to take with them. He sat on one in the buckboard cart, burying the other among their bundles far back. As they pulled through the gate of Chorna Sosna, children smelled the bread from many feet away and came running, calling "Bread!" and the only bag saved in the struggle was the one underneath him.

So people in the Ukraine were just as hungry. My father remembers horses with skin draped smoothly over their bones, and vertebrae he could count with his eyes. He remembers people stealing from the collective farm's produce, knowing that if they were caught they would die, and that if they didn't steal they would die also.

From the time he arrived at the farm, Peter's struggle was not just with circumstance, but also with the minds of people. He was not, as was Julia, a Russian by birthright, and he could not claim to belong there, or even to love Stalin. Julia's mother and her sister Nastka distrusted him, and even Julia herself had begun to feel bitter, to see Peter as a man who ran forward and could not love the place he came to. As an outsider, Peter knew he would die if he did not endear himself to the people, and so he befriended old men, speaking old Ukrainian that new Russians did not use, telling stories of the old Cossack army, playing sad Russian folk songs on his violin.

These are times my father remembers best: the day off every ten days when the people drank black-market vodka and sang sad songs, and when Peter played the violin, laying his jaw on the chin rest, closing the lids of his eyes. My father's sister Vladka danced with her friends to a song about a sailor, and they cried when he lost his lady friend, and they asked for the song again. These were times, too, that Julia pointed to when Peter wanted to leave, when he said he was not safe here for long. He said that once the old men were dead, so would be old Ukrainia, and his knowledge of it would no longer save him; young Stalinists would approach him then, would tell him to embrace the "new life," and when he refused he would die. Julia called Peter a fool, said he was born one, that he could not recognize safety when it came. But even my father, the youngest child and just six by then, knew how the children watched him, played with him but watched him, always from the corners of their eyes.

And so the war outside their ranks broke in on them, in the way that war does, splitting whole families into factions, chalking out borders between them. Peter told his wife that they had to escape before winter, while they were still strong for the effort, that they had to go back to Poland, where at least they were citizens, and at least belonged. Julia took a long wooden pestle to his body, and he put up his arms, shouting, "*Głupia,* what are you doing." And she reported his escape plans to the NKVD, hoping that if Peter was killed, she would be permitted to stay alone as a widow. Peter heard of all this in time to beware, but it was obvious by then that the family would not be saved.

Fall came on, turning the trees and dropping the last berries to the ground. Most of the goods Peter and Julia had brought with them

— silks, mostly, and crocheted things — were gone now, had been traded for food. Still Julia said they must stay, they could survive here together, picking berries all around and mushrooms in the woods. Young village overseers watched the back of Peter's head, and as the old men grew older, Peter took to looking at the tops of trees, measuring how many leaves had fallen, and how far to winter. Peter was looking up like that with his eyes, and his children were picking mushrooms beside him, when John spoke tightly at his shoulder. "Dad, don't. Please don't."

Peter looked down. John's lips quivered and his eyes crept in at the corners. Peter said, "Don't what, Janek? Son, what's wrong?"

"Don't hang yourself, Dad. Don't look at the trees. Just don't."

My father remembers that it was the farm's day off and he was in the straw loft of their quarters, sitting with Peter and John, with Vladka and Pietrek, when Julia's sister Nastka came in downstairs. She began to speak to Julia words she had obviously spoken before, saying that if Julia hadn't the courage herself to kill Peter, she should go to Moscow and ask Philip to do it. Merely reporting on Peter had done nothing, she said; he was still alive, still wanting to leave. Upstairs, John crawled to Peter and said, "Dad, did you hear that?" No one else moved in the straw until Nastka left, and then, as his children went outside, Peter climbed down the ladder to his wife.

Hours later, my father says, his parents called the children — to play a game, they said. Julia stood at one end of a long table, Peter at the other, and they said that this was a chess game, and they were kings of two countries — Russia and Poland — and that the children were faithful subjects, standing exactly in the middle. Who, they said, would travel to Moscow with the King of Russia? And who, with the other king, to Poland? For three rounds of the game, the parents shouted, "Come to me!" and first John and then the other children crowded to their father's end, but on the fourth, the daughter Vladka looked back to Julia standing alone, and she turned and walked, and stood looking up at her mother. Julia took Vladka's hand and, speaking over her head, said, "Children, you'll see Mommy again sometime."

Peter stood watching, then turned his face to his sons. "No," he said. "Kids, if you come with me, you won't see your mommy again." He told his sons to go to Julia, to say goodbye to her, to kiss Vladka. Peter walked to Vladka himself and stooped, and brought her head in to his chest. That night the Kuszes took leave of one another, and my father's family was after that all male.

Their escape through the Soviet Union was a long one. The authorities were looking for a man and three boys, and in Kiev the clan had to split into even smaller parts. Peter put John in charge, showed the boys a great boulder on the edge of town where he and they could leave notes. Even if it took years, he said, for any of them to get back there, no one else would come to this rock, and the notes would be safe. Then he sent his sons to the railway yard to tell the guards there they were lost from their parents. The boys left Peter and, with John leading them, went to the station and then on to a children's home fenced in with barbed wire.

Their months there were cold, and their food hardly enough to sustain them. Their clothes were taken from them and they wore only underthings, sleeping in concrete barracks which must once have been for prisoners. Finally, boys of John's age were sent away, a few at a time, to work camps, and John told Pietrek and Dodek that it was time to get word to their father. At evening, John scraped through the barbed wire and ran, and Pietrek waited, then leaned his body into the barbs and screamed. The guards ran to him and did not see John, ducking away on the trolley passing by. The next day's train brought Peter, severe in a good Soviet suit, speaking severe Russian to the overseers. By morning, the men of the family were together, and on the run, again.

The remainder of the war was, to my father, a series of the same: splitting apart and coming together, across the borders of countries, through the gates of concentration camps and work farms. While governments fought for ideals and for land, Peter and his sons fought not to lose one another, and to be still alive at the last. They did not see Julia or Vladka again, and after the war was over between countries, there was still the struggle of being Displaced Persons among thousands of others.

In 1950, after five years of shuffle between DP camps in Germany, Peter and my father managed to get emigration visas to the United States, and at the last minute connived to take Pietrek along. By then, John had joined the French Civilian Organization and had to stay in France without them. Months later, in New York, my father received a letter from John, who had escaped from an experimental hospital and had managed, before he was caught again, to send a plea for his brother to come get him. John had checked himself into the hospital in order not to starve, and had found himself the subject of psychological and drug-related experiments. My father was too young and too poor then even to care for himself, and never heard from John again. When I was grown, John's letter showed up in the bottom of a box of mementos, and I watched my father weep for John, who had surely died, and for what he himself had not been able to do to save him.

The move to New York made things no easier than had the first move to Russia. The three men spoke no English, and the city was overcrowded with thousands of other refugees all looking for the same few jobs and places to stay. Peter was too old and too tired by then to take easily to a new language; he grew discouraged and yearned to return to Poland. From what my father says, this feeling was common among immigrants.

But Dad did make it, did eventually join the army, did move to California, where he met my mother. Two years after he married her, my father drove for three days cross-country to get Peter, older by then and still speaking only Polish, feeling more than ever the cold in New York. In Los Angeles, Peter slept on the Murphy bed while my parents shared the couch folded out.

My mother was shy and very reserved in those days, and, as she says, very much in awe of my grandfather. Because they spoke different languages, she could not tell him so, but she had heard and dwelt on the stories from my father and from Pietrek, of the war and how their father had kept them all alive. For her, the stories were legends, and when she finally met her father-in-law, she had no thought of what to say. And though my father told all this to Peter, the old man interpreted Mother's quietness as dislike; to him, my mother must have symbolized this whole new country, the language he could not understand, the emotional reserve that passed for good breeding.

Peter was awkward in L.A., and weary. He tired easily and slept in any space, and was arrested in the park for drunkenness on a day when he had only sat down to close his eyes. To the old man, all police were still NKVD, and he must have been very afraid. My father's English was still quite poor, so he sent my mother after Peter, to defend him to the police. At home, Peter looked long at his son and said, "You wouldn't even come get me from jail." And one morning, while my father still slept, Peter handed his apartment key to his daughter-in-law and left through the front door. My parents spent many years looking for him, and even now we look under cemetery listings for the name "Peter Kusz, Sr.," but none of us has ever found him again.

And so it was no wonder to me that my father's impulse all my growing-up years had been to keep the family whole at whatever cost to himself. We had prevailed, as he said, like a family, keeping together, but his part in the effort had often called him away, to someplace separate from the rest of us, where he managed his grieving alone.

First, he had been away on the North Slope when Mom had found me in the snow half-eaten among sled dogs, and my father's only image of the accident had been the blood on her clothes when he had arrived at the hospital eight hours later. He stood against the wall then as she spoke what the surgeons had said, that I would likely die today, or tomorrow, or a day after that, and his parka grew heavy on his shoulders and he closed his eyes to stay conscious. He had done what he could, he said, to keep us whole, yet he was not, had never been, close enough by. But on the third day, when I woke up in intensive care, I heard his voice first and was glad, and asked him where were my eyes. In a month, when the stitches were off and I could see through the eye I still had, my father stayed behind us once more, looking for work, while my mother boarded the plane with four children, heading for Seattle, where I would have many months of surgery, and would receive many letters from my father.

We had counted the Seattle months as hard, for me, and for my mother and siblings, but in retrospect they had been equally hard for my father, separated from us again and without even a paycheck to send along. He had written of too many men seeking too few jobs, of writing his letters in the truck between union calls, not wanting to waste gas driving home. He wrote these things gently, needing support but fearing the extra burden he gave us. "You must not pay too much attention," he said, "whenever I sound a bit discouraged. I am sure that things will work out. It's just that sometimes I feel this is only a bad dream I'd like to wake from." Long afterward he told me of buying a bottle of brandy, and of drinking it on the floor till he slept. He wrote: "Perhaps when I start working my attitude will change, but at present the idea [of] me being here without any of you near me, makes it a bit tough, even though I know, that should you be here in these depressed surroundings [it] would probably make me feel worse, knowing that I can't help any of you out of the bleak situation." He promised to build us a house after the crisis, "such as you had in mind — a 45 by 35 foot, two stories house, you won't even get cabin fever." And over all he called us to keep faith, to overcome hopelessness, to believe that these things would pass if in the meantime we had kept one another from falling.

He had gotten work by the time I had returned to Alaska for more surgery. It was summer then, and his job was in town, and he spent much time upholding me, the one he assumed must feel the most alone now. He came to the hospital often, and stayed as late as he could, carrying a chessboard under his arm. I had come to dread surgery by then, to cry at the smell of ether, and I would spend days before each operation wanting only to lie down, to sleep and sleep; my father would set up a chess game for the pre-op hours, knowing I could not concentrate on the pieces, or he would bring me halvah or chocolate that I could not eat anyway until surgery was over. It was a Polack's way, he said, to do always something when nothing was to be done.

One year I had developed a drop-foot after I was propped up too long by sandbags during an operation. I could feel my foot and lower leg, but I could not move them, and the ankle sagged to the side, inert. After a long while, when the leg muscles began to atrophy and my therapists gave up trying to restore them, I was given a walking brace so I was at least mobile. Dad, though, said that a one-eyed person should have two legs, and that from now on he was my therapist, that I had a standing appointment every day. For many hours we sat side by side, my leg stretched out in front of us, and we talked to my big toe, telling it to move left, then right. He made me push up my glasses, look hard down past my knee, and move the toe, move it with my eye. For months we did this, talking to a dead toe, shining a light on it and staring. The day it shifted, moving just barely closer to the next one over, he stayed sitting and said, "Do that again." I looked hard at it and it moved again, a little, just a little, and then Dad was gone, shouting for my mother, calling her in. After that, we moved to other toes, and to the whole foot, and to the ankle, and although none of the leg was ever very strong, it always moved after that without my eye.

And it was these, I think, the few things he could make visibly better, that had saved him as a father; from war, he had learned survival with his hands and his mind, and he told me once that sometimes we must look away from hard things and pray, before we turn back and do them. One July, he took me to the hospital for surgery the morning after, and my face broke when the I.D. bracelet shut together over my wrist. Dad said to the admissions clerk, "Take that off. We're going raspberry picking." At the railroad yard he offered me his finger, and I held it as we crossed the tracks, fitting the smooth grain of my hand over the rough one of his. Dad lifted the leaves of the bushes, talking: "See? You have to look underneath. They think they're hiding, but we know they're there." He found a fat berry, and called me with the family whistle. This one was too good to save, he said. He pressed it flat enough to fit between my teeth, which barely opened now since I had lost my jaw joint. He laughed at me and turned back to the bushes. "Why are you standing around," he said. "They won't just hop into your bucket." In the evening, we went back to the hospital, to the room they saved for me near the nurses, and the last things I ate before fasting time were raspberries Dad chose out from inside his pail.

He was a generous father, one who brought us pencils in college, and hid dollar bills and quarters around our apartments just to feel he was helping; and now that I was grown I had followed him to a strange city and taken him shopping all day, reminding him, when he said, "You don't have the time to be here," that this was the way he had taught us, the way we all knew to be faithful.

Dad grinned then, said he was glad I had come, and not to yell too much at the nurses.

"I won't," I told him. "It doesn't seem like I'll have to."

My father said, "Good thing, too. I'd hate you to get sued by a nun."

At the hospital that night, we sat all together on his bed, speaking of other things than operations. My father said again, "It's good that you came, it's what your mom would have done," and I said yes I knew that, I remembered the last time. Tomorrow we would collect here again in his room, the surgery having been a success, and much less intolerable than the first; but before that, for tonight, there was still the turning of our faces aside, the gathering together of faith; I started to sing in Polish, a sailor's song to a mermaid, and my father sang, too, pushing hair off his forehead, keeping time with a closed hand. When the chorus was over, Dad began again and I followed, giving heart to the sailor's voice, asking his mermaid love to rise back from the bottom of the sea. The words were well fit for a traveler man choking on loss; they came in deep vowel sounds from the throat, steady and long, as if he could not take that sorrow, or as if he could, perhaps, but did not want to.

EPILOGUE: COVERING OLD GROUND

I bought an octagonal window today; it stands leaning against the wall of my living room. It is small, the size of two faces looking out, with beveled glass in the shapes of flower petals, and leaded lines fanning outward like beams of the sun. Some of the glass petals are glazed, some white, some clear, and the way they are cut gives the sense of many layers, opening from the center and widening out. Of all the windows like it in the store, I chose out the one with the smoothest wood framing, all the same fine grain, no nicks or chips. It is exactly like the one my mother envisioned years ago when we drove together past small cabins, rebuilding them in our minds and placing round windows just there, high in the front wall under the peak of the eaves.

I called my father last month when I first

decided to buy this window. "I'm homesick for carpentry," I said. "I want to build a cabin to set it in." Dad laughed into the phone and said okay, we could put one up next summer, but wasn't I thinking a little backward. I told him the price of the window, how little it cost compared to what we could find in Alaska, and he whistled, appreciating it, saying, "Buy two. And bring them both home when you come."

Two years ago, when the oil boom went bust and Alaskans could find too little work, I took a job in Minnesota, teaching writing to students at a small private college. It was among the hardest things I could have done just then, leaving home, and I considered not doing it at all — or at least not now, when Leslie and Ian were still in school and Dad lived alone in the big house, three years past his last heart surgery but still too unhealthy to work anymore. Bethel was married by then and quitting college for a while, planning a move to Portland, Oregon, the city her husband was from; Mike said there were jobs there and living was cheap, they could both return to school when they had earned enough money. It should not happen like this, I thought, Bethel and I both leaving at the same time, but the jobs I could find at 7-Eleven or as an adjunct teacher would not pay my own bills, still less let me help out the others. "I could work as a secretary," I told my father, "maybe in an office somewhere." He said that was absurd, everyone was looking for those positions, and besides, I was trained as a teacher, and with summers off, I could always come back home. So Bethel and I were to leave the same month, about a week apart, and we cleaned our apartments in Fairbanks and drove with our things down to Delta. Dad blessed us well and the others smiled when they thought we were looking, but I knew that, however hard it would be for me to go, it was harder still to be the ones left behind.

We packed up my station wagon, a smaller, newer version of the one we had driven to Alaska the first time, and for Charity we dug out my old treasure chest, the leather one with the mirror in the lid. Together, Leslie and I filled it with "nostalgia items": children's books from our shelves, Mom's old green comb, an Etch-A-Sketch, a drawing pad, pencils and markers and crayons. Charity was eight and well into our family's feeling for music; she put in Dad's Walkman and Leslie gave her some headphones, and we set up the back seat like a nest for her, laying out pillows and a sleeping bag, leaving room for her legs to stretch across.

Dad drove me to get "road food," insisting

that I take along his green picnic cooler, and we bought cheese and bread and apples, and small bottles of soda, coffee for the thermos, granola bars. In the end the cooler wouldn't fit in the car, so I carried the food in a bag, squashing it down between seats. "Look at all this stuff," my father said, looking in through the door. "You packed it as well as I would have." He considered himself the expert on filling up a car, remembering, I suppose, our trip up the highway, those nights of which Dick Conger had wanted a photo, when Dad and Mom had emptied the trailer for bedtime, piled our things under tarps, then packed them all back every morning, a thousand family possessions in twelve feet of space. Now Dad circled my car, looking through the windows at computer accessories and file boxes, books and photo albums, blankets and clothing and cassette tapes. A big road atlas and Milepost lay on the seat, and a CB radio shaped like a phone; and my father said, "This is good. But I wish we could fit the green cooler."

Ian was working in Fairbanks, but the rest of us were there in Delta, and we cut rhubarb leaves and wore them like hats, taking pictures of ourselves making sultry kiss-lips on the steps. The edges of the leaves drooped like huge green elephant ears cut and stuck on our heads, and Dad sat Charity and me on a fencepost, handing me a fireweed bouquet and shouting, "THAT'S IT, NOW SMILE."

"She can't," Bethel said. "There's bees in those flowers."

We did a lot of our standard family things — cooking out, hunting mushrooms, singing the Polish songs. We played Trivial Pursuit and Pictionary, and the others forbade Bethel and me to be partners, saying, "You win too much. You reach each other's minds." Bethel looked superior and said they were jealous, and in the end I said, "Come on, this is the last time. We might not be on the same team for YEARS." The others thought that comment was below the belt, but they let us play together in the end.

It was chilly and raining, but Charity talked us into swimming in the pond. We put on old shorts and walked down the mud path, stepping over deep moose prints filled with silty water. The pond was cold and we inched into it, stepping in knee-deep and gasping, then lowering ourselves slowly down, grimacing. "No," Charity yelled. "Do it all at once, like this," and she held her nose and collapsed in, coming up again and shuddering. "All at once," she shouted again. "It feels warm now."

"Then how come you're shaking." Dad

grinned, taking a picture. A few feet away, Leslie and I were still crouching in, covered by now up to our hips, and she said to me, "This is good. I won't much feel like doing this after you're gone."

At the last, Dad tied my spare tires and luggage to the car roof, wrapping it all in a yellow shower curtain and strapping the cords down tight. We drove off humming road songs, without the heart to sing full-voice. By the time I reached Minnesota, the shower curtain was in ribbons, trailing behind us in the wind.

We have spoken on the phone nearly every day since — myself, and Leslie or Ian in Fairbanks, or Dad in Delta, or Bethel and Mike in Portland. Leslie goes to Delta for me to spy on Dad, sending word of how he is eating. "He saves all his food till I visit," she says. "I think we should give him a lecture." It hit eighty below last winter, and to keep the house at sixty degrees Dad had to feed the fire every forty-five minutes, getting up from sleep and walking deliriously out to get the logs. He got sick and we all became worried, feeling impotent and much too far away; since then, we have kept him in stove oil, sending a man around and having the bill mailed to me. The small oil stove won't heat the whole house, but it does cut the wood-stoking down to every few hours; as soon as we can, we plan to buy baseboard heating, the kind that turns on with a thermostat.

I am going through old photographs, and Dad mailed me the negatives he could find at home. I copy the best ones and send them around, telling the others, "This was the day Dick and Esther first saw the big house," or "I forget his name, but this is a kid from Children's Hospital." There is a field within driving distance from here where the sandhill cranes stop for mating dances on their way north to Fairbanks. Leslie says I should tie pictures and a letter to one and she'll grab it when it arrives, and send a reply back down with the fall migration. I hunted up Dick Conger's phone number, remembering he was a photographer, and I called him in Arizona, asking if he still had his photos. "Twenty thousand," he said. "I kept them all. If you come visit, I'll show you." He is seventy-eight, but his voice was strong, and I told him I'd be there this spring.

Dad sends me books he has read, and Ian sends picture postcards, writing poems or stupid jokes on the backs. Leslie buys "good writer's pens" and mails them with notes to me and Charity. "I miss you," she says. "When are you coming home?" I've discovered UHF television here, and I tape old movies and mail them to Dad. He watches sometimes two a day, he says, and asks me when I can send more. "I'm on the last three," he tells me, "and I'm saving them till Leslie comes." Bethel and Mike came here for Christmas, and she sang a new message for my answering machine. "We wish you a Merry Christmas," it said. "But we're not answering the telephone." It still plays when someone calls, and all my friends whine that the holidays are over.

My phone bill is more than my rent, but I budget for it. The family asks how I'm doing, and I complain a lot. "I can't get used to it," I tell them, "the way spring comes so soon here. And when it does, people meander to the lakes. They just close up their houses and go." It's the same way in Oregon, Bethel says. People buy their houses all finished and they work sometimes in their yards, but mostly their summers are languid, full of barbecues and lawn chairs, and little white shorts and sandals. As for us, we still get building fever, that sense that summer is here and must be utilized, spent hammering nails or stuffing fiberglass in rapid motion, before snow comes and catches us still unprepared.

Other things, too, are hard. Charity and I live in a duplex with neighbors, and other people's windows face onto our back yard.

Going back there to sit, we have to comb our hair and put on "public" clothes, I wear an eyepatch, we speak in quieter voices than we'd like. I've never been out in my nightgown. Looking out in any direction, we can see no farther than fifty feet before the horizon is broken by a building or a car. My father says, "Oo, I couldn't live like that anymore; I heard three trucks driving past on the road yesterday, and I thought THAT was a lack of privacy."

There are car washes everywhere here, and everyone uses them; even the "dirty" cars seem clean to me. The day we arrived with the shower curtain hanging in yellow shreds over the roof, people in other vehicles stared at us, then looked away when we stared back. We had hit a mud slide in Canada and nearly skidded over a cliff, and in the three thousand miles since, bugs had collected in the mud, so many that they looked like black whiskers growing out of dead skin. Charity loved it that first time we put in our quarters and drove through the car wash, and now she asks about twice a week if we can do it again. We roll up the windows and sit there, and when the huge blue brushes start to turn and move in, she holds both fists to her chest and yells, "Here they come!" It's almost better, she tells my father, than video movies or TV.

I would not have expected ethnicity to matter much, but somehow it does. The population here is mostly Scandinavian, tall, silent, reserved people who respect one's own privacy, but who are so much more stoic than we are that it's hard for me to distinguish the moods in their faces. Six months after we moved here, Charity and I visited a friend in Chicago who said, "You look homesick. I'm taking you to the Polish neighborhood for lunch." We parked the car there, passed down the sidewalk toward the deli, and were immediately surrounded by loud, sturdy people, with round faces and big noses and red balls of cheeks pushing up to their eyes. There were men like my father with short thick fingers and pants hanging low, and others like Ian, taller but hunching forward, both hands in their pockets up to the wrists. The women were mostly as large as I or my sisters, with smooth pink faces and heavy hair around them, and flat bottoms and square hips, standing on wide, solid feet in their shoes. They were the kind of women, as Leslie would have said, who looked as if they could push a car, or dig a hole, or carry a cord of wood to the house; and here, suddenly after months, they were all around me, arguing or laughing in groups, waving their hands in broad gestures. To have come there so abruptly — among people who looked like me, whose faces were so easily readable, who were speaking my father's familiar language — was such a relief somehow that for a moment I felt faint, and was glad when we sat down to order. That day I bought "real" sausage and mailed some to Dad, and Leslie says he cut off tiny slices for weeks, chewing it slowly and grinning.

Even the pleasant things have been difficult to grow accustomed to. We were poor when we arrived, but when we had a few dollars and decided to entertain ourselves, Charity and I would buy a newspaper and feel daunted by the number of choices we found there. Charity had enrolled in a public school for the arts, and she said, "Let's narrow it down. Something I can talk about in class." Even so, the selection was too big: musicals and stage plays, concerts, ballet, gallery openings, an exhibit of fiber art at the civic center. In Alaska, each one would have been special, a single event in a long month of waiting for it to come, but in their abundance each was diminished somehow, and we felt called to pass over things we might have looked eagerly forward to at home. In the end we closed our eyes and pointed, then bought tickets to the theater.

And still I am disoriented, most of all by the land. I do like the city, the central district, very much. St. Paul is old by our standards, the buildings all made when architects looked to Europe for ideas, laying bricks and molding scrollwork, making intricate patterns with windows, letting the light come in. The neighborhood I live in across the Mississippi is just as old, and in places where the asphalt has worn off, the original brick pavement shows through, bright red against the black-top. I am a little awed by those bricks, for they must have been laid at a time when there was no pavement at all in Alaska, and even the asphalt which covers them now is probably older than the most ancient road-work at home. Having come from a building family, I have called home amazed at the cost of the buildings, telling my father, "There are houses here with turrets and little round rooms, things you'd never afford to build yourself." Yet, when I drive around gaping, I become easily lost, for whereas in a forest I can tell true north without looking, I am utterly dysfunctional here. It has some-thing to do with freeways, I think — how, to go west, one takes an off-ramp east; re-gardless of the reason, Charity moans, "Oh, no," when I decide we should drive some-where new. "We'll take all day to go three miles," she says. "And then we'll never get back."

This spring I got building fever more strongly than ever, and out of curiosity I looked in the phone book for supply stores, driving over to one while Charity was still at school. It was astonishing. I walked in and stood confounded in a vast supermarket of a hardware outlet, full of more and better things than all the places we had shopped in for years. I felt as my father described when he arrived in this country and went to his first grocery store, gawking at the mounds of food and no breadlines, the casual hands of shoppers picking over the fruit. "Five kinds," he had said. "Five kinds of apples alone," and people allowed to touch them, choosing exactly the ones they liked best.

So here I was experiencing that awe, that same urge to stuff my car full of goods and be off, hoarding it all in my kitchen. Instead, I merely passed down the aisles, counting off things to call home about: designer doors and tile, carved railing spindles, enamel faucets in a hundred colors, even candy-apple red — all for many times less than we paid for utilitarian pieces at home. I saw the octagon window there and held it up to a lamp. The bevels shone like prisms, refracting the light into stars.

I thought about that window for months, of all the places we could have used it back home, all the cabins we had built before from parts we had found at the dump — old greenhouse windows and splintered boards, bent nails and torn Visqueen, and rusty lengths of stovepipe Dad hammered the dents out of. In the trailer days in Delta, we had put up a shack we called just "the cabin," a sixteen-foot box with a tar-paper roof and a woodstove, and it had been our hideout, the place we spent the night in to get away from the trailer. Friends coming to visit had stayed there, and others whose own houses were still being built, and we children had been allowed to have slumber parties, so long as we were careful lighting the lanterns. After time, we had built the big house and people visited us there instead, and when a man we knew had no housing ready for the winter, Mom and Dad had offered him the cabin, telling him, "We can move it onto your land, and you can at least be warm while you're building." It had been good to see the place used fruitfully again, yet for years after we helped David drag it away, the empty space had seemed sad, the dirt pressed down and bare.

In the end, after long thinking on the subject, I phoned Dad, and that was when he laughed. "You buy a window," he said, "and then build a cabin for it? That's a Polish way of thinking."

"It sounds hasty," I agreed, "but I've been thinking this for a while. We're coming home for the summer, and I want to build a cabin. On that corner where the other one was, the one we gave to David." We had spoken of this before, I reminded my father, how good it would be to have another small place, something framed in and covered over and standing again on the old ground.

Dad didn't argue, didn't even mention his "condition." "Okay," he said. "What size?"

"Small, like the other. Maybe sixteen by sixteen."

"One floor?"

"One floor. No water, that would be expensive, but there's electricity close, and oh, I really want this window . . ."

So everything is set, at least in our minds. It is January now, the trip home is in June, and we have been talking about the cabin for months, planning it small so we can finish quickly. Bethel won't make it up this year, she doesn't have the cash, but Leslie will spend weekends in Delta, and maybe Ian will, too, and Dad and Charity and I will work the rest of the week, figuring walls on the clipboard. We all worry about Dad, how much work he can do, but the idea of building again seems to have lifted him somehow; he still breathes hard answering the phone, still sounds weak when he's been stoking the stove, but his words themselves seem expanded, much brighter, as if he has reason now to look forward.

We all feel that way. It has been a good thing to speak again of carpentry, to haul out Mom's house plans and leaf through them. Charity wants to build a tree fort nearby, a secret place like the ones we others built all those years. My father tells her this is fine, she can have the wood scraps and some nails, as long as she doesn't hurt any birch trees. He says he is walking the land more, strengthening his legs for the work. I am lifting weights, broadening my arms, hoping I can take more of his share. I have no depth perception, so have never been excellent with a hammer, but I think this year I'll use one more often than before, hiding the bent nails from my father. And I have the octagonal window sitting in the living room, taking up space in the corner.

If I could, I would drive up instead of fly, and I'd take a truck filled with goods from the builder's store — clear windows and carved molding and railing spindles for a porch. I'd bring a new front door for Dad's house, too, one of the ones with etched glass and brass hinges and a heavy round doorknob like a fist. Mundane things are cheaper here, too, so I'd strap down bundles of fiberglass and electrical wire, and a new hammer for myself. I've always been partial to a twelve-ounce, and I can get one here the way I like it, heavy steel with a flat head and perforated rubber on the handle. All these are merely wishes, but they feel good in the evening, and on the phone my father listens and dreams with me, asking, "So what else do they have?" In reality, we will build the cabin fast, as always, with splintery rough-cut boards from the mill. It may even be that when summer comes Dad will be worse, or we will all be too tired, or too short of money to build. I speak of this sometimes to Dad, wondering if he would be disappointed. "I'd be upset myself," I tell him. "But there's always a chance it'll fall through."

Of course, Dad agrees, plans change; we lived for years in that trailer, and we'd expected a house the first month. For now, we just imagine a cabin, buy little windows, talk the big talk. "But if summer comes," my father says, "and we don't build, so what? We make potato pancakes and put that window in your room upstairs." He says we have the big house, and enough land for privacy, and anything else is just extra. "Remember, Tochka," he tells me, "after all the long work, we have what we need. We never were called to build kingdoms." It's an old phrase of his, those words about kingdoms, and he has spoken it for years, since before our move north, before my accident, before the thousand substitutions of new plans for old. My father means, and the rest of us concur, that hopes are white stones shining up from the bottoms of pools, and every clear day we reach in up to the shoulder, selecting a few and rearranging the others, drawing our arms smoothly back into air, leaving no scar on the water.

THORNDIKE PRESS hopes you have enjoyed this Large Print book. All our Large Print titles are designed for easy reading, and all our books are made to last. Other Thorndike Large Print books are available at your library, through selected book-stores, or directly from the publisher. For more information about current and up-coming titles, please call or mail your name and address to:

THORNDIKE PRESS
PO Box 159
Thorndike, Maine 04986
800/223-6121
207/948-2962